4-2-75

FEATHER FASHIONS AND BIRD PRESERVATION

Feather Fashions
and Bird Preservation

A Study in
Nature Protection

ROBIN W. DOUGHTY

University of California Press
Berkeley, Los Angeles, London

UNIVERSITY OF CALIFORNIA PRESS
BERKELEY AND LOS ANGELES, CALIFORNIA
UNIVERSITY OF CALIFORNIA PRESS, LTD.
LONDON, ENGLAND
COPYRIGHT © 1975, BY
THE REGENTS OF THE UNIVERSITY OF CALIFORNIA
ISBN 0-520-09478-6
LIBRARY OF CONGRESS CATALOG CARD NUMBER: 72-619678
PRINTED IN THE UNITED STATES OF AMERICA

Contents

Tables

Acknowledgments

An oil spill in San Francisco Bay in January, 1971, galvanized more than 4,000 people into clean-up operations. The *San Francisco Chronicle* reported that Robert T. Orr, of the California Academy of Sciences, was pleased at the turnout compared with a similarly large spill in 1937 about which "nobody seemed to care very much." Accelerated landscape change brought about in the last fifty years by new technology and exponential population growth has served to make resource degradation and depletion conspicuous and, of late, newsworthy. It has not always been so.

Only a relative handful of people became concerned about the spectre of extinction that hung over the woods of Petoskey, Michigan in 1878 at the last great nesting of passenger pigeons (*Ectopistes migratorius*), and that hovered over cart-loads of dead and dying eskimo curlews (*Numenius borealis*) shot on the plains of Kansas in spring. The public did not notice the disappearance of the ruff (*Philamochus pugnax*), osprey (*Pandion haliaetus*) and black tern (*Childonias niger*) as breeding birds in the United Kingdom a century ago. However, people who did notice spoke out sharply against the imperiled state of wildlife. That so-called age of extermination marked the beginning of a serious attempt to change attitudes to nature and to preserve remnant populations of wildlife.

Opposition to bird destruction in particular came from two organizations founded in England and the United States which planned and carried out a crusade to protect wild birds, notably those killed for millinery ornaments. In early discussions of the issue of wearing bird feathers, members of these groups—the Royal Society for the Protection of Birds and the Audubon Society —encapsulated cherished themes about man and birds, and about man's duties to the creatures and the natural environment. Their pronouncements were broadcast by popular periodicals and the daily newspapers. The arguments they contained served to awaken a general interest in bird and nature study. Speeches were made in state and national chambers to curtail the importation of plumage before World War I in the United States, and in 1921 in England. Ideas put forth became part of the "land ethic" articulated by persons like Aldo Leopold, forester and conservationist, which has today become so central to the current renaissance of concern for environmental quality.

Problems of humanly-induced landscape change and the impact of man on biota have been the focus of inquiries by geographers for many decades. Students of an historical and cultural bent have discussed tastes in landscape and the ethos binding mankind to his hearth, homeland, and assemblages of plants and animals. This book is intended to continue this tradition. The original manuscript is located in the Library of the University of California, Berkeley.

I wish to express my deep appreciation to all those who have encouraged and assisted me in this study.

At Berkeley, I am indebted to Dr. James J. Parsons, Dr. Clarence J. Glacken and Dr. A. Starker Leopold for their constant helpful comments and suggestions. I acknowledge the provocative comments of Dr. Carl O. Sauer and Dr. Daniel B. Luten. I thank my colleagues Rowan Rowntree, Robert Reed and Tom Vale for constructive criticism.

In Washington, D.C., I express thanks to Dr. Oliver H. Orr, Library of Congress, Dr. Alexander Wetmore, Dr. Richard L. Zusi, Dr. Richard Banks and Mrs. Claudia Kidwell, Smithsonian Institution, for helpful suggestions and for reading drafts of my thesis. To Dr. Lee M. Talbot for his interest and encouragement in my research and to Dr. Dale Jenkins for facilities so generously donated to me in the Office of Ecology I am extremely grateful.

In England, I thank Miss Phyllis Barclay-Smith, Secretary, International Council for Bird Preservation; the staff of *Royal Society for the Protection of Birds,* especially Miss Dorothy Rook; and the staff of the *Royal Society for the Prevention of Cruelty to Animals,* especially Mr. Roland P. Ampleford. I thank Mrs. Joanne Williams for typing various papers related to wildlife protection. Also I have appreciated the help of Mr. Jack Marquardt, Librarian, Smithsonian Institution, and staff members of the National Archives, the New York Public Library, and Customs House Library in London.

I wish to thank the Smithsonian Institution, National Science Foundation and the University of California, Berkeley, for financial assistance during this study.

To Linda whose unflagging support has enabled me to continue when the way appeared burdensome—my debt is immense.

Abbreviations

AOU   American Ornithologists' Union
BL   *Bird-Lore,* publication of National Audubon Society
BNN   *Bird Notes and News,* publication of RSPB
RG   Record Group of National Archives data
RSPB Royal Society for the Protection of Birds (after 1904)
SPB   Society for the Protection of Birds
SPCA Society for the Prevention of Cruelty to Animals

Introduction

At the French Court of the resplendent Marie Antoinette "a woman's head was in the middle of her body, and society had the appearance of an extravagant fancy ball." This "featherhead," as her brother Joseph nicknamed her, set the halls of Versailles aflame in a riot of color as varied plumes rippled and swayed upon the heads of noble ladies acting out social graces and dancing to courtly music. A fad for ornamental feathers was conspicuous in the reign of Louis XVI after 1775 and infected the aristocracy of several European capitals a decade later. It was sparked off by the queen, who upon a whimsy, is supposed to have placed a number of ostrich and peacock feathers in her coiffure one evening which drew compliments from the king.[1]

This *grande finale* of extravagance and sumptuosity discovered bird plumage to be an attractive and individual form of decoration which had become prized as symbolic of high status. Rose Bertin, jocularly called "Minister of Fashion," invented *poufs*, or piled hairstyles, beloved of the French queen. Aided by Leonard, Her Majesty's hairdresser, Rose fashioned unique compositions of feathers, stuffed birds, flowers and *objets d'art* to crown the billowing hair of noble ladies. This madness for piled hair topped with feathers reached absurd proportions as women were reputedly forced to kneel on the floors of carriages or had to ride with their heads out of windows [2] to accommodate feathered coiffures.

A lady at court likened feather trim, upwards of a foot high on the head, to "a moving garden of bright-colored flowers, gently caressed by the zephyrs." [3] Satirists lampooned this foppery which

---

1. Augustin Challamel, *The History of Fashion in France: The Dress of Women from the Gallo-Roman Period to the Present Time* (London, 1882), p. 161.
2. Emile Langlade, *Rose Bertin: The Creator of Fashion at the Court of Marie-Antoinette* (London, 1913), pp. 48–49.
3. Challamel, *History of Fashion*, pp. 166–167. Julius M. Price, *Dame Fashion* (London, 1913), p. 4.

changed in type, texture, and color so frequently that courtesans grumbled about its expense and talked of ruination. James Gillray, noted London caricaturist, depicted smart ladies of the 1790's with cargoes of feathers three times as high as their heads seated in open sedan chairs. One anonymously written satire entitled "Feathers" derided English ladies who:

> Are not content with looking like a jay,
> But they must dress as lightly and as gay;
> Nay, ev'ry tail, of ev'ry bird they rob,
> And with the lightest feathers wing the nob;
> Like horses move in the funereal train
> Beneath their plumes, and shake the plaited mane.
> Now, since to ornament the frolic fair,
> There's not one pretty bird whose rump's not bare;
> Do not the ladies more or less appear,
> Just like the birds whose various plumes they wear? [4]

Although Marie Antoinette's tragic end rendered plumage unfashionable, feather trim never disappeared completely from French dress. It was revived and achieved notoriety in the last decades of the nineteenth century. The blaze of color and sea of plumes of Louis XVI's court never returned under the Empire, though Empress Eugénie in the late 1850's made an unsuccessful bid for a monopoly on fashion. By the beginning of the last century, however, feather wearing was a tradition at courts of Europe and among the well-to-do. In England and America, the demand for feathers increased from the late eighteenth century as more and more women were willing and able to follow styles suggested by actresses, fashion houses, and a proliferation of fashion magazines and home journals.[5]

The United States followed the styles of London and Paris. High-ranked officials in colonial Virginia sported flamboyant Cavalier hats trimmed with ostrich plumes. The genteel costume of

4. Louis Octave Uzanne, "Weapons and Ornaments of Women," *Cosmopolitan* 41 (1906): 405–414. See also *The Feathers, A Tale: or, Venus Surpassed by a Beauty in Grosvenor Square. Inscribed to a Certain Fair Plumed Dutchess* (London, 1775).

5. Edmond Lefèvre, *La Commerce et l'Industrie de la Plume pour Parure* (Paris, 1914) cites the following journals important in disseminating styles: 1768, *Journal de Goût;* 1785, *Cabinet des Modes;* 1796–1831, *Journal des Dames et des Modes;* 1799–1824, *Ladies Monthly Museum;* 1800–70, *La Vie Parisienne;* 1829–1834, *Lady's Magazine.*

the Carolinas contrasted with the sombre Puritan garb of the New England colonies, where all gaudy dress was forbidden under ecclesiastical law. In 1634, Massachusetts proscribed slashed sleeves, beaver hats and bands, ruffs, silks, and gold or silver thread. This legislation remained in effect late into the century, when Puritan merchants in New England (despite scoldings from the pulpit) began to wear tricorne hats with a cargo of plumes and ribbons.[6]

Despite prohibitions, some women appear to have worn feathers quite early in New England's history. William Morrell, a clergyman with a critical eye for the country, was sent to the Plymouth colony in the 1620's. He seems to have been the first to mention feathers used by ladies.

> The fowles that in those bays and harbours feede,
> Though in their seasons they doe else-where breede,
> Are swans and geese, herne, pheasants, duck and crane,
> Culvers and divers all along the maine:
> The turtle, eagle, partridge, and the quaile,
> Knot, plover, pigeons, which doe never faile,
> Till sommers heate commands them to retire,
> And winters cold begets their old desire.
> With these sweete dainties man is sweetly fed,
> With these rich feathers ladies plume their head,
> Here's flesh and feathers both for use and ease
> To feede, adorne, and rest thee, if thou please.[7]

After the Revolution the young Republic turned to France for fashionable styles. Marie Antoinette's whims were emulated in communities along the eastern seaboard. Benjamin Franklin seems to have had trouble in persuading his daughters to forego plumes which merchants' and bankers' ladies were donning, following French styles in all their trifles.

Ornamental plumage had been popular in Europe since the time of the Crusades. Earlier uses, however, drew upon relatively few kinds of birds compared with the scores of species employed

6. Edward Warwick, Henry C. Pitz and Alexander Wyckoff, *Early American Dress* (New York, 1965), pp. 70–89, 99–116. Elisabeth McClellan, *History of American Costume, 1607–1870*, new edition (New York, 1937), pp. 48, 75–80, 135 ff, and glossary, 617. A background to U.S. sumptuary laws is provided by Elizabeth B. Hurlock, *The Psychology of Dress: An Analysis of Fashion and its Motive* (New York, 1929), pp. 63–70.

7. " 'New England' in 'New England's Plantation'," *Collections of the Massachusetts Historical Society* I (1792): 126–39, quote p. 129.

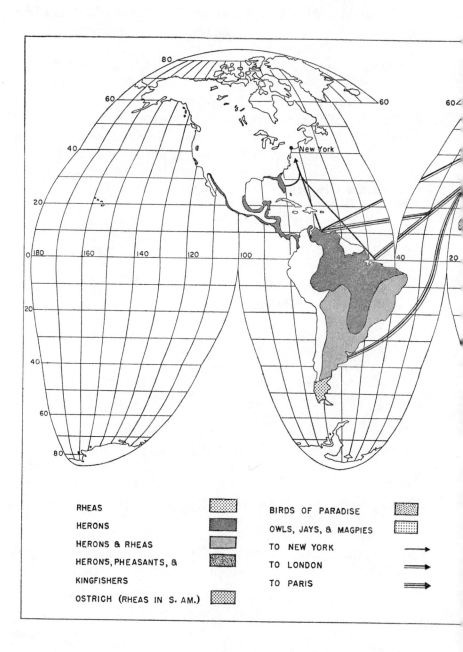

RHEAS

HERONS

HERONS & RHEAS

HERONS, PHEASANTS, &

KINGFISHERS

OSTRICH (RHEAS IN S. AM.)

BIRDS OF PARADISE

OWLS, JAYS, & MAGPIES

TO NEW YORK

TO LONDON

TO PARIS

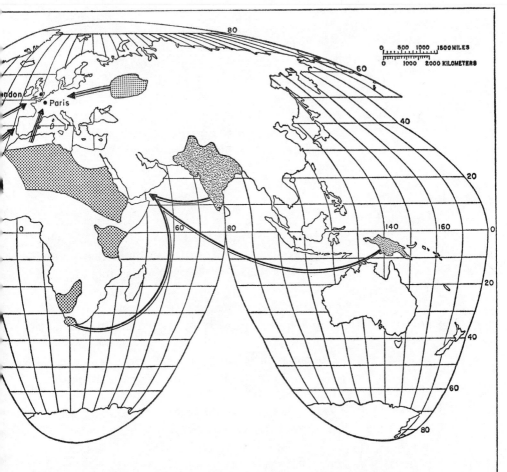

MAJOR SOURCE REGIONS OF PLUME BIRDS
IN THE LATE 19TH CENTURY

by nineteenth century milliners. Colorful, strangely shaped or patterned feathers were generally expensive because they were difficult to obtain from overseas. Little was known about the distribution and life histories of handsome birds of tropical regions which supplied many of them. In the case of the ostrich, attempts had not been made to produce abundant trim by taming or ranching birds. The rarity of certain plumes lent them especial value. For instance, on at least one occasion, Henry VIII wore feathers of "some Indian bird" each of which was four and one-half feet long and extremely expensive. But the quantities of plumage supplied to these earlier courts in Europe did not compare with the amounts which poured in from all continents to meet demands of the nineteenth century's fashion-conscious, middle-class, urban women.[8]

A limited number of birds were the mainstay of milliners during, but particularly before, the nineteenth century. The ostrich (*Struthio camelus*) was esteemed for its plumage by Romans and Greeks. Hunting scenes in remains of Roman villas include ostriches among game animals captured or killed. Dignitaries wore their feathers as head ornaments. Ostriches were occasionally used to pull Roman chariots and to provide public entertainment at circuses.[9]

After the collapse of the Roman Empire, information about the use of ostrich plumes in Western Europe is sporadic until the late Middle Ages. They appeared regularly on headgear in France in the fourteenth century, and robber barons are said to have seized them, so highly were they regarded. By the middle of the sixteenth century, elaborate use of feathers was relegated more to jousts and tourneys at which noblemen sported trains or excrescences of sumptuous plumage. White ostrich feathers from the wings of the male bird were most valued. They came from birds hunted in Northern Africa and reached Europe through Italy, notably Venice.

In his nine-volume work on the *Natural History of Birds* written in the 1770's, Georges-Louis Leclerc, later Comte de Buffon (1707–88), devoted considerable attention to ostriches:

---

8. John A. Repton, "Observations on the Various Fashions of Hats . . ." *Archaeologia* 24 (1832): 168–189.

9. Frederick E. Zeuner, *A History of Domesticated Animals* (New York, 1963), pp. 476–477. Julius De Mosenthal and James E. Harting, *Ostriches and Ostrich Farming* (London, 1877), pp. 13–15.

It is well known what prodigious consumption is made of them in Europe for hats, helmets, theatrical dresses, furniture canopies, funeral decorations and even for female ornaments; and, indeed, it must be allowed, that they have a fine effect, both from their natural and their artificial colours, and from their gentle waving motion.[10]

Ostrich farming began in the final decades of the nineteenth century in Cape Colony and North Africa, and spread to Australia, Europe and the United States. The ostrich and its flightless counterpart in South America, the rhea (Rheidae spp.), are important to the debate about artificially rearing birds for their plumage. The voluminous literature on this subject indicates that millinery interests suggested the setting aside of commercial ranching areas as an alternative to the ostrich's possible extinction.[11]

Peacocks (*Pavo* spp.) provided early and significant *plumes fantaisies,* as the French millinery trade called the feathers of birds other than the ostrich. Indian peafowls were known beyond their natural confines on the Asian subcontinent and Ceylon as much as 3,000 years ago. Phoenician traders carried them to Mesopotamia and to the Mediterranean; rulers in Asia Minor often kept them in parks and gardens. In Europe they were rare and extremely valuable until Alexander the Great made the peacock better known in the Mediterranean. Peacocks came to Greece from Persia, Media, and Babylonia and were kept as sacred birds in the Temple at Samos. The "eyes" on their tail feathers, seen to symbolize the stars in the heavens, made them favorites of Hera, the Goddess of the firmament.[12]

Hortensius, Cicero's contemporary, regaled guests with roast peacock, and fly swatters made from peacock tails became widespread throughout Italy. Victory Hehn, in his classic work on the diffusion of fauna and flora throughout the world, noted that

10. *Natural History, General and Particular,* translated by William Smellie, new edition (London, 1812), Vol. 11, p. 387.

11. An overview of ostrich farming in the United States is provided by Robin W. Doughty, "Ostrich Farming American Style," *Agricultural History* 47 (1973): 133–145. Elizabeth K. Mitchell. *The Ostrich and Ostrich Farming: A Bibliography* (Cape Town, 1960), has citations to all facets of rearing and to the sale of plumage.

12. Zeuner, *History of Domesticated Animals,* pp. 456–457. Victor Hehn, *The Wanderings of Plants and Animals from Their First Home,* James S. Stallybrass (ed.) (London, 1885), pp. 263–270, discussed the spread of peacocks in the Mediterranean basin. Jean Delacour, *The Pheasants of the World* (London, 1951), pp. 311–322 referred to the bird in classical literature.

European names for the peacock began not with the Greek '*t*' but the Latin '*p*', "a clear proof," he believed, "that the bird was introduced into barbaric Europe, not from Greece or the East, but from the Apennine peninsula." [13]

Charlemagne kept peacocks and pheasants on his estates, an example followed by the Normans in England. In decoration, however, the ostrich came to supplant the peacock, thereby relegating the peacock—a bird with "the plumage of an angel, step of a thief and voice of the devil"—to the pleasure garden and shrubbery, until Marie Antoinette brought its feathers back into vogue. It is suggested that people looked upon the bird with disfavor in the nineteenth century because of the ignominious and tragic end of its mistress, the French queen.[14]

Hehn painstakingly analyzed the etymology of various tamed and domesticated birds, among which was the common or ring-necked pheasant (*Phasianus colchicus*). Acclaimed as fine eating, it was bred and reared frequently in aviaries and parks in Roman Italy. The term "phasianus" refers to its home in western Asia from the Caspian lowlands to the foothills of the Caucasus (the Georgian Soviet Republic). Tradition holds that the Argonauts brought this exotic bird with spectacular plumage from the land of the Colchis, through which wound the River Rion (classically Phasis). The pheasant lived along its banks from whence it was carried to peninsular Greece.[15]

One authority on pheasants, Jean Delacour, recognizes 16 genera with 49 species. They belong to the subfamily Phasianinae, and are characterized by their large size and the specialized ornamental plumage of the males. Adapted alike to dank woodlands

13. Hehn, *Wanderings of Plants and Animals*, p. 266–267.

14. Alfred Newton, *A Dictionary of Birds* (London, 1893), p. 699, commented that the peacock "can hardly be accounted an inhabitant of the poultry-yard, but rather an ornamental denizen of the pleasure-ground or shubbery." Jules Forest, "Les Oiseaux dans l'Industrie à Travers les Ages," *Revue Scientifique* 35:2 (1898), pp. 174–175, mentioned that from the fourteenth century to the reign of Louis XVI sumptuary uses of peacock plumes were replaced by the ostrich, although several noble houses continued to bear them as heraldic devices. Idem, "Le Paon à Travers les Ages," *Bull. Soc. d'Acclimatation* 43 (1896): 337–344, outlined the Oriental use of peacock plumage and stated that the old name for plumassier was "chappellier de paons" or as Lefèvre (p. 219) stated, "paonniers." The profession was apparently introduced into France from Italy in the thirteenth century. The plumassiers formed a corporation approved by Henry III in the sixteenth century; also, see Pierre Larousse, *Grand Dictionnaire Universel du XIX Siècle* Vol. 12 (Paris, 1874), p. 1202.

15. Douglas Dewar, *Game Birds* (London, 1928), p. 45 ff.; Hehn, *Wanderings of Plants and Animals*, pp. 274–276; Zeuner, *History of Domesticated Animals*, p. 458.

and bleak plateaus up to 16,000 feet, pheasants became popular as game birds and were carried from their Asian domain into Western Europe and the United States. They are considered an easy species to transplant, more so than any other bird.[16]

Pheasants were incorporated into millinery work before, and especially after, the time of the plumage debate. Skins of eight different species were frequently confiscated by customs officials after the enactment of the British Plumage Bill in 1922 prohibited their importation into England. Both in England and America they were commonly made into hat ornaments and artificial fishing flies. From 1860–1900 the Société d'Acclimatation of France attempted with some success to introduce Chinese and Indian species to areas in France; and ornamental pheasant societies were founded in England, France, and the United States to raise birds for exhibition and commercial purposes.

Skins of the striking Impeyan Pheasant (*Lophophorus impejanus*), found from the Himalayas to Central China, sold for as much as $20 each on the London Market. During 1876, between 200 and 800 were auctioned every month in that city. The Impeyan Pheasant, although a hardy upland bird, proved difficult to raise in Western Europe. Another variety, the Reeves Pheasant (*Syrmaticus reevesii*), a native of the wooded uplands of north-central China, proved more amenable to transplantation and bred freely in England in the 1860's. Marco Polo mentioned this arresting bird with its central tail plumes reaching up to five feet in length. The unusual headdress of Henry VIII may possibly have been of this or a related species.[17]

Two other bird families deserve mention as important in ornament before the nineteenth century. They are the birds of paradise (Paradiseidae) and herons (Ardeidae). Magellan's circum-global expedition carried back bird-of-paradise skins to Europe in 1522. While in the Moluccas, two specimens of *Paradisea minor* were said to have been given to the crew for the King of Spain. In 1498, the Portuguese established a base at Goa and twenty years later had explored the Malay Archipelago, reaching New Guinea in 1512. It seems likely, therefore, that they knew of

16. *Pheasants of the World*, pp. 23–29.
17. Charles William Beebe, *A Monograph of the Pheasants*, 4 vols. (London, 1918), is a classic. Information about different species was derived from Vol. I, p. 111 ff., p. 134; Vol. 3, p. 143 ff. Seizures alluded to in England come from Customs House and RSPCA records.

the "Birds of the Sun" before Magellan's voyage. Belon, travelling in the Levant in 1546, described plumes worn by Janissaries in terms usually reserved for the birds of paradise. It appears possible that they were carried by caravan routes to the Middle East, before Portuguese incursions into the Indian Ocean.[18]

By 1600, numbers of *P. minor* and *apoda* entered Europe regularly. In the next century, Comte de Buffon described six separate species. Their plumage was admired for its dazzling colors and airy lightness. Four species became common in European and American ornament during the nineteenth century; and in the early twentieth century colonial governments appear to have exported more than 80,000 birds a year before World War I.[19]

Herons and egrets furnished upstanding tufts, or sprays, for use on military helmets and hat ornaments during the eighteenth and nineteenth centuries. The Ardeidae, consisting of 15 genera and 64 species (particularly 8 species belonging to the genus *Egretta*) became the focal point around which people rallied to end the use of wild birds' plumage by the millinery industry. The crown, upper breast, lower neck and dorsal region of various herons provided elongated lanceolate and aigrette plumes (which are long and narrow with barbs held together in the lanceolate plumes and become loose fine feathers with long barbs and degenerate barbicels in the aigrette plumes peculiar to the genus *Egretta*).

One large white bird sought by plume hunters was the white heron, or grande aigrette (*Casmerodius albus*) a species of wide distribution in both the Old and New Worlds. A subspecies, *Casmerodius albus egretta* known as the great (-common, or American) egret,* ranged from the United States to Patagonia. Belon (1555) gave the name "aigrette" to the herons, and the plumage trade applied the same name to the long delicate plumes taken from adult birds, particularly the large white heron, in the breeding season. These dorsal plumes were between 35 and 50 cm. long and consisted of thin and widely spaced first order barbs

* Nomenclature follows the American Ornithologists' Union, *Checklist* . . . Fifth edition, 1957, with revisions of 1973.

18. E. Thomas Gilliard, *Birds of Paradise and Bower Birds* (London, 1969), pp. 15–20, 21, 216, 231. Gilliard provided an extensive bibliography and based much of his historical material upon E. Stresemann, "Die Entdeckungsgeschichte der Paradiesvögel," *Journal für Ornithologie* 95 (1954), pp. 263–291. See also Newton, *Dictionary of Birds*, pp. 37–40, who drew Belon's remarks from *Observations de plusieurs singularitez etc.* III, Chap. 25.

19. Gilliard, *Birds of Paradise*, p. 30.

(rami) attached to the shafts or rachis. They are without second order barbs (radii), or barbules, that help hold the vane together. The resulting plume has a texture as soft as silk, is flexible, yet able to keep its stiffness.[20] There were several qualities of "long whites" or "longues" as they were called by the trade. The best were 40 to 50 cm. long, of a shining whiteness, and had long unblemished barbs with full unworn tips. However, a high fraction of aigrettes came from Latin America and Eurasia and were actually inferior quality feathers which were passed off under different guises.[21]

A small white or little egret (*Egretta garzetta*) from southern Europe, south and central Asia, parts of Africa, Japan and China, has a New World counterpart *Egretta thula* called the snowy egret, of which two subspecies have been recognized in the United States. These diminutive white egrets bear exquisitely recurved dorsal breeding plumes supplying the trade with valuable "crosse" aigrettes. The name reportedly came from the curved nature of the 12-to-20-cm.-long webs, which swept up from the back of the bird.

Alexander Wilson, pioneer of American ornithology, described the ornamental sprays of the snowy egret as:

> Long silky plumes, proceeding from the shoulders, covering the whole back, and extending beyond the tail, the shafts of these are six or seven inches long, extremely elastic, tapering to the extremities, and thinly set with long slender bending threads or fibres, easily agitated by the slightest motion of the air; these shafts curl upwards at the ends. When the bird is irritated, and erects these airy plumes, they have a very elegant appearance.[22]

Each egret was said to yield 40 to 60 plumes suitable for ornament. The best quality feathers came from Mexico, Central America and northern South America. These birds had longer and shorter crosse plumes, and some provided "fausse crosse," a

20. Newton, *Dictionary of Birds*, p. 192, f.n.; A. A. Voitkevich, *The Feathers and Plumage of Birds* (New York, 1966), pp. 5–8 and fig. 1.

21. The brilliance of aigrettes was emphasized by Alfred E. Brehm, *Bird Life: Being a History of the Birds, its Structure and Habits* (London, 1874), "These feathers are manufactured into plumes, worn by the Hungarian magnates, and by their splendidly-dressed soldiery in their schakos. . . . Ostrich feathers look heavy and—however pure and clean they may be—dirty in comparison with those of the White Heron," pp. 796–797.

22. *American Ornithology: or, the Natural History of the Birds of the United States* (Philadelphia, 1808–14), Vol. 7 (1813), p. 122.

set of plumes which failed to curve sharply into a cross-like position and were correspondingly cheaper to purchase.[23]

Jules Forest, a prolific writer on the plumage industry and an avid supporter of attempts to breed wild birds, including herons, in captivity, maintained that aigrettes fell under sumptuary legislation in France. He furnished few details to support his assertion, but information from other sources suggested that heron feathers were symbols of authority among eastern potentates. Returning Crusaders reportedly carried them back to Europe as spoils of war. They were worn on knights' helmets and later set in jeweled clasps or brooches on the headdress of courtly ladies.[24] Buffon provided interesting information about the use of aigrettes in France:

> Belon is the first who gave the name of *Aigrette* (tuft) to this small species (Little Egret) of white heron, and probably because of the long silky feathers on its back; these being employed to decorate the lady's head-dress, the warrior's helmet, and the sultan's turban. They were in great request formerly in France, when our doughty champions wore plumes. At present, they serve for a gentler use; they deck the heads of our beauties, and raise their stature: the flexibility, the softness, and the lightness of these feathers, bestow grace on their motions.[25]

French military officers sported aigrettes late into the nineteenth century; and in England, Queen Victoria confirmed an order issued for the discontinuance of the wearing of "osprey" plumes, as they were called. This order of 1899 replaced the aigrettes with ostrich plumes in the British Army, after consideration of a statement furnished to Lord Wolsely by protectionist groups, notably the Society for the Protection of Birds (SPB). In the nineteenth century, prizes were offered for successfully raising herons in captivity, along guide lines developed for the ostrich.

23. Jules Forest, "Les Herons—Aigrettes," *Revue des Sciences Naturelles Appliquées* 40 (1893): 201–208, 256–267, covered the trade preferences for and geographical distributions of white herons. Lefèvre, *L'Industrie de la Plume,* pp. 159–165, dealt specifically with the aigrette garzette (*Egretta garzetta*). Other pertinent remarks can be found in articles by A. Menegaux and by Jules Forest (see Bibliography).

24. Forest, "Les Oiseaux dans l'Industrie," p. 175; and Lefèvre, *L'Industrie de la Plume,* p. 7. Plumed headdresses are illustrated in R. Turner Wilcox, *The Mode in Hats and Headdress* (New York, 1945), pp. 59, 61.

25. *Natural History of Birds,* Vol. 7, pp. 373–374 (or *Nat. Hist.* 18, pp. 373–374).

A polemic ensued about the methods used to collect heron plumes and about the ways they were treated and prepared for millinery.

Man has worn the plumage of birds for a very long time. What is novel about feather fashions at the beginning of this century is the prolonged and considerable comment the harvesting of birds evoked. Never before had opposition to feather wearing been so organized, vehement, or widespread. Never before had it even been deemed important enough to merit more than passing attention. The sentiments it aroused and movements it sparked off are with us today. The following chapters describe and seek to understand the development of the plumage dispute, set in the context of trends in nineteenth-century fashion. They will relate an incipient bird protection movement to new and revamped ideas about nature and man's relation to his environment.

1

Feather Wearing and Bird Protection in the Nineteenth Century

Birds' feathers had been worn frequently as hat and bonnet trimmings by ladies of status in Western Europe before the nineteenth century. As the Victorian century progressed, however, women of more moderate means, following the suggestions of *modistes,* who had customarily catered to a clientele of aristocrats and courtesans, adopted avian trim. Paul Nystrom, an expert on women's fashions, recalled that, "In almost every ten-year period throughout the century, large additional groups of people were able to expand their standards of living beyond bare subsistence levels. . . ."[1] Expectations of middle class ladies, especially towards the end of the century, included fine clothing and stylish accessories. Bird plumage contributed interesting colors, fascinating shapes and assemblages to dress hats at garden parties, and proved attractive trimmings on fans, gowns, capes, parasols and muffs at theatres, bazars, and elegant gatherings.

Journals such as *Graham's Lady's and Gentleman's Magazine* (1826–1858), *Godey's Lady's Book and Magazine* (1830–1898), *Peterson's Magazine* (1842–1898), the *Delineator* (1873–1937), and *Harper's Bazar* (1867), did much to stimulate a popular interest in dress and accessories, and anticipated seasonal changes in outdoor and indoor wear.[2]

1. *Economics of Fashion* (New York, 1928), pp. 224–303, quote p. 229.
2. Theodore B. Peterson, *Magazines in the Twentieth Century,* 2nd edition (Urbana, 1964), pp. 2–6, states that the era of modern national magazines began about 1880. The 700 periodicals existing in the United States in 1865 had grown to some 3,300 by 1885. Growth was stimulated by low-cost mailing privileges. The

Ladies' journals multiplied in kind and in circulation as the century progressed. By the 1880's half a dozen periodicals entered hundreds of thousands of homes across America. The *Delineator*, for example, tripled its circulation during the decade before 1885, when its publishers claimed 80,000 readers; by 1892 it had nearly half a million subscribers and was one of the most popular fashion journals in the country.[3] Before the Civil War, 100,000 people received *Godey's Lady's Book*, a strongly sentimental, biographical and fashion-conscious magazine which was merged with *Argosy* in the 1890's. Other publications appeared later in the century; these included *McCalls* (1870), *The Ladies' Home Journal* (1883), *Good Housekeeping* (1885) and *Vogue* (1892). Most of them reported styles in clothing and ornament (including feathers) from the fashion centers of London, New York and Paris.[4]

The desire to be fashionable led scores of thousands of women to milliners for something eye-catching and elegant. If plumes were costly looking, then ladies demanded them by the crateload, and the elegant trimmings pictured regularly in journals meant that bird populations all over the world fell under the gun. The unprecedented abundance of ornamental plumage, the range of birds which supplied it, created a spectre of suffering and extinction over the breeding grounds of many species. After the middle of the nineteenth century, the sight of stuffed seabirds, finches' wings and waving sprays on hats touched the consciences of people, and sore consciences helped create the movement to banish the use of ornamental feathers. The cavalier manner in which birds were sacrificed on the altar of vanity began to arouse feelings of disgust and outrage, not admiration.

---

use of the rotary press in the '80's helped produce fine quality copy quickly and abundantly.

    Graham's Magazine was one of the first journals in the United States to use fashion plates, and had achieved a circulation of 40,000 by 1842. *Godey's* became a landmark with more than 100,000 copies printed regularly before the Civil War. See also James P. Wood, *Magazines in the United States: Their Social and Economic Influence,* 2nd edition (New York, 1956), pp. 53–54, passim.

    3. Frank L. Mott, *A History of American Magazines,* 5 vols. (Cambridge, Massachusetts, 1938–1968) 3: 481–490.

    4. *Ladies Home Journal* was a monthly with a circulation of close to one million in 1900. When Edward W. Bok took over editorship of the magazine in 1889 he broadened its appeal and included statements against killing birds for hat decorations. See Peterson, *Magazines in Twentieth Century,* pp. 6, 11–12.

Plumage in Nineteenth-Century Fashions

Many authorities on fashion have described the changing styles in women's clothing decade by decade through the last century; others have talked about cycles of fashion, which make changes in clothing predictable. Cecil Willet Cunnington, for example, was attentive to feminine dress in England and contrasted the "Romantic" 1830's with the "Revolting" 1860's. He believed that the sentimental and illusory quality of dress in the first period clashed with the exhibitionism of the second; both traits served, however, to attract men's attentions during the century.[5]

With sentiment, exhibitionism, or a confusion of both prevailing, women donned feather trimmings in every decade of the last century, particularly after 1850. In this later period, every hat worn on the street could almost be counted upon to boast a pair of wings. Inspired by Roman mythology, these "Mercury wings," of doves, blackbirds, swallows and seabirds were regarded as coquettish and attractive when placed jauntily on the side of the head. Ostrich feathers, heron and bird of paradise sprays were commonly used. In the 1880's and 1890's, women's hats bore owls' heads with blank staring eyes, small birds in attitudes of "earnest incubation," and hummingbirds perched on artificial flowers.

In 1886, on two late afternoon excursions through uptown shopping areas of New York, Frank Chapman (1864–1945), ornithologist and bird preservationist, noted that three-quarters of the 700 women's hats he counted displayed feathers. The feathers came from 40 different kinds of native birds, including sparrows, warblers and flycatchers. Chapman said, however, that in many instances bird identification was made impossible due to mutilation.[6] In Paris, at about the same time, dresses were edged with swallows' wings, downy tufts of marabou and glossy-smooth grebe skins. In London, one fashionable lady was observed in a gown hemmed with the heads of finches, and, unpardonable sin, the plumage of the robin redbreast.[7] Cunnington believed that the

5. *Feminine Attitudes in the Nineteenth Century* (New York, 1936), p. 2 ff; idem, *English Women's Clothing in the Nineteeth Century* (London, 1937), pp. 95, 169, 254, passim. A recent discussion of cycles in fashion is made by Marilyn J. Horn, *The Second Skin: An Interdisciplinary Study of Clothing* (Boston, 1968), pp. 222–229.

6. "Birds and Bonnets" (Letter to the Editor), *Forest and Stream* 26 (25 February, 1886): 84.

7. See *Harper's Bazar* 26:38 (September, 1893), p. 775. Comments from various newspapers include: "A large hat, which will appeal to the sympathies of bird

passion for bird and animal decorations in the 1880's reflected sadistic cravings that "seemed to take the place of those flagellations and funeral-orgies of the past." [8] He suggested the trend had sexual origins.

In the latter years of the nineteenth century the idealized female silhouette shifted attention away from the fullness of the lower body (exemplified by the crinoline and bustle) to the upper body, neck and head. Feathers upon enlarged hats and bonnets lent height to upper features and provided dignity and elegance. They were also necessary to soften and fill out body and dress contours and to highlight the face. Through an infinite variety of color and shape, plumage conveyed a novel attractiveness and individuality to head wear.[9]

In fact, the excesses of the 1890's represented the culmination of a long trend in fashion. The French Revolution had ushered in an era of simplicity and comparative austerity in dress which played down feather trim. After the downfall of Marie Antoinette, the 24 feather-dressers and plumage-mounters in Paris fell upon hard times in the trend to neoclassical dress. A turn to Romanticism however, and the Restoration of the French monarchy revived the more extravagant costumes in elite circles.[10] As more people began to follow Dame Fashion's dictates, and when hat sizes began mushrooming in the 1820's, women increased the demand for feathers. At that time, ostrich material was fashionable but expensive; as late as 1869, high quality plumes in New York sold for between $4.50 and $9.00 each, more costly than other feather ornaments.[11]

The best ostrich stuff, said to be pulled from birds hunted in North Africa, entered Europe through the ports of Livorno and

---

lovers, is massed with blush roses . . . on one side of the hat is a bird, also of the same soft pink color. He is partially lying on his side . . . and has an appealing expression" (*New York Times*, 18 April, 1897 p. 14, col. 3). A satirical editorial in the *Independent* 58 (1905): 190–192, lampooned the fad: "women, birds and butterflies belonged originally to the same species. . . ." Little girls liked plumes on their hats, a form of "nuptial flight," revealing ambitions but ignorance about style!

8. *Feminine Attitudes*, pp. 250–251.

9. Anne Buck, *Victorian Costume and Costume Accessories* (London, 1961), p. 120, commented about the various ways feather trim was used: "In the second half of the 1870's, and in the 1880's, whole birds as well as parts of birds were used for the trimming of bonnets. Feathers were much used in the millinery of the 1880's, not only as trimmings but also as the fabric of the whole hat, particularly in the toque forms."

10. Augustin Challamel, *History of Fashion*, p. 177.

11. *Harper's Bazar* 11:41 (October, 1869) p. 643.

Marseilles. In 1807, an estimated 509 kilos were imported into France,[12] where 30 years before, Comte de Buffon had reported a high demand for the plumes of this "winged camel of the desert." Before the mid-1860's, when ostrich farming began to be practiced in Cape Colony, the feathers of this bird were esteemed as much for their relative scarcity and expense as for their beauty. This plumage could be cleansed and colored easily, and hundreds of thousands of pounds of ostrich plumes came annually into Europe and into North America in the 1880's. Ostrich feathers remained popular despite a slump in South African farm trade in the early 1890's, and complaints from some manufacturers that Cape plumage was rather poor in quality.[13] The Boer War (1899–1902) served to turn attention to other species when shipments from the Cape of Good Hope became unpredictable.

Shortly after Queen Victoria's accession to the English throne in 1837, bird of paradise and egret "ospreys" became popular. In the 1850's, bonnets opened more at the brim, and a little later, young ladies took to wearing larger hats. Both developments occasioned a more liberal use of ornamental feathers. By 1875, English headgear carried entire birds, often placed in striking poses. In the eclectic tastes of the period it was a customary belief that no lady's toilet was complete without a fan of marabou, peafowl, pheasant or pigeon plumage mounted often upon a tortoiseshell handle.[14]

12. Magnien and Deu, *Dictionnaire des Productions de la Nature et de l'Art.* . . . 2 vols. (Paris, 1809), 2:1 p. 388.

13. The *American Textile Manufacturer*, commonly called the *Textile Colorist*, was a monthly trade journal devoted to the practical aspects of texile making. It began publication in 1875 and its first volume (number 12) contained remarks about ostrich feather dyeing. Many other articles devoted to feather coloration over the years were derived from German magazines; one published in 1880 states that the finest ostrich plumes came from Egypt and the poorest from new farms established in South Africa. In 1912, the Union Government imported North African ostriches (*Struthio c. camelus*) into Cape Colony to improve the quality of the Cape product through selective breeding. From 1860 to 1910 efforts had been made to improve South African feathers. After a promising start, the bottom dropped out of the ostrich feather market (beginning in 1914) and research was curtailed. South African farms never recovered from the trade set-backs due to the First World War and changes of fashion. Peak exports of over one million pounds weight valued at three million pounds sterling in 1913 were never repeated, but plummetted to one-tenth of that weight by 1918. See South Africa, *Department of Agriculture,* "Breeding Experiments with North African and South African Ostriches," *Bulletin* no. 3 (1919).

14. Anne Buck, *Victorian Costume*, pp. 166–167, 177–178, 181. Lucy Barton, *Historic Costume for the Stage* (Boston, 1935), p. 471, has traced a similar demand for feathers in later Victorian times: "There was, among milliners, a growing

An article appearing in *Chambers's Journal* in 1863 noted that "humbler" plumage, suitable for bed stuffing, was plucked from geese (live-plucking incensed members of humane groups), or obtained from poultry, eider ducks, and the "sooty petrel, found in great numbers near Bass's strait, in Australia." Quills for writing (the cleaning of which was a secret reportedly known only to the Dutch) were made from goose wing-feathers and from "crows." [15] The *Chambers's Journal* article reminded readers that most treasured for decorative purposes were:

> The long plumes from the wings and tail of the Ostrich. The best are imported from Algiers; they also come from Tunis, Alexandria, Madagascar, and Senegal. On the continent, the feathers of the emu are favorites; as well as those of the ibis, bird of paradise, marabout, peacock, pheasant, plotus, vulture, eagle, swan, turkey, and heron. Some feathers are very costly; the heron plumes which the Knights of the Garter wear cost from fifty to one hundred guineas, owing to their scarcity. The hussars wear the large feathers of the egret. The Chinese mandarins mount the peacock's plume. (P. 128)

The article named twelve birds employed in ornament; however, a generation later this represented only a fraction of the number of different birds used by millinery firms in Europe and in North America.

Table 1 gives an indication of the ways in which birds and their feathers were worn in the United States in the late nineteenth century. Editors of New York fashion columns in *Harper's Bazar* [16] paid close attention to feathers. Plumage was most prominent in autumn styles and upon bonnets and round hats imported from France.

---

interest in ornithology. In 1869, for instance, one *artiste* turned out a confection of black lace with a 'bird's nest of golden-hued moss on the forehead, with three tiny pearly eggs in it', and another creation adorned with both beetles and a humming-bird. Aigrettes as well as Ostrich plumes were much in demand, and as the eighties advanced wings and breasts of bright woodland songsters, and finally complete birds."

15. An article entitled "Feathers—Their Nature and Uses," *Penny Magazine* 10 (1841): 357–358, 363–364, had noted earlier that swan and crow quills made fine pens.

16. The journal was "designed to be a Family Journal, in the true sense of the word . . ." with a concern for the household circle and advance news in fashion. *Harper's* New York staff arranged to have electrotypes and fashion proofs of *Der Bazar* (Berlin) shipped over to America. After a profitable start in 1867, the magazine remained a weekly until 1901 when it began losing money. The extra "a" in Bazar was added in 1929. See Peterson, *Magazines*, pp. 218–220.

TABLE 1
Feather Millinery Reported in Harper's Bazar, 1875–1900

		Millinery in New York	Birds
1875	Fall	Birds and small wings, bandeaus and sprays on imported French hats.	Hummingbirds, pigeons; wings of larks, blackbirds and starlings; sprays of birds of paradise and "bronze" species.
1878	Winter	White trim on bonnets.	Marabou.
	Summer	Heads and wings as wall hangings.	Peafowl and white pigeons.
	Fall	Colored novelties for headwear.	Tanagers and orioles.
1881	Winter	Breasts on bonnets and dresses; small bonnets entirely of feathers, and feather collars for street wear.	Grebes, pheasants and "small stuffed" types.
	Spring	Grey birds on medium poke bonnets, feathers on large flared round hats.	Doves with other grey colored species and ostrich plumes.
	Summer	Aigrettes, long colored plumes and pompons.	Herons and ostriches.
	Fall	A profusion of feathers, especially breasts, wings, and parts on turbans, large round hats and upon the sides of bonnets.	Fourteen types named, including scarlet ibis, kingfishers, paroquets, hummingbirds and the impeyan pheasant.
1884	Winter	Feather fans, nodding plumes for younger girls; and sealskin hats with feather borders, wings, heads, and breasts.	Ostriches, pheasants and hummingbirds.
	Spring	Aigrettes on small dress bonnets.	Herons, marabou and hummingbirds.

TABLE 1 *(continued)*
Feather Millinery Reported in Harper's Bazar, 1875–1900

		Millinery in New York	*Birds*
	Fall	Dresses bordered with smooth soft feathers and birds' heads. All imported bonnets carry feathers for a "wind blown" effect while aigrettes lend height to some.	Ostriches, partridges, guinea fowl and usual species.
1887	Spring	Some breasts and wings added to ribbon trim; algrettes.	Ostriches and herons.
	Fall	Feather revival on close fitting bonnets and round hats; tails and quills.	Domestic fowl, pheasants and parrots.
1890	Winter	Novelty capes of coqs' plumes tasseled with bits of plumage.	Domestic fowl.
	Spring	Feathers on large round hats with short aigrette trim and cavalier plumes.	Ostriches and herons.
	Fall	"Hats will be feather-laden all winter. . . ." Prince of Wales plumes and neck ruches.	Ostriches, swallows, blackbirds, and owls' heads.
1893	Spring	"Mercury wings and Mephisto aigrettes appear larger and more exaggerated than those of last year. . . ."	
	Fall	"Valkyrie" effect of mercury wings *in extremis.* Dinner gown of black duchesse "bordered with tiny swallows with outspread wings."	Parrots, ducks' breasts of yellows, greens, blues.

TABLE 1 (*continued*)
Feather Millinery Reported in Harper's Bazar, 1875–1900

		Millinery in New York	Birds
1896	Winter	Grebe skins with furs and feather turbans, wings, tails, and quills.	Grebes, parrots, and ostriches.
	Spring	Bonnets dazzling in feathers and flowers; aigrettes.	Herons and others.
	Summer	Lavish use of feathers, wings and plumes.	Peafowl, "dark" birds, birds of paradise.
1899	Summer	Fad for whole birds on walking hats; wings, feathers on golf hats and horse-show costumes.	Pigeons, ostriches and many others.
	Fall	Feather heaped windows.	Seabirds and grebes.

Spectacular effects and varied colors were obtained by combining whole birds and different feathers with other ornaments. White terns on winter bonnets in early 1878, for instance, changed to browns and russets in fall fashions of that year. Milliners anticipated motley browns and ragged effects in 1884; *Harper's* suggested that lady readers should re-arrange old bird pieces, in positions that today appear grotesque, to suggest the "unkempt" look. Parrots' wings and tails supplied surprising blues and greens in 1893 and in the same decade owls' heads became popular. Feathers provided strong colors and robust decorations for ready-to-wear street hats. Less durable dress hats displayed fragile goura sprays, tiny wings and soft marabou aigrettes and pompons. Upstanding aigrettes added height and bearing to the lady wearing them; sweeping ostrich plumes were graceful and could be flamboyant; nodding plumes on young ladies suggested a hint of mischief.

In 1896 *Harper's Bazar* expressed an unusual concern for bird preservation in reporting New York fashions. It said:

> Feathers and plumes still wave from edifices which women wear on their heads, and it really seems as though it were time a

crusade were organized against this lavish use of feathers, for some of the rarest and most valuable species . . . will soon be exterminated if the present craze continue.[17]

The magazine continued to keep readers abreast of continental and domestic fashions with feathers until well after the turn of the century.

The Feather Trade: Some Facts and Figures

After the 1880's the fad for ornamental plumage caused a proliferation of establishments engaged in dealing in plumage and in manufacturing feather ornaments, and led to the development of new techniques of treatment both at home and abroad. In 1888 Alexander Paul, a feather dyer, published *The Practical Ostrich Feather Dyer* (Philadelphia) which he claimed was the first book of its kind in the English language. According to Paul, until 1875 feather coloration had been an art confined largely to France. His book described twelve recommended dyestuffs, and provided information about every step in producing resistant, uniform and bold colors in feathers. All plumage needed cleansing; after being sorted and looped on threads, bundles of feathers were soaked in a soap solution, rinsed, bleached, starched, beaten and then dyed. Different feathers were treated in different ways according to their intended uses.[18] Thirty years after the appearance of Paul's book, feather coloration remained largely in the hands of professionals. The *Textile Colorist,* a monthly founded in Philadelphia in 1879, kept dyers abreast of the latest techniques of cleansing and dyeing plumage, especially of ostrich material.

In 1900 headwear for women and children was a handicraft industry dependent upon supplies from importers and wholesale distributors. Approximately 83,000 people, mostly women, were employed in the United States in making and decorating hats, mostly by firms located in New York City.[19]

17. 29 (February, 1896): 663.
18. Feather dyeing was treated in detail by Charles B. Pellow, *Dyes and Dyeing* (New York, 1918) especially pp. 131–140. Lefèvre, *L'Industrie de la Plume,* provided a fascinating account of methods of feather treatment, pp. 237 ff., 265–301.
19. Details of the New York millinery trade of the period can be found in Mary Van Kleeck, *A Seasonal Industry: A Study of the Millinery Trade in New York* (New York, 1917). She admitted that it had "whimsical irregularities," and working conditions were often poor and seasonal. The increasing use of automobiles compelled wearing of close fitting bonnets and simple millinery which was unprofitable to trimmers. Two seasons were most marked; one from Easter to Independence Day, and the other from Labor Day to Thanksgiving. Employment statistics appear

Designing and trimming womens' headwear was a skilled operation requiring experience, a strong aesthetic sense and a good
eye. As a standard hat trimming, bird plumage could be worked
into eight basic forms, excluding mounted birds. The plumes of
ostriches, herons, birds of paradise, goura pigeons, egrets and "vultures" could be made into aigrettes. Pads and bands came from a
number of birds including barnyard fowl, pheasants, parrots and
pigeons; wings, breasts, pompons and quills were supplied by a
host of species, particularly gaily-colored ones.[20]

American buyers visited Europe regularly to meet with middlemen. As agents, these men sent advance word to local brokers to
have samples of plumage ready for inspection. A story from *The
Millinery Trade Review* recounted that in Paris at the turn of the
present century one could often see men peddling bicycles along
the city's narrow streets with enormous collections of boxes
strapped to their backs. Every now and then a driver would dis-
mount and dart into an off-street doorway. His boxes or "cuvettes"
contained samples of feathers and artificial flowers to set before
prospective foreign buyers. Middlemen oversaw the transactions,
becoming guarantors to Parisian brokers, facilitating the exchange
of foreign currency, and checking each buyer's credentials.[21] In
England, drawing an analogy from the hide and skin trade, ship-
pers and overseas agents cabled details of impending shipments to
brokerage firms in London where dealers were in touch with
millinery agents who anticipated styles for each season.[22]

Set forth in tables 2 and 3 are statistics on plumage imported
into the United Kingdom and into the United States during the
craze for feathers. It is not possible to compare them with runs
on gulls' trim, birds of paradise, or herons which fashion magazines talked about from season to season. At best, these statistics
distinguish between ostrich and other ornamental plumage, and
supply little information about the other kinds of birds shipped
from country to country. Moreover, plumage categories changed
at times, making meaningful figures difficult to compile.

---

in Lorinda Perry, *The Millinery Trade in Boston and Philadelphia* (New York,
1916), pp. 5–7.

20. See Charlotte R. Aiken, *Millinery* (New York, 1922), table, p. 74; and Anna
Ben Yusuf, *The Art of Millinery* (New York, 1909), pp. 177–188.

21. "The Drummers in Flowers and Feathers," 25:1 (January, 1900), 111–112.

22. Cuthbert Maughan, *Markets of London* (London, 1931), pp. 86–87. A recent
sketch of the London feather market was given by J. Penry-Jones, "Feathers," *Port
of London Authority Monthly*, 33 (April, 1958), 91–94.

Subject to vagaries of supply and demand, United States' imports of feathers were customarily expressed in dollar values, whereas British statistics appeared in weight and monetary value. Comparisons between the two countries are difficult to make due to a discrepancy in import categories. Total figures cannot be given even for feathers entering America, as one heading combines some feathers with other millinery items. England's statistics are easier to follow and are tabulated mostly in poundage weight (table 2).

Imports of ornamental plumage into the United Kingdom increased steadily until the First World War. Shipments of ornamental feathers from France grew from 250,000 pounds annually in the 1880's to 360,000 pounds in the 1890's and topped 500,000 pounds between 1900 and 1910. However, imports from the same country plummeted from a record 2.2 million pounds in 1913 to less than one-tenth that amount in 1920. A special Anglo-French agreement permitted imports of some ornamental plumage to continue during the War, which terminated all plume shipments from Germany and Austria-Hungary, both major exporting regions.

Subtracting South African exports of ostrich material from import figures, nearly 40 million pounds (or 20,000 tons) of ornamental plumage was carried into the United Kingdom between 1870 and 1920. This figure is less than half the quantity (over 50,000 tons) that T. Gilbert Pearson, energetic conservationist, discovered entering France between 1890 and 1930.[23] His total, however, possibly included imports of ostrich plumage, which are omitted from this overall British figure. Both estimates represent scores of millions of birds killed all over the world.

United States' imports, expressed ordinarily in dollar values prior to 1920, were divided into three categories: "crude," "dressed" and "artificial" feathers and downs. In the 1860's, ornamental feathers were lumped with artificial flowers and other items not necessarily made of feathers. After 1913, feathers "suitable for millinery ornaments" were combined with manufactured flowers and fruits; both listings cloud actual values of ornamental feather imports. After the 1870's, duties levied on crude feathers were generally lower than those on dressed and finished materials. Thus, in the first decade of the century, it appeared that most

23. *Adventures in Bird Protection* (New York, 1937), p. 272.

TABLE 2
Imports of Feathers into the United Kingdom

Decade	Types	Major source regions (in thousands of lbs.)		Total imports (in thousands)
1872–1880	Ornamental feathers and downs, including ostriches	Cape Colony farms India		2,444 lbs. 7,471 £
1881–1890	(as above)	Cape Colony (1885 + mainly ostrich India [a] France (1885 +) Holland (1885 +	 1,197 455 1,547 693	 6,746 lbs. 13,837 £
1891–1900	(as above)	Cape Colony (mainly ostrich) British E. Indies France Holland United States Latin America [b]	 3,162 1,044 3,619 1,687 481 81	 10,732 lbs. 11,692 £
1901–1910	(as above)	Cape Colony (mainly ostrich) Brit. E. Indies France Holland [c] United States Egypt Venezuela	 5,175 202 4,903 1,416 314 175 36	 14,362 lbs. 19,923 £
1911–1920	(as above, excluding ostrich after 1912)	France	3,833	 7,397 lbs. 9,376 £

TABLE 2 *(continued)*
Imports of Feathers into the United Kingdom

Decade	Types	Major source regions *(in thousands of lbs.)*	Total imports *(in thousands)*
1921–1930	Ornamental undressed feathers, ex- excluding ostrich		193 lbs. 81 £

SOURCE: U.K., Board of Trade, *Statistical Abstract* 1876–1890 (London, 1891) and Customs Stat. Office, *Annual Statement of the Trade . . . with Foreign Countries . . .* (London, 1889, etc.).

a Figures incomplete after 1885, see P. L. Simmonds, *Journ. Soc. Arts* (1885), p. 849.

b Includes incomplete statistics from Brazil, Colombia, Venezuela and Argentina.

c 1906 statistics are inconsistent with imports from Germany suddenly increasing to over 250,000 lbs. annually, while others from Netherlands show dramatic declines.

ostrich plumage came into the country in a crude state to be worked up by domestic firms. For that reason and partly to avoid possible confusion with feathers for bedding, table 3 is directed only to such obvious millinery items as processed plumage and finished birds shipped mainly from the United Kingdom, Germany and France.

Paris was an important source for British and American ornamental plumage and was the center for processing and finishing feather millinery. The city drew much of its raw material from other regions of France, the colonies and from areas in Eastern and Southern Europe. Paris and London supplied the bulk of both treated and untreated feather millinery imported into the United States. For some years after 1902, crude feathers valued at over $2 million were shipped annually into America. By 1907, they had doubled in value; and by 1910 over $7 million worth of birds' skins and plumage, other than ostrich, were listed in statistics of national commerce. Fractional values of ornamental material came directly from such places at China, Mexico, Brazil, and Argentina.

TABLE 3
Imports of Feathers into the United States

Decade	Types	Source region (values in $1,000)		Total (in $1,000)
1872–1880	Ornamental dressed feathers			1,018 [a]
1881–1890	Ornamental dressed feathers, colored or manufactured			
	Ostrich	(1884 +)	290	
	Other	(1884 +)	2,453	
				3,073
1891–1900	(as above)	France (1893 +)	3,341	
		U.K. (1893 +)	925	
		Germany (1893 +)	616	
		Mexico (1893 +)	101	
				6,079 [b]
1901–1910	(as above)	France	7,930	
		U.K.	149	
		Germany	2,588	
				10,896
1911–1920	As above, however categories changed in 1914 to Feathers for millinery ornaments incl. artificial flowers, fruits, etc.			
				20,819 [c]

SOURCE: U.S. Bureau of Statistics, Dept. of Commerce and Labor, *The Foreign Commerce and Navigation of the U.S.* (Washington, D.C., 1870, etc.).

[a] During this period, crude feathers, paying only 25% duty (compared with 50% for dressed material) increased in value from $545,000 in 1872 to $1,357,000 in 1880.

[b] Imports from France in 1896 were valued at $758,000 and 472,000 lbs. of plumage left the U.S. for Germany in more than one million pounds of crude and prepared feather exports. Most material was shipped through New York, Baltimore and Boston.

[c] Statistics include birds exempted under 1913 Tariff regulations. Dressed feathers dropped sharply from $820,000 in 1914 to $56,000 in 1920. Crude feathers other than Ostrich fell from $7.0 million to $1.5 million between 1910 and 1920.

Nineteen thirteen was an important year for imports of feathers into the United States. Congressional restrictions upon certain plumage millinery took effect in October, 1913, but not before over $6 million worth of raw ostrich feathers and $2 million worth of other birds' plumage had been imported. Additional amounts of dressed material, mainly from France, amounted to $1.7 million and other feathers and flowers brought the total to over $12.5 million in that year.

Comparing English and American import values for the decade 1901–1910, almost 20 million pounds sterling of duty free ornamental plumage entered England, much of it to be transshipped to the Continent and North America; compared with dutiable plumage amounting to $74.7 million for three categories of feathers imported into the United States. The higher English figures resulted from the fact that New York, unlike London, drew heavily upon native birds.

What kind of birds were displayed at London and New York feather sales and in what quantities? No exhaustive list of birds used by the trade has been compiled, and such a compilation would be a laborious task, involving analysis of original customs declarations, interpretation of milliners' lists and a search of trade and ornithological literature. In his research of the plumage problem, William T. Hornaday recorded 61 families and species that he believed were threatened with extermination by the London and continental feather markets. New York milliners submitted a list of 79 birds for official approval after the Shea-White Plumage Act of May, 1910, prohibited from sale any bird native to the state, or members of families to which they belonged.[24] Customs authorities in the United Kingdom confiscated at least 100 different kinds of birds upon the enforcement of the 1921 Act limiting imports of plumage. Some of these were no doubt curios and personal effects of travellers not intended as clothing accessories. In the United States, William E. D. Scott reported that J. H. Batty and associates, shooting for northern firms in Florida in the mid 1880's, were taking almost anything with feathers and up to 150

24. William Hornaday in "Supplement to Brief" before U.S. Congress, House, Ways and Means Committee. *Hearings on Schedule N—Feather Millinery*, 62nd Congress, 3rd session, House Document 1447 (Washington, D.C., 1913), p. 5315. For the New York situation see *BL* 12:3 (June, 1910), pp. 128–129, and idem (December, 1910), pp. 265–266. A list of birds was given on page 266, and can be compared with another one in *The Millinery Trade Review* 36 (September, 1911), p. 95.

TABLE 4

Extracts from London Auction Sales 1890–1911 [a]

Species	Date	Numbers of birds [b]
Herons, egrets	1905–1907	490,000
	1897–1911	
	39 sales	1,125,000
Sooty terns	1908	
(*Sterna fuscata*)	3 sales	51,200
Lyre bird	1907	180 tails
(*Menura superba*)	2 sales	
Kingfishers	1906–1907	50,000
	3 sales	
Hummingbirds	1904–1911	152,000
	8 sales	
Birds of paradise (espec. *apoda* and *rubra*)	1904–1908	155,000

SOURCE: *BNN* I (1903) etc.; also Boucard, *The Humming Bird,* Vol. I (1890), pp. 8, 16; ibid., Vol. 1, (1891) pp. 32, 58, 62–63.

a A note in *The Auk* (1888) pp. 334–335) contained a "Public Sale" list of one London firm which was believed to contain more birds than all ornithological collections in the United States: "Besides about 16,000 *packages* and *bundles* of 'Osprey,' Peacock, Argus and other Pheasants, Duck, 'Paddy,' and Heron feathers, we note several thousand *mats* and *handscreens,* while under the head of 'various bird skins,' we figure up between 7,000 and 8,000 Parrots, shipped mainly from Bombay and Calcutta, but including some from South America; about 1000 Impeyan and 500 Argus Pheasants; about 1000 Woodpeckers; 1450 'Penguins' (Auks and Grebes?); some 14,000 Quails, Grouse and Partridges; about 4000 Snipes and Plovers; about 7000 Starlings, Jays, and Magpies; over 12,000 Hummingbirds; about 5000 Tanagers; 6000 Blue Creepers and 1500 other Creepers (probably family Coerebidae); several hundred *each* of Hawks, Owls, Gulls, Terns, Ducks, Ibises, Finches, Orioles, Larks, Toucans, Birds of Paradise, etc. . . . ." The passage concluded: "Last year the trade in birds for women's hats was so enormous that a single London dealer admitted that he had sold 2,000,000 of small birds of every kind and color."

b Similar incomplete sets of figures are repeated in Parliamentary Debates and Committee Hearings on the plumage question.

birds per day. It is a safe estimate to say that at least 50 species of North American birds were taken for trade purposes.[25]

25. See *The Auk* 4 (1887) pp. 276–277. Scott reported that Batty had at least 60 men working for him on the Gulf Coast in 1886. When he contacted him in May,

The Royal Society for the Protection of Birds (RSPB) made frequent comments in its journal about London auction sales. Given the paucity of trade figures in London libraries and archives, and taking into account the RSPB's scant regard for feather industry spokesmen, the detailed statistics in table 4 must be taken with reserve. They are intended to be conservative when actual numbers of birds have been calculated from plumage sold by weight.

Bird Protection and American Natural History Literature

The plumage debate gave birth to two bird protection organizations in England and in America, namely the Royal Society for the Protection of Birds and the Audubon Society. The issue brought the plight of many birds to the attention of the public and caused people to support laws for the protection of birds other than game species. Well-known ornithologists, church dignitaries, scientists, writers and others campaigned to end what they considered a profligate waste of creatures ecologically important to human welfare, and traditionally part of the matrix of myth and folklore in Western society.

Initially restricted to the well-to-do and better educated people, this anti-plumage movement focused upon the propriety of feather wearing. Socially prominent ladies discouraged their friends and servants from donning plumage on religious and moral grounds. From the correspondence columns of local and national newspapers, middle class urban Britons and Americans learned about the dimensions of the feather trade. Articulate protests of influential spokesmen called for renewed interest in wildlife, especially birds. Their campaign can be set in the larger context of a "back to nature" movement at the close of the nineteenth century, when feeding, building homes for and watching birds became praiseworthy in suburban eyes.

In America, Peter Schmitt, historian of urban life of the period, has called this movement a response to an "arcadian myth." Nature, as opposed to the land, was regarded as the spiritual force which refreshed the inner man seeking the peace and quiet of

---

Scott discovered that he was shooting knots, sandpipers, sanderlings and turnstones over decoys, as well as Wilson's plovers and least terns. In addition, boat-tailed grackles, gray kingbirds, owls, particularly the barred owl, hawks, and small birds were shot. Scott concluded from talks with one of Batty's men that, "Mr. Batty was constantly purchasing and trading with native and other gunners for plumes and round and flat skins of all the desirable birds of the region," p. 277.

the country "beyond the trolley lines" without relinquishing the amenities of city life.[26] The symbols of wild nature, rather than its actual presence, appealed to city dwellers. Birds according to Schmitt were important in this nature movement because they delighted the human eye with their anthropomorphic traits, were instructive to children and provided a link with the mysterious and slightly frightening wilderness. Bird calls and migrations recalled a pristine past and were part of the "Book of Nature" from which mankind had drawn so many lessons.

Bird study was therefore important in the return to nature movement and was popularized by many writers of the period. Philip Hicks, commenting upon the development of the natural history essay in American literature, stated that, "among the branches of natural history, ornithology has always held first place in the affections of those who have given literary expression to their observations." [27] In studying the natural history essay, Hicks traced its origin to the works of Henry Thoreau and its full development and popularization in the twentieth century to the writings of John Burroughs.

In general, however, the natural history essay has declined in literary importance, becoming suffused with the kind of sentimental anthropomorphism exemplified by the essays of the Reverend William J. Long. Several bird-loving authors began to sacrifice the accuracy of observation to moral and religious lessons, involving a kind of "Christian ornithology." [28] This "sugar coated" natural history writing was especially prevalent at the turn of the century when Ernest Thompson Seton and Burroughs were at the heights of their fame. Members of humane organizations believed that a child's normal development was based upon an early contact with nature, and Bird Day became an integral part of the school calendar in several states.[29] The anti-plumage campaign drew from

26. Peter J. Schmitt, *Back to Nature: The Arcadian Myth in Urban America* (New York, 1969), pp. xv–xxiii.

27. *The Development of the Natural History Essay in American Literature* (Philadelphia, 1924), p. 8.

28. Schmitt, *Back to Nature*, pp. 36–38, had in mind Edith Patch's *Bird Stories* (Chicago, 1921) which went to seven printings in the 1920's. Also, Charles Abbott, *Bird-Land Echoes* (Philadelphia, 1896) and other authors displayed sentimental attachments to birds which possessed many human traits; reference to Neltje Blanchan and Gilbert Trafton is made by Schmitt, pp. 35, 197, f.n. 7.

29. The idea of Bird Day was attributed to C. A. Babcock, superintendent of schools, Oil City, Pa., who suggested that it be extended nationwide. J. Sterling Morton, Secretary of Agriculture, was impressed with this request; he believed that

and added to this current of nature lovers and amateur ornithologists, who were noted for their concern about bird study and wildlife depletion.[30] What could be more enjoyable than a morning ramble through nearby fields armed with opera glasses and bird pictures, renewing contacts with "wild" America?

Early Sentiments for Bird Protection in America

A literary tradition a century older than the Audubon Society sympathetically deals with birds and their well-being. William Bartram and Alexander Wilson expressed a desire to preserve beautiful winged creatures which so well revealed the design, goodness and harmony of the natural order of things. These two "birders" were especially struck with the beauty and usefulness of birdlife and effectively communicated their beliefs to their own and to succeeding generations.

William Bartram (1739–1823) opened his *Travels through North and South Carolina, . .* (1791) in a lyrical vein:

> This world as a glorious apartment of the boundless palace of the sovereign Creator, is furnished with an infinite variety of animated scenes, inexpressibly beautiful and pleasing, equally free to the inspection and enjoyment of all his creatures (P. xiv).

This remarkable Pennsylvania naturalist, who influenced Coleridge and Wordsworth, portrayed man as the caretaker of creation. He saw goodness in animals, and the power, wisdom and beneficence of God in birds.[31] Bartram was struck by the attachment animals had for each other and was convinced that we should be "merciful to them, even as we hope for mercy." This, he considered, was appropriate Christian conduct which differed from the Cartesian view of animals as machines.[32]

Bartram discovered in wildlife a deep religious significance and

---

it could "hardly fail to promote the development of a healthy public sentiment toward our native birds." Morton concluded: "Let us have Bird Day—a day set apart from all the other days of the year to tell the children about the birds." It was successfully celebrated in Oil City and was started in Iowa in 1896; other states also took an interest in Bird Day and the National Education Association took up the matter in 1884; see T. S. Palmer, "Bird Day in the Schools," U.S.D.A., *Biological Survey, Circular* No. 17 (Washington, D.C., 1896).

30. Schmitt, *Back to Nature*, p. 34.

31. Page xvi, for details about William Bartram, see William and Mabel Smallwood, *Natural History and the American Mind* (New York, 1941).

32. Bartram, *Travels*, pp. xvi–xviii, xxiv–xxv, 101.

bird song stimulated him to moods of exhilaration, piety and goodwill. He associated birds' melodious notes with "the reanimating appearance of the rising sun," leading to a joyful worship of God:

> Ye vigilant and faithful servants of the Most High! ye who worship the Creator, morning, noon and eve, in simplicity of heart! I haste to join the universal anthem. My heart and voice unite with yours, in sincere homage to the great Creator, the universal sovereign.[33]

The Fransican ring of these descriptions of landscapes and wild animals in the *Travels* suggests a serene acceptance of a designed, ordered and varied world. In it, birds are God's messengers, exemplars of innocence, and the regulators of the agricultural seasons.[34]

Alexander Wilson (1766–1813), a friend and scientific associate of Bartram's ascribed a similar religious significance to birdlife in his classic text on American ornithology. Wilson found in waterbirds, "a wisdom of design never erring, never failing in the means it provides for the accomplishment of its purpose." [35] Birds revealed to him "an amazing diversity in habit, economy, form, disposition and faculties . . . [sufficient to] overwhelm us with astonishment at the power, wisdom and beneficence of the Creator!" [36] Wilson reiterated Bartram's discovery of the attributes of God in birdlife, as well as the traditional notion that there is a design and a teleology in nature, put there by an artisan deity or Creator. For Wilson, ornithology could play a didactic role in ethical and religious matters. He believed it led man "by such pleasing gradations, to the contemplation and worship of the *Great First Cause,* the Father and Preserver of all, [it] can neither be idle or useless, but is worthy of rational beings, and doubtless agreeable to the Deity." [37] Certain species—for example, the painted bunting (*Passerina ciris*) with its dazzling hues—aroused a "delicacy of feeling" in the most savage breast and hardened heart.[38] Songsters such as the mockingbird (*Mimus polyglottos*), hermit thrush (*Hylocichla guttata*) and many warblers offered

---

33. Ibid., p. 100.   34. Ibid., p. 285.
35. *American Ornithology* (Philadelphia, 9 vols., 1808–1814) 7, p. v; or Ord's 2nd edition, 1824, vol. 7, p. i.
36. Ibid., 1, p. 3.   37. Ibid.   38. Ibid., 3, p. 69.

hymns of praise to the "Fountain of light and life." [39] Like Bartram, bird songs left an indelible mark on Wilson. He believed that American birds were unsurpassed in sweetness, melody and variety of their songs.[40]

Lacking the drama so vital to Audubon's work, Wilson's homely accounts of the "inoffensive" ruby-crowned kinglet (*Regulus calendula*), "affectionate" fly-catchers and other birds, conveyed to his readers the same atmosphere of primitive and wild America that Audubon, his acquaintance and successor on the Kentucky frontier, would later describe so boldly. Wilson admired American birdlife, the primitive American scene and the wealth of a continent of which he was so proud.[41] In this regard, he took strong issue with Buffon's idea that much of the New World fauna was degenerate. He believed that birds were living examples of the vitality and beauty of untouched American nature.[42]

Possessing a talent for accurate and painstaking description and painting, Wilson understood the need to collect and to classify. He thought that by concentrating in field observations on the chain of being, that "beautiful gradation of affinity and resemblance" in nature,[43] he could contribute to the progress of ornithology in America. Wilson procured bird specimens for scientific purposes but was averse to endless collections or mindless destruction, and stressed more than Bartram the economic importance of birdlife to mankind.[44] He argued for bird protection on utilitarian grounds. The bluebird (*Sialia sialis*) snaps up the insect destroyers of fruit; kingbirds catch flies; and woodpeckers devour harmful grubs. A poem about the eastern kingbird (*Tyrannus tyrannus*) emphasized its economic significance, the companionship it offered, and argued for its preservation. A farmer was about to shoot the bird for eating honey bees:

> Ah friend! good friend! forbear that barb'rous deed,
> Against it valor, goodness, pity plead;

39. Ibid., 4, p. x.   40. Ibid., 1, p. 2.

41. Robert Cantwell, *Alexander Wilson Naturalist and Pioneer* (Philadelphia, 1961), p. 241.

42. Wilson, *American Ornithology* . . . I, pp. 34, 50; 3, p. 33; 7, p. vi; or Ord, 1924 edition, p. ii. For a discussion of the concept in Buffon see Clarence J. Glacken, *Traces on the Rhodian Shore* (Berkeley and Los Angeles, 1967) pp. 681 ff., 698, f.n., 122. A major thrust of Buffon's contention was that pristine nature was wild and disordered and needed the hand of man to improve it.

43. Wilson, *Ornithology* I, pp. 3–4. For a discussion of the great chain of being, see Arthur O. Lovejoy, *The Great Chain of Being: The Study of the History of an Idea* (Cambridge, Massachusetts, 1948).

44. Cantwell, *Alexander Wilson*, p. 139; also Wilson, *Ornithology*, I, p. 37.

If e'er a family's griefs, a widow's woe,
Have reach'd thy soul, in mercy let him go!
Yet, should the tear of pity nought avail,
Let *interest* speak, let *gratitude* prevail;
Kill not thy friend, who thy whole harvest shields,
And sweeps ten thousand vermin from thy fields;
Think how this dauntless bird, thy poultry's guard,
Drove ev'ry Hawk and Eagle from thy yard;
Watch'd round thy cattle as they fed, and slew
The hungry black'ning swarms that round them flew;
Some small return, some little right resign,
And spare *his* life whose services are thine!
. . . I plead in vain! Amid the bursting roar
The poor, lost KING-BIRD, welters in his gore.[45]

Wilson, the poet, personalized his birds to a large degree. He popularized bird study, at the same time impressing the scientific circles of Philadelphia with his knowledge and the accuracy of his field observations. In sum, for Wilson, customarily referred to as the "Father of American Ornithology," birds were cheerful companions. They exhilarated mankind, soothed him, attended to his health and subsistence by preventing the increase of "those supernumerary hosts of insects that would soon consume the products of his industry." [46] They exemplified in their color, song and behavior, religious and moral lessons and revealed in their abundance and diversity the wealth and grandeur of the New Continent.

Sentiments similar to those of Bartram and Wilson are found in the work of the great luminary of American ornithology, John James Audubon, whose genius was widely celebrated a generation after his death (in 1851). His devotees saw in Audubon a man battling against the commonplace to erect a monument to nature —American nature. In the final decades of the nineteenth century, Audubon was popularly regarded as an epitome of correct American feeling and reasonable action in his love of nature and quest for bird protection in America. In fact, Audubon was an immigrant, a bankrupt and a social outcast in his two adopted towns, Henderson and Louisville, Kentucky.

The small group of natural scientists, headed by William Brewster, that gathered to discuss American ornithology, including

45. Ibid., 2, pp. 72–73.   46. Ibid., 5, p. viii.

Audubon's work, in Cambridge, Massachusetts in the 1860's, had among its participants, the founders of the American Ornithologists' Union (AOU). This body of bird scientists worked closely with Audubon groups on the plumage issue.[47] The five volumes of Audubon's *Ornithological Biography* (1831–1839) infected these men and others of a biological bent with a delight in observation and a curiosity about details of the lives of America's avifauna.

From his earliest years, birds fascinated this bourgeois French emigré who discovered that:

> A grand connected chain does exist in the Creator's sublime system, the subjects of it have been left at liberty to disperse in quest of the food best adapted for them, . . and are not in the habit of following each other, as if marching in regular procession to a funeral or a merry-making.[48]

Accordingly, Audubon followed no "regular procession" in his *Ornithological Biography*. Interspersing regional vignettes distilled from his "Journal" with descriptions of the life habits, distribution and taxonomy of each species, Audubon ended with a short explanatory note about the species' colored, life-size portrait in *Birds of America*.

In the first half of this century, more than ten volumes about Audubon have been produced or reprinted in the United States.[49] Curiosity has persisted about the character of the man, his life and talent as a bird and animal artist. His enthusiasm, perseverence and dedication to birds have been held up to young people as worthy of emulation. His presumed championship of the perservation cause, however, appears to many more an invention of posterity than a passion of his life.

Audubon enjoyed collecting natural objects, whether as a truant from school or an escapee from the drudgery of his retail stores in Kentucky. Outdoor exercise, hunting, and sketching the trophies of the chase consumed much of his time. In his *Biography*, he stressed the usefulness of many birds to man as insect destroyers. However, its pages possess plentiful accounts of bird destruction,

47. Charles Batchelder, "An Account of the Nuttall Ornithological Club," *Memoirs Nuttall Ornithological Club* No. 8 (Cambridge, Massachusetts, 1937).
48. *Ornithological Biography* (Edinburgh, 5 vols., 1831–1839) I, p. xix.
49. Francis H. Herrick, *Audubon the Naturalist* (New York, 1917) I, pp. 12–15 ff provides evidence of the spread of Audubon's name as a "household word."

some of them at Audubon's hand. He noted that large numbers of passerines, including the mockingbird, grackles, blackbirds and the snow bunting (*Plectrophenax nivalis*) were eaten or used as cage birds.[50] He observed that the carolina paroquet (*Conuropsis carolinensis*), "always an unwelcome visitor to the planter, the farmer, or the gardener," was killed in great numbers. He wrote, apparently without remorse, that, "I have seen several hundreds destroyed . . . in the course of a few hours, and have procured a basketful of these birds at a few shots. . . ."[51]

In his later years Audubon became more explicit in condemning wanton bird killing. On his visit to the Natashquan River of Labrador in June, 1833, he condemned the slaughter of ducks, murres and gulls, considering its considerable egg trade to be jeopardized by collectors.[52] He berated the Eggers of Labrador, "the pest of the feathered tribes," for their destructive activities. Local natives who raided the rookeries for eggs were more leniently treated,[53] perhaps because they were apparently meeting only subsistence needs of fisher-folk.

In general, however, Audubon had no qualms about shooting birds and large numbers of them. He admitted taking hundreds of red-winged "starlings" (*Agelaius phoeniceus*) is the course of an afternoon, although he did not regard them as good eating.[54] Of Canada geese (*Branta canadensis*) he said: "We continue to shoot until the number of geese obtained would seem to you so very large that I shall not specify it," and exclaimed "Oh that we had more guns!"[55] Some twenty pages later in describing the activities of the "cruel sportsmen" who gunned down hundreds of clapper rails (*Rallus longirostris*) near Charleston, his derogatory remarks appear more the product of petulance born of envy than a concern for the survival of the species. The chuck-will's-widow (*Caprimulgus carolinensis*) and Mississippi kite (*Ictinia misisippiensis*), at which he "could not resist the temptation . . ." to shoot, provide other examples of Audubon's cavalier approach to bird protection.[56]

The debt we owe Audubon lies primarily in his magnificently

50. *Ornithological Biography*, I, pp. 37–39, 73, 113.   51. Ibid., I, p. 136.
52. Alexander B. Adams, *John James Audubon* (New York, 1966), p. 409. See also Robert C. Murphy, "John James Audubon (1785–1851): An Evaluation of the Man and His Work," *New York Historical Society Quarterly* (October, 1956).
53. *Ornithological Biography*, 3, pp. 82–86.   55. Ibid., 3, p. 16.
54. Ibid., I, p. 350.   56. Ibid., 2, p. 111.

colored album, *Birds of America*. With a sense of history, he created a detailed, convincing impression of the natural world, doing so with a command of design, coloration, and composition "that established him as the greatest bird painter the western world has known." [57] The vivid descriptions and personal anecdotes in his *Biography* (modified by MacGillivray in syntax and grammar), together with his paintings, revealed an enthusiasm for birds that was infectious. Though Thomas Nuttall may have had a keener ear, "there has never been a keener eye" than Audubon's, or a greater singleness of purpose. So stated John Burroughs, born himself with the woodsman's vision. He caught "bird fever" from a casual opening of Audubon's work in 1863. [58]

The sentimental character of birds assumed a particular importance in the works of John Burroughs (1837–1921). In his early writings on natural history, he associated the sight and sounds of various species with personal moods and recollections, and with the passage of the seasons. This was especially marked in his most poetic period, from the appearance of his first book, *Wake Robin* (1871), to *Birds and Poets* (1877). By the turn of the century, Burroughs had developed a more scientific interest in the natural world and paid close attention to accurate detail in observations and descriptions.

Ornithology interested him from early youth, when he derived pleasures in bird observations on rambles in the Catskill mountains of New York state. The mechanics of bird study were simple. "First, find your bird; observe its way, its song, its calls, its flight, its haunts; then shoot it (not ogle it with a glass), and compare with Audubon." [59] This "instant" approach to ornithology was not typical of Burroughs; for in his notebook (May, 1865), he indicated that he did not shoot birds for fear of "outraging the woods" and breaking the spell of intimacy between man and nature. His basic desire was to enter into birds' lives and translate the meanings of their songs; however, he was not averse to collecting specimens with a gun. [60]

Burrough's capacity for painstaking and sympathetic observa-

57. New York Historical Society, *The Original Water-Color Paintings of John James Audubon* (New York, 1966), I, p. xi.
58. *Wake-Robin* (New York [1st edition, 1871], 1877), pp. 240–241.
59. Ibid., p. 231.
60. Clara Barrus, *The Life and Letters of John Burroughs* (Boston, 1925) I, pp. 115–116.

tions, respectful to science and religion and delivered in unpretentious language, made him the "nature guru" of a cohort of lady nature lovers before World War I. A great popularizer of bird study, "his nature-books express the joie de vivre of the intelligent, healthy outdoor man walking over his acres in the sunlight and the breeze." [61] By defining standards for natural history writing, Burroughs made coherent the concern for birds and bird protection in the works of his literary forbears—Henry Thoreau, Nathaniel P. Willis, Wilson Flagg and Francis Higginson. He viewed nature pantheistically, sought to reconcile dualism between matter and spirit, and was able to communicate his strong affection for birds to an emerging audience interested in natural subjects.

Man as an Ecological Dominant: A General View

The concern for bird protection manifested early in the nineteenth century by birdmen and natural history writers was part of an increasing concern about landscape alteration and destructive environmental change. Interest in the grand themes of man's relationship to nature in eighteenth century writing had narrowed to observations of all life forms by the nineteenth century. Biologists and earth scientists began to perceive clearly that human activities reverberated throughout all realms of nature.

Comte Buffon, in *Des Époques de la Nature,* believed that there were seven epochs of earth history. Human "assistance" of nature characterized the last. Considered by some to be the greatest of all natural historians of the eighteenth century, Buffon foresaw destructive tendencies in human endeavors but emphasized the benefits accruing from purposeful and intelligent use of the land in fulfillment of the biblical injunction to "complete creation." [62] Sir Charles Lyell in the first edition of his *Principles of Geology* (1830–33) believed that mankind was not merely an observer but had a selective role to play in influencing earth processes. Stripped of Buffon's optimism (from which a *tout est bien* vision of civilization and a view of progress as inevitable could be derived) and giving mankind more of center stage than did Lyell, the American, George P. Marsh (1801–1882) emphasized man's power to effect physical and biological change. In the preface to *Man and Nature* (1864), Marsh's objective was "to point out the

61. William S. Kennedy, *The Real John Burroughs* (New York, 1924), p. 5.
62. Glacken, *Traces on the Rhodian Shore,* pp. 655–705.

dangers of imprudence and the necessity of caution in all operations which, on a large scale, interfere with the spontaneous arrangements of the organic or the inorganic world. . . ." [63] From
a sojourn in Europe and from travels in the Middle East, he had
witnessed the devastating effects of man-induced landscape change.

A century before Marsh's work, agricultural writers in America
had proposed solutions to wasteful agricultural practices. Samuel
Deane, Solomon Drown, John Lorain and others had led the fight
against poor husbandry, monocropping and topsoil erosion. In
Marsh, however, the ancient idea of nature designed by a Creator
was blended with an awareness of the consequences of man dis-
regarding his role of stewardship. Many of Marsh's warnings of
the effects of forest clearance, of over-grazing and of plant and
wildlife destruction had become stark realities of the American
scene by the 1890's.

Marsh devoted several pages of *Man and Nature* to bird destruction. Citing Arthur Young, he noted the hail of shot unleashed
upon French birdlife with the Revolution. He noted, too, the
negative effects of "new circumstances" as in the case of nocturnal
bird migrants flying against a lighthouse on Cape Cod,[64] or the
effects of increased shipments of American game to European
city markets.[65] A diplomat from Vermont, Marsh depicted man as
a predator and exterminator of birdlife, including species whose
beauty of plumage "as a military and feminine decoration, threat-
ens to involve the sacrifice of the last survivor of many once numerous species." [66] Marsh feared that wild birds hunted for their
meat or plumage were declining "with a rapidity which justifies
the fear that the last of them will soon follow the dodo and the
wingless auk." [67] Twenty years after he had penned these words
concerted efforts were beginning to be made to make sure that his
prophecy was not fulfilled. For some wild animals, these efforts
came too late.

A vision of wildlife scarcity gripped natural scientists and American sportsmens' associations in the 1880's. The bison and passenger pigeon were offered as proof of depletion, and the sporting fra-

63. *Man and Nature*, p. *iii*. For a dicussion of man and nature in the nineteenth
century I am indebted to a paper by Clarence Glacken entitled, "Man's Place in
Nature in Recent Western Thought," in Michael Hamilton (editor), *The Little
Planet* (New York, 1970), pp. 163–201; idem "The Origins of the Conservation
Philosophy," *Journal of Soil and Water Conservation* 11:2 (March, 1956), 63–66.

64. *Man and Nature*, f.n. p. 94.   66. Ibid., p. 95.
65. Ibid., p. 97.   67. Ibid., p. 97.

ternity was urged to exercise restraint before the dwindling herds
of big game.[68] James Trefethen in his study of the origins and
development of the Boone and Crockett club organized to crusade
for wildlife preservation in 1887, has pointed out that waterfowl
was the mainstay of the market hunter, except for a time in the
1870's. He noted too that by the end of the century evident declines in numbers of ducks and geese could be attributed directly
to overshooting, as the effects of widespread reclamation and
drainage were to be felt in later decades.[69] In the '80's, New
York City, for example, received market game shipped from
Minnesota, where spring and fall shooting of waterfowl, upland
game and shorebirds was relentless.[70]

This fear of a general wildlife scarcity which accompanied the
concern for birdlife was in part caused by the improvement of
firearms for animal killing. In the mid-1870's, choke-bored,
breech-loading shotguns began to be sold commercially; in 1893 a
repeating shotgun became available; and in 1904, an automatic
loader appeared on the market. These weapons made spectacular
kills possible. George O. Shields, the editor of *Recreation Magazine,* described the perpetrators of these kills as "game hogs".[71]

An essay in *Forest and Stream* (17 September, 1885) prophesized
the pauperization of the avifauna of the United States. It en-
visioned a canoe excursion of a boy and his aging father in the
year 1950. Smaller passerines like finches, orioles, and other "min-
strels of the year" had almost disappeared, consumed by "the
stomachs of men and the bonnets of women." Men had "tickled
their maws" with the flesh of snow buntings, and years ago:

> A fashion . . . raged so virulently that if a bird had handsome
> plumage or even shapely form, his sweetest song and his prettiest

68. Marvin Kranz, "Pioneering in Conservation: A History of the Conservation
Movement in New York State, 1865–1903," Unpublished Ph.D. (Syracuse, 1961), has
traced the chronology of game preservation in New York State. High society took a
hand in this field as early as 1844 when wealthy hunters organized the New York
Sportsmen's Club following prophesies of doom for game animals in the State.
In 1874 this club became the New York Association for the Protection of Game,
limited to 100 prominent people. William Murray and Verplanck Colvin extolled
the scenic qualities of the Adirondacks as primitive and inspiring in the 1860's, and
began to interest others in the tourist potential of many wild areas.

69. *Crusade for Wildlife* (Harrisburg, Pennsylvania, 1961), p. 162.

70. E. B. Swanson, "Use and Conservation of Minnesota Game, 1850–1900," unpublished Ph.D. thesis (Minneapolis, 1940), pp. 43–78, 132.

71. Trefethen, *Crusade,* p. 163, Peter Matthiessen, *Wildlife in America* (New
York, 1959), pp. 165 ff., 177. For comments on firearms see Paul W. Parmalee,
Decoys and Decoy Carvers of Illinois (DeKalb, 1969), p. 10, and Hornaday, (1913
and 1931).

ways could not save his life from the savage skin hunters who invade all parts of the land, more cruel, rapacious and destructive than all beasts and birds of prey (p. 142).

Crows were virtually the only game birds left in the imaginary 1950, and one or two red foxes remained alive to be hunted repeatedly by landowners, who were careful not to fatigue them too much. Raccoons and opposums had become extinct, and with forest clearance mountains had become savage sterile treeless rocks "not giving so much as a home to the eagle." Marsh drainage had proceeded apace and herons and kingfishers no longer frequented the few remaining water bodies.

> "Let us return," said the old man. "This is all so changed from what it was when I was a boy that I cannot bear to look upon it. The ax and fire—man's greed and carelessness and spirit of wanton destructiveness have spoiled it all" (p. 142).

He concluded: "I cannot but be glad that in a few years my eyes will be shut forever from the sight of this 'abomination of desolation.' "

This essay is almost contemporary in its concern and despair over man-made environmental change. Its message was clear to weekly readers of the *Forest and Stream*—that by his unrestrained greed mankind was beggaring the American scene. The periodical expressed distaste for plume and market hunters who shot for monetary gain. Such "pot shots," it suggested, contravened the finest traditions of sport hunting.

Humane Organizations Interested in Birds

Societies on both sides of the Atlantic, founded to combat cruelty to animals and foster in children a love of brute creation, took an early interest in bird protection and became vocal in support of the anti-plumage movement. Henry Bergh (1811–1888), philanthrope, founder of the American Society for the Prevention of Cruelty to Animals (1866) and a similar society for children, and George T. Angell (1823–1909), who was responsible for the Massachusetts SPCA (1868), actively supported the first national society for bird preservation in the United States. Both men were honorary vice-presidents of the Audubon Society, and other vice-presidents held important positions in state and local humane associations.[72]

Ernest S. Turner, in a provocative overview of the birth and development of ideas to curb cruelty to animals in England, has said that the Christian tradition fostered, at best, a mental respect for beasts. European hagiology is full of strange alliances between man and beast, for which seventeenth century humanism had little charity. Late eighteenth century romantic poetry marked, for Turner, a turning point in appreciation of animals; devotion to Nature included compassion for birds and beasts.[73]

A traditional delight in hunting as a preparation for manhood and as an excuse for fun and conviviality proved an obstacle to the better treatment of animals for a long time. Animal baiting and fighting appalled essayists Alexander Pope, Joseph Addison and Eustace Budgell who argued whether, "Man had any more right to carve up the brute creation than he had to bait or otherwise abuse it." [74] Englishmen had a callous regard for livestock and domestic beasts well into the nineteenth century because bull and bear baiting offered a chance for wagering, as did cock and dog fighting.

With the passage of Martin's Act (1822), Britain began an up-

72. The following important people in the American humane movement were also vice-presidents of Grinnell's Audubon Society: Mrs. W. Appleton, Boston, Massachusetts, helped Angell found the Massachusetts SPCA. Miss Adele Biddle, Philadelphia, Pennsylvania, was co-founder of the American Antivivisection Society. Mr. Leonard H. Eaton, Pittsburgh, Pennsylvania, was elected president of the American Humane Society 1891–1892. Mr. Abraham Firth, Boston, Massachusetts, became secretary of the Massachusetts SPCA and president of the American Humane Association. Mr. G. E. Gordon, Milwaukee, Wisconsin, was president of the American Humane Association, 1885–1887, and co-sponsor of the AOU supplement in *Science* (26 February, 1886) devoted to bird protection. Mrs. Lilly L. Tifft, Buffalo, New York, organized a branch of the American SPCA (1868). Miss Anne Wigglesworth, Boston, Massachusetts, supported the American Humane Association. Mrs. Caroline E. White, Philadelphia, Pennsylvania, was influential in Pennsylvania humane campaigns and founded the Women's Pennsylvania SPCA; she was also a director of the American Humane Association, and pioneer of antivivisection in the United States. Sources: Sydney H. Coleman, *Humane Society Leaders in America* (Albany, New York, 1924), and Roswell C. McCrea, *The Humane Movement* (New York, 1910).

73. *All Heaven in a Rage* (New York, 1965), p. 70. Turner named poets with compassion for animals, as Wordsworth (*Hart-Leap Well*, 1800), Coleridge, Blake, Burns, and Cowper. The latter devoted poems to the hare, halibut, cat, spaniel, swallow, nightingale, bullfinch, glow-worm, silkworm, grasshopper, parrot, sparrow, goldfinch and robin. Charles D. Niven, *History of the Humane Movement* (New York, 1967), pp. 53–55, passim, believed that the Quakers were helpful in fostering appreciative sentiments towards animals.

74. Turner, *All Heaven*, p. 48.

hill fight against ill-treatment of animals, making cruelty to them punishable under the law. A small band of gentlemen founded an SPCA in 1824, nearly foundering under financial difficulties before achieving much in the way of animal protection. Progress was painfully slow until Princess Victoria became the Society's patron in 1835; and in 1840, as Queen, she bestowed upon it the title of "Royal Society." Her Majesty insured the survival of the RSPCA by taking an active interest in it throughout her reign. People who had sneered at its officers as a bunch of meddlesome kill-joy fanatics began to take seriously campaigns against livestock beating, baiting, and droving.[75]

In the 1870's, a group of women became prominent in the RSPCA. Among them was Baroness Burdett-Coutts, vaunted to be the richest lady in the land and a close friend of Queen Victoria. She was an active supporter of the infant Society for the Protection of Birds, and while interested in other philanthropic causes, headed a Ladies' Committee for humane education dedicated to interesting school children in animal protection. She supported Bands of Mercy founded in both England and the United States to foster in children a love of animals.[76]

Ties between Baroness Burdett-Coutts and two other SPCA officials, Henry Bergh, son of a wealthy New York shipbuilder, and George Angell, a prominent Boston barrister, were close. The "enlightened" spirit sweeping America in post-Civil War days welcomed the new humane organizations. One of Bergh's biographers, Zulma Steele, remarked that his work for animals complemented movements for women's rights, temperance, prison and poor reform. She said:

> War profiteers and industrial tycoons began to look askance on sordid city slums and other national sore spots which tarnished

75. Edward G. Fairholme, *A Century of Work for Animals* (London, 1934), pp. 83–90, passim, reported that the RSPCA was concerned about the practice of putting out birds' eyes to make them better songsters. In 1863 Prince Edward and Princess Alexandra consented to become RSPCA patrons. Edward became president of the Society in 1893.

76. Turner, *All Heaven*, pp. 230–232, stated that essay writing among school children was thought to strengthen humanitarian sentiments. By 1889, Turner reported that 1,000 schools were sponsoring essay competitions in England with prizes to be presented by members of the Royal Family. Miss Angela Burdett-Coutts presided over a ceremony in 1869 to inaugurate new premises of the RSPCA in Jermyn St., London. At the event were some of England's most notable people, including Lord Harrowby, Ladies Melville, Beauchamp, Duckett and Gomm, and the Bishop of Gloucester.

America's Gilded Age. Beer barons and railroad kings were persuaded, reluctantly, to spend part of their fortunes upon hospitals and missions, and to found libraries, colleges and art museums. . . .[77]

The new wealth and its stimulus to philanthropic endeavors brought with it a taste for English blood-sports, the loves and lusts of the country squire, and even an attempt to popularize Spanish bull fighting in America.[78] Reform was destined to be slow in the sphere of animal treatment, if only because game battues and trap shooting of live pigeons were pursuits deemed proper to gentlemen, and thus were acceptable to American *bon vivants.* "Sparrow" shoots occupied the leisure time of many middle-class Americans, and women were no strangers to the gun. The mania for collecting birds, nests and eggs gripped both countries and natural history buffs made great show of their zoological cabinets and collections of skins. Such attitudes hastened the disappearance of birds and impeded progress towards preservation.[79]

In the United States, objections to this wildlife carnage and callous treatment of animals were made on the grounds that blood letting had debauched the British aristocracy and set a poor example for the lower classes. The lesson of the French Revolution was open to all. It was held that cruel treatment and indifference to brutes coarsened human sensibilities and in the long run debilitated human nature. These statements were not lost upon those who were to campaign most keenly against feather fashions.[80]

From the start, humane societies in America included birds as among those creatures needing protection. *Our Dumb Animals,* a

77. *Angel in Top Hat* (New York, 1942), pp. 3–4.

78. Ibid., p. 4, and Turner, *All Heaven,* pp. 84–103.

79. Apart from collectors, Turner (pp. 193–200) reported that bird catchers were taking finches as children's playthings, songsters were used in competitions, some exhibited in fights with other birds or placed with cats and dogs. It was estimated that in 1854, 400,000 larks arrived annually in the London market.

80. Speech by Rev. E. N. Kirk before Massachusetts SPCA, March, 1869, and printed in *Our Dumb Animals* 2 (June, 1869) p. 1. Bergh's views on pigeon shooting are expressed by Zulma Steele, *Angel in Top Hat,* pp. 218–234. The demoralizing effects of such activities see ibid., pp. 7–8, 161, 219, 230. Turner, pp. 90–95, 176, 179–200, passim, reported similar expressions from England about the degradation of human nature from field sports. Particularly strident was a passage from the *Echo:* "We must have kingly kings, and noble noblemen and gentle gentlemen, or revolution will come upon us." p. 182.

weekly journal speaking for "those who cannot speak for themselves," was launched by Angell from Boston in June, 1868, and immediately took up the cudgels for birdlife. In its first issue, a poem entitled "Boys, Spare the Birds" admonished young readers not to injure wild birds nor to take their eggs. Instead, youngsters were encouraged to feed winter visitors to the backyard and learn how useful songsters were in attacking insect hordes.[81] Angell's journal had a religious bent; its aim was, "to educate all, and particularly children to a higher humanity, and to inspire a deeper reverence for the Great Creator of all these wonderful forms of animal life, and a more profound consciousness of our duty in regard to them.[82] Killing butterflies or even spiders was morally reprehensible because all things were created by God. He had made animals as companions of man. Especially shocking to Angell were reports of the wanton killing of bison from cars on the railroad to California.[83]

Our Dumb Animals, which circulated 200,000 gratuitous copies of its first number and published 20,000 thereafter, spoke out against wearing birds' plumage as early as 1869. It printed a poem about a gull on a lady's hat which paralleled the concern for seabird slaughter in England.

> Ah, let them but remember, child,
> That every bird they slay
> Might, had it lived, have saved some ship,
> In some wild night or day.[84]

The thrust of the magazine's anti-plumage sentiment came after 1875, however, when tales of hummingbird millinery arrived from Paris and news of Baroness Burdett-Coutt's efforts to halt feather wearing in England were matched by the report from the home front that C. C. Haskins was organizing an "Army of Bird Defenders." [85] Haskins' group had first been announced in a childrens' periodical, *St. Nicholas,* in 1873. The goals of the group, which seems to have foundered quickly, were similar to Angell's

---

81. See *Our Dumb Animals* 1 (June, 1868), p. 7; 1 (August, 1868), p. 18; 1 (January, 1869), p. 59; (March, 1869), p. 78.

82. *Our Dumb Animals* 1:7 (December, 1868), p. 49.

83. Ibid., 2:12 (May 1870), p. 120.   84. Ibid., 2:3 (August, 1869), p. 31.

85. Ibid., 8:1 (June, 1875), p. 7.

Bands of Mercy, whose members sought to help insectivorous birds and to show compassion for "the lower races" in order to become better men and women.[86]

Robert Welker, an authority on bird study in the nineteenth century, has shown considerable respect for the didactic and moral tone of the monthly *St. Nicholas* and its weekly counterpart *Youth's Companion* (began by Nathaniel Willis in 1827). The latter magazine contained a natural history section with affectionate stories about mercy to birds and animals. Under new management, its circulation grew to over 300,000 readers in the mid-1880's when Bradford Torrey, bird lover and writer, became a junior editor. Welker concluded that these periodicals for young people may have been uniquely influential in promoting bird study and appreciation among boys and girls.[87]

Adults were also propagandized on behalf of birds. Mention has been made of the importance of literary birdmen in writings about nature and natural history. They were not alone in their sympathies for wild creatures. Jules Michelet (1798–1874), the great French literary historian, penned a book called *The Bird* (1856) which sought to portray "the bird in the bird," avoiding human analogies. He wrote it "specifically in hatred of sport" and as a book of peace. Mankind, especially farmers, persecuted feathered creatures through ignorance and a deficient sense of history. Full of pathos and reminiscence, Michelet's work was unusual in its devotion to birdlife and modified anthropocentrism.[88]

Michelet's inspirational and subliminal treatment of birdlife had been captured in England earlier in the century by the artist George F. Watts (1817–1904). This painter of ideas found the taste for ornamental plumage defective because, he believed, "no fashion can be in good taste that seems to imply contempt for the

86. Robert Welker, *Birds and Men* (New York, 1955), p. 182. The Band of Mercy of America is mentioned in *Our Dumb Animals* 19 (December, 1886), pp. 59, 63. Angell was president and suggested that teachers be given a gold badge of membership; regular members received a certificate, a copy of "Twelve lessons on kindness to animals," and 52 Band of Mercy songs and hymns. By December, 1886, there were 5,162 branches in the United States and Canada, with 400,000 members. In England, *The Band of Mercy Advocate* 1 (January, 1879), included a catechism on humanity to animals, poems and hortatory messages to young readers; later the movement was taken over by the RSPCA. McCrea, *Humane Movement*, p. 94, believed that the first Band of Mercy was established by Mrs. Caroline Smithies of Wood Green, England in 1875.

87. Robert Welker, *Birds and Men*, pp. 179–181.

88. *The Bird* (New York, 1869), was the first part of a trilogy followed by *L'Insecte* and *La Mer*. References are to pp. 17–18, 55–56, 82, 213.

beautiful arrangements of created things." [89] All successful art was, for Watts, a translation of some page of the "Book of Nature." G. K. Chesterton discovered a deep humanitarian significance in Watts' "The Wounded Heron," a painting exhibited at the Royal Academy in 1837. It portrayed for him, "The suffering of a stricken creature; it depicts the pathos of dying and the greater pathos of living." [90]

Watts painted a late work, "A Dedication" (1899), variously named "The Mourning Angel" or "Shuddering Angel," "to all who love the beautiful and mourn over the senseless and cruel destruction of bird life and beauty." [91] It showed an angel hovering over a dais strewn with remnants of shattered birdlife taken for the plumage industry. Watts strongly objected to cruelty to animals. He refused to paint the famous actress Lily Langtry's portrait until she had divested her bonnet of feather trim. His sympathies also extended to the human realm, as he agreed to lend his name to a ladies anti-tight-lacing society. Watts became a member of the British RSPB and upon his death in 1904 the Society eulogized his work for birds.

The intense and prolonged reaction to feather wearing at the close of the nineteenth century was part of a renewed interest in all facets of the natural environment. Many urban Americans were becoming knowledgeable and anxious about the misuses of natural resources. Agriculturalists knew about the problems caused by deforestation and land clearance, particularly about top soil exhaustion and loss. Sportsmen were vexed by the disappearance of game animals from many eastern states. On a broader front women and children could be heard voicing disapproval of cruelties practiced on domestic beasts. In their scheme of things, man had duties as well as rights in his treatment of brutes, and was responsible to God for their humane treatment.

Birds were important in this feeling for nature. They struck a responsive chord in the minds and hearts of many people. Natural historians such as Bartram and Wilson, and nature writers such as Thoreau, Higginson, Flagg and others, had shown affec-

89. M. S. Watts, *George Frederic Watts* (London, 1912), 3 p. 204.
90. G. K. Chesterton, *G. F. Watts* (London, 1904), p. 47.
91. The 54 inch by 28 inch oil canvas is housed in the Watts Gallery at Compton, Guildford, Surrey. Lilian Mackintosh, the artist's ward, posed as a sorrowful angel; after completion the work was exhibited in Manchester, Newcastle and in London (Royal Academy) in 1905.

tion for birds and concern for their well-being. By watching and caring for birds of the field and garden it was believed that children could be led closer to nature. For some bird lovers "our feathered friends" were also "little people" who instilled by force of their everyday activities human virtues. Killing them for their plumage was murderous and barbaric, betraying the finest, most civilized human sentiments.

As time passed, more voices joined with that of the ardent preservationist William Hornaday (1854–1937), who declared that: "We are weary of witnessing the greed, selfishness and cruelty of 'civilized' man toward the wild creatures of the earth. We are sick of tales of slaughter and pictures of carnage." [92] Hornaday made this remark in 1913 when the movement to preserve wildlife was in its ascendancy. Scarcely five years before, according to Hornaday, no comprehensive code of sporting ethics had been drawn up in America.

As early as the 1880's, calls were being made for changes in attitudes to the environment and its animal denizens. A ground swell of interest was shown in nature as an economic good not to be misused, as a fount of relaxation, as inspiration, and as a teacher. These themes blossomed on both sides of the Atlantic with the dawn of the twentieth century. The feather trade at that time was preparing to fight for its existence, and was seeking ways to counter bad publicity by disclaiming protectionists' charges of cruelty and extermination. It was taking stock of its strengths in the business and political fields and was preparing a rear-guard action against any legislation likely to curb the free flow of plumage.

92. Hornaday, *Our Vanishing Wildlife,* p. x.

2

The Debate Over the Plumage Trade (1880-1920)

Between 1880 and 1920 attitudes towards the trade in plumage ebbed and flowed in England and in the United States. Feather merchants and millinery establishments faced a growing clamor for embargoes against feather imports. Restraints enacted in England and the United States followed prolonged and exhausting debates between anti-plumage groups and industry spokesmen. One interpretation of final constraints upon ornamental feather imports holds that humanitarian principles and a growing appreciation of nature and wild creatures prevailed over narrower materialistic and economic goals.

In England, however, another view suggests that except for the austerity and simplicity of ornament engendered by World War I, coupled with the imponderable caprices of Dame Fashion herself, feather wearing doubtless would have continued in vogue. Tactics adopted by plumage interests in the United Kingdom were effective in delaying controls. Industry spokesmen held up legislation against plumage for twelve years, and when it did come in the form of the 1921 Plumage Bill, the Royal Society for the Protection of Birds deemed it more regulatory rather than prohibitive in nature.[1] During the decade following the passage of the 1921 Act, customs officials confiscated quantities of ornamental feathers. Bird defenders argued, however, that these seizures

1. See *Bird Notes and News* 9 (Summer, 1921) p. 41. The journal of the RSPB abbreviated to *Bird Notes* and now simply *Birds*, will be referred to in subsequent citations as *BNN*, standing for its original title *Bird Notes and News*.

and the relatively few prosecutions stemming from them were but small fare compared with the quantities of feathers still entering the country. United States' plumage laws were more comprehensive than British ones, and attempts to outwit them brought fines. A mysterious appearance of ornamental quills in American department stores occurred during and after the Second World War despite regulations prohibiting them; some people regarded the event as a tribute to the power of fashion and a measure of the ineffectiveness of legal restraints.[2]

This chapter identifies different factions in the plumage dispute on both sides of the Atlantic. It considers the issues involved, the arguments stemming from them, and the methods used to arouse, sway or assuage public opinion and to promote political action at home and abroad.

The substantive arguments and rebuttals for and against ornamental feather-wearing shifted through time. Trade representatives, for example, claimed early on that made-up or artificial feathers provided the bulk of hat trimmings. To answer charges of cruelty, they maintained later that farms existed in South America and India where plume birds nested and from which their moulted breeding plumes were collected and shipped to Europe and to the United States. Trade opponents regarded these claims as specious; or at best, a concoction of fable and fact calculated to reassure a concerned public about the innocence of an industry engaged in the ruthless and indiscriminate exploitation of scores of wild birds species. Governmental committees investigating the merits of conflicting claims found available information scarce and often fragmentary.

A number of English aristocrats, out of the pages of Debrett, closed ranks behind moves in the 1880's to discourage the use of ornamental plumage.[3] Members of the Linnean, Selborne and

2. See Richard H. Pough, "Massacred for Millinery," *Audubon Magazine* 42 (1940): 395–404. Legal loopholes were exploited until 1951. The original bi-monthly journal of the Association of Audubon Societies was named *Bird-Lore,* became the *Audubon Magazine* and at present is named simply *Audubon.* Henceforth the magazine will be referred to as *BL.* The stress on smuggling in Britain does not imply that smuggling did not occur in the United States; it did.

3. Dorothy Rook, "Protecting Britain's Birds," *BNN* (1966): 65–69. She listed the Duchess of Portland, the Baroness Burdett-Coutts, Margaret, Ranee of Sarawak as supporters of the S.P.B., all of them "the very kind of people who might have been expected to wear the fatal plumes . . ." p. 65. When His Majesty chartered the Royal Society in 1904 three duchesses, three earls, a marquess, viscount and three bishops were listed as vice-presidents of the S.P.B.

Zoological Societies, the RSPB, joined by local natural history and humane organizations, protested strongly against the wanton destruction of birds for purposes of ornament. With support from professional and popular wildlife organizations, ornithologists such as Alfred Newton (1829–1907), professor of zoology and comparative anatomy at Cambridge; Dr. R. Bowdler Sharpe of the British Museum; and Lord Lilford, president of the British Ornithologists' Union appealed publicly for an early end to plumage use.[4] William H. Hudson (1841–1922), noted naturalist and author, allied himself with the infant SPB by contributing to its leaflet program, which alerted the public to the potential disaster to birds from feather fashions.[5]

In the United States, too, scientists and authors spoke out against the plumage trade. During the final two decades of the nineteenth century, individuals from all walks of life allied themselves with a growing Audubon movement on this issue. As early as 1876, Joel A. Allen (1838–1921), co-founder of the American Ornithologists' Union (AOU), lamented the destruction of native bird species whose feathers only served the whims of middle-class urban ladies.[6] An erudite man in the natural sciences, Allen enlisted the support of fellow ornithologists, naturalists and concerned laymen to oppose millinery factions. Nature writers, members of sporting groups, the clergy, womens' organizations and humane societies campaigned before an indifferent or antagonistic

4. The first Plumage Bill introduced into the House of Lords by Lord Avebury in 1908 carried with it the support of the Linnean, Zoological and Selborne Societies; see House of Lords, *Parliamentary Debates,* 19 May, 1908, 3–11. A public meeting held in March, 1914, in support of a similar bill was sponsored by the Zoological, Avicultural, Animals' Friends Societies; the RSPB, RSPCA, British Ornithologists' Union (BOU), the Society for the Promotion of Nature Reserves, Preservation of the Fauna of the Empire, Our Dumb Friends' League; *BNN* 6 (1914), p. 14.

5. Hudson wrote at least six leaflets printed by the Society for the Protection of Birds: No. 3, *Osprey, or Egrets and Aigrettes;* No. 10, *Feathered Women;* No. 14, *Lost British Birds;* No. 25, *Letter to the Clergy;* No. 28, *The Trade in Birds' Feathers;* No. 73, *On Liberating Caged Birds:* Several biographies are devoted to this domiciled Englishman, raised in Argentina of American parents. He grew up fascinated by birds and sensitive to the nuances of nature. See Richard Haymaker, *From Pampas to Hedgerows and Downs* (New York, 1954).

6. Allen's first article lamented the decrease of birds due to "natural causes" (the inevitability of deforestation and drainage) and especially to the excessive use of firearms of the "sporting community." See "Decrease of Birds in Massachusetts," *Bull. Nuttall Ornith. Club'* (Sept., 1876): 53–60. A good historical article by Allen, "On the Decrease of Birds in the United States," *The Penn Monthly* 7 (Dec., 1876), 931–944, alluded to pressures on Florida herons sought for their plumes. Egging in tern colonies had reduced their numbers, Allen believed. He reported that Herring Gulls had begun to nest in trees through persecution (p. 937).

public, to press home the point that feather wearing caused needless suffering and sharp numerical declines to many kinds of birds.

Robert Welker has emphasized the importance of nature writers in impressing the public, especially young people, as to the
benefits of wildlife appreciation and protection.[7] John Burroughs,
Ernest Thompson Seton, Olive Thorne Miller, Florence Merriam
Bailey and others popularized bird study early this century. They
contributed to *Bird-Lore,* the bimonthly journal of the Association of Audubon Societies. The magazine was owned and edited
by Frank M. Chapman, who fought hard to instill sensitivity about
feather wearing.[8] Burroughs addressed the plumage issue in the
following terms:

> False taste in dress is as destructive to our feathered friends as
> are false aims in science. It is said that the traffic in the skins of
> our brighter-plumaged birds, arising from their use by the mil-
> liners, reaches to hundreds of thousands annually. I am told of
> one middleman who collected from the shooters in one district,
> in four months, seventy thousand skins. It is a barbarous taste
> that craves this kind of ornamentation. Think of a woman or
> girl of real refinement appearing upon the street with her head-
> gear adorned with the scalps of our songsters! [9]

7. *Birds and Men* (New York, 1955). Welker deals with the bird protection movement up to the end of the nineteenth century in the latter part of his book
(Chapters 14, 15 and 16).

8. The first edition of *Bird-Lore* consisting of 6,000 copies, was published in
February, 1899. John Burroughs wrote its first nature vignette called "In Warbler
Time," (pp. 3–5). Chapman intended the journal "to fill a place in the journalistic
world similar to that occupied by the works of Burroughs, Torrey, Dr. Van Dyke,
Mrs. Miller, and others in the domain of books," p. 28. Others promising to contribute articles on birds were: Annie Trumbull Slosson, Florence A. Merriam,
Joel A. Allen, William Brewster, Henry Nehrling, Ernest Seton Thompson, Otto
Widmann. The first edition had sections for teachers and students, and for young
observers. The call for a popular bird magazine had been made by Witmer Stone
to the AOU Committee on Bird Protection in 1898. Chapman pointed out the fact
that over 70,000 bird texts had been sold since 1893 by New York and Boston
publishers; therefore, the need for this journal was apparent. Fifteen local Audubon
Societies were listed in Vol. 1:1, p. 29, and the feather campaign was mentioned in
the very first issue in a report of the Massachusetts Audubon Society, p. 30. Insights
into Chapman's activities are found in his *Autobiography of a Bird-Lover* (New
York, 1933) and in Elizabeth S. Austin, *Frank M. Chapman in Florida: His Journals
and Letters* (Gainesville, 1967).

9. *Signs and Seasons* (Boston, 1886, 1914), p. 214. This passage was adapted from
an article "Birds-Enemies," *Century Magazine* 31:2 (1885), 270–278, which was re-
viewed in *The Auk* 3 (1886), pp. 142–3. It roundly castigated Burroughs for his
attack on ornithologists as causing bird declines. "Can it be that our friend is so
entirely unconscious of the wholesale slaughter of birds for millinery purposes as his
silence on the subject would seem to indicate?" The review concluded "It is to
be hoped that when next Mr. Burroughs assumes the role of public censor he will
have a fair degree of acquaintance with the subject he takes in hand."

Burroughs, affectionately known as "John O'Birds," criticized Thompson Seton and others for undue anthropomorphism and sensationalism in essays about animal life and behavior. Whatever the justice of his criticism, such popularisers of bird study as Seton, George Trafton, and Bradford Torrey encouraged children to take a healthy interest in nature by instilling an understanding, couched perhaps in emotional images, of "our feathered friends," which probably helped make feather wearing repugnant to many readers as they grew older.[10]

These "faddist and sickly sentimental" groups, as plume dealers and trade representatives of London and New York put it, were overreacting to a well-established and reputable industry offering gainful employment to scores of thousands of workers in the fashion centers of the Western world. Feather importers, brokers, manufacturers and millinery houses were the principal trade propagandists. Members of the Textile Section of the London Chamber of Commerce, the New York Millinery Merchants' Protective Association, and the Chambres Syndicales and the Association of Feather Merchants and Manufacturers of Paris, vigorously defended themselves against attacks they considered unjustified.[11] They struck out at "misguided elitists" with "neither truth nor the support of the public" on their side. Some apparel trade journals, fashion magazines and scientific periodicals argued in favor of the plumage industry or gave space to its supporters.[12]

10. Burroughs, "Real and Sham Natural History," *Atlantic* (1903), pp. 298–309. The nature-faking dispute was placed in the broader context of the natural history essay by P. M. Hicks, *The Development of the Natural History Essay in American Literature* (Philadelphia, 1924), pp. 126–156. The best known biography of Burroughs is that by Clara Barrus, *The Life and Letters of John Burroughs*, 2 vols. (Boston, 1925).

11. Lefèvre, *l'Industrie de la Plume* (Paris, 1914), pp. 226–228. In 1798, 25 plumassiers were known in France. In 1862 there were 120, and 280 in 1870. Among feather groups Lefèvre listed: La Chambre syndicale des Négociants en plumes brutes; La Chambre syndicale des Fabricants de plumes pour parures (1893); La Chambre syndicale des Fabricants de plumes fantaisies pour modes (1904); La Chambre syndicale des Fleurs et Plumes (1858); La Chambre syndicale des Teinturiers en plumes; La Chambre syndicale des Fournitures générales pour fleurs et plumes; La Société de Secours mutuels des Fleuristes et Plumassiers (1852); La Société pour l'assistance paternelle des enfans employés dans les industries des fleurs et plumes (1866); Caisse patronale de Secours de l'industrie des Plumes pour parures; and Caisse de Secours Immédiat aux ouvrières plumassières.

12. Feelings often ran high between the two factions, as reflected in correspondence to the editors of *The Times* of London and New York. In an exchange between Nov. 18 and 29, 1897, in the *New York Times* a trade defender suggested that an anti-Audubon Society should be formed to counteract the mock sentiment of Audubonists.

"But as 'constant dropping weareth away the hardest stone,' and reiterated mis-

Charles F. Downham, manager of a firm dealing in feathers, was
an articulate defender of the trade in England. He spent long
hours before Parliamentary committees refuting arguments forwarded by plumage groups. Some members of both Parliament
and Congress, representing trade interests, disdained what they
viewed as the hysterical outbursts of well-intentioned but over-
zealous ladies' societies.[13]

Before discussing the substantive positions for or against the
plumage trade, a word about relevant source materials is necessary. Information about the feather issue abounds. Newspaper
articles, popular essays, professional papers, government monographs, Parliamentary debates and historical studies of wildlife
conservation movements in both England and America provide
direct and indirect coverage of the controversy, especially between
1900 and 1920. In England, the RSPB published a series of leaflets
outlining specific claims of the trade and rebutting them one by
one.[14] Charles F. Downham, *The Feather Trade: The Case for the*

---

statements in the end gradually affect the thoughts or beliefs of those who hear
them," so too the crusade against bird millinery, exaggerated and distorted as it
was, hurt the interests of the feather dealers. So reasoned Harold Hamel Smith,
Aigrettes and Bird Skins (London, 1910), p. 15. As editor of *Tropical Life*, he gave
space to the trade in his journal. Charles W. Farmer, Secretary of the New York
Millinery Merchants' Protective Association, defended the trade in columns of the
Millinery Trade Review and elsewhere. *The Draper's Record* devoted sympathetic
attention to the trade interests. The *Bulletin de la Société d'Acclimatation* (Paris)
gave ample coverage to trade and protectionists. Helen Berkeley Lloyd, "Fashions
in New York," *The Delineator* 67 (1906): 7–11, believed the magazine was being
unjustly blamed for recommending the use of feathers, when all it did was to record
their vogue; surely a case of inertial guidance. The Port of London Authority came
out against the Plumage Bill (1914) on account of loss of revenue from storage dues,
see *Parl. Debates—Commons* 59, 9 March, 1914, par. 979–982.

13. Downham read a paper to the London Chamber of Commerce in November,
1910, which was published in part in the *National Review* (November, 1910) and
later as a monograph entitled *The Feather Trade: The Case for the Defense* (London, 1911). He argued his case in the columns of *The Times* (London). See 4 Nov.,
1910, p. 16, col. 3; 4 April 1913, p. 5, col. 6; 3 Jan., 1914, p. 4, col. 2; 6 March
1914, p. 10, col. 5. Downham put the trade's case to the Select Committee of the
House of Lords on the Importation of Plumage Prohibition Bill, on 24 June, 1908;
and (together with other representatives of the Textile Trade Section of the London
Chamber of Commerce) before the Inter-Departmental Conference on the Destruction of Plumage Birds, on 1 March, 1911. He was appointed a member of the
Plumage Committee in 1921.

14. Almost half of some 80 leaflets published by the RSPB, were devoted to the
plumage issue, beginning in the 1890's with no. 1 called "Destruction of Ornamental-
Plumage Birds" to "Imported Plumes for Millinery: Attempts to Evade Prohibition,"
published in 1925. The Society introduced a brochure "Murderous Millinery" complete with a colored plate of five plume species, to bolster a resolution against
feather millinery at the International Conference of Women in Edinburgh, July, 1938.

Defense (1911), promoted succinctly and in detail the case for the plumage trade. Shortly after Downham's publication, the RSPB, in *Feathers and Facts: A Reply to the Feather-Trade* (1911), responded in kind to trade statements. *Hearings* of a Select Committee of the House of Lords on the Plumage Bill of 1908 [15] contains a wealth of information, as do the *Minutes* of an Interdepartmental Conference on the Destruction of Plumage Birds sponsored by the Colonial Office between 1911 and 1913,[16] and, also the unpublished information of the Plumage Committee [17] appointed by the Board of Trade to make recommendations about additions to and subtractions from the schedule of birds drawn up under the British Plumage Act of 1921.

In the United States, the National Association of Audubon Societies, in its leaflets and circulars and through the columns of its journal *Bird-Lore,* played much the same role in the controversy as the RSPB did in England. William T. Hornaday (1913, 1931) denounced the industry in vitriolic language. In their autobiographies, Frank M. Chapman (1933) and T. Gilbert Pearson (1937), both Audubon Society officials who were prominent in bird protection, provided evidence of plume-bird destruction and helped direct the campaign to oust the plumage industry from the American scene. Hearings of Committees of the House and Senate and pages of the *Congressional Record,* especially those covering the debate on the Tariff Act in 1913, are replete with facts and arguments about feather wearing.

In France, much of the literature on the controversy tended to be sympathetic to the trade's position, reflecting the interests of an old and lucrative Paris feather market. The *Bulletin* of the Société d'Acclimatation gave ample coverage of the history of the ornamental feather trade and accounts of egret, pheasant and ostrich farms can be found in its columns.[18]

15. Referred to in future as Lords Select Committee.
16. Referred to as Colonial Office Hearings.
17. Abbreviated to P.C., Correspondence or Minutes.
18. Jules Forest published at least fifteen articles covering all aspects of the plumage trade—its history, significance to France and the problems it faced. The few complete books devoted to the trade are in French. The most comprehensive is by Edmond Lefèvre, 1914. Short monographs by Justin Montillot, 1891, and E. Morin *La Plume des Oiseaux* . . . 1914, expressed sympathy for the trade. Morin was vice-president of the Chambre Syndicale des fabricants de plumes fantaisies pour modes. Henri A. Ménégaux of the Museum d'Histoire Naturelle, Paris, wrote several articles considered by the RSPB to be overly gracious to the trade, *BNN* 4 (1911), p. 77.

Utilitarian Arguments in the Plumage Dispute

In his address to the British Association in 1868, Alfred Newton, a Cambridge University zoologist, made a plea for a closed season to protect colonies of breeding seafowl from the guns of "sportsmen" and millinery agents bent upon procuring the heads and wings of Kittiwakes (*Rissa tridactyla*) nesting along the chalk cliffs of Flamborough Head, Yorkshire, and elsewhere.[19] Newton thought that some seabirds were useful and most were innocuous. For example, the Lapwing (*Vanellus vanellus*), an inland-nesting wader, helped clear grubs from farmers' fields. Moved by the professor's concern and by lobbying from local groups, Mr. Christopher Sykes, Member of Parliament from the East Riding of Yorkshire, introduced a Sea Birds' Preservation Bill into the Commons in February, 1869.[20] Taking notice of ancillary humanitarian arguments, Sykes claimed that seabirds were useful to farmers in following the plough and devouring harmful insects from the upturned sod. Merchant seamen heard the calls of these "Flamborough pilots" and steered clear of shoals and cliffs when heading to port in fog billowing in from the North Sea. Fishermen followed gulls in the belief that wheeling flocks indicated schools of fish; according to Newton, the extermination of the gulls was an economic bane the fishing industry could ill afford. Based mainly on such utilitarian arguments, the seabird bill passed both Houses of Parliament and received Royal Assent on 24 June, 1869.

The initial move to protect plume birds in England focused upon marine species; in America, ornithologists, witnessing similar demands for gulls and terns along the Atlantic seaboard, emphasized also the especial utility of insectivorous birds. J. A. Allen's essay in *The Penn Monthly* (1876) was a masterful synopsis of natural and man-made agents of bird destruction. He used both economic and aesthetic arguments to push for the protection of non-game birds. Action came from the AOU's Committee on Bird Protection, established in 1884, which began collecting data about the agricultural benefits of passerines and birds

19. "The Zoological Aspect of Game Laws," *British Association*, Section D. (1868), in S.P.B. *Third Annual Report* (1892–1893), Appendix: 24–31.
20. House of Commons: *Parl. Debates* 3 series, vol. 194, 26 Feb., 1869, pp. 404–406. The history of the Bill can be followed through the session. Ibid., 5 March, 9 April, Lords 1st Reading 13 April, Passage 11 May, Royal Assent 24 June, 1869.

of prey. These studies were counterweights to the claims of millinery agents that many birds were noxious, and to the activities of southern European immigrants, accustomed to snaring, netting or shooting birdlife at home, and who viewed birds with a gourmet's eye.[21] In April, 1885, the same AOU Council proposed that the American, Dr. C. Hart Merriam, be made head of the Department of Economic Ornithology (which later developed into the Biological Survey) in the Division of Entomology, Department of Agriculture, to study in depth the relationships of birds to agriculture.[22] Under his direction, research into food habits of many passerines was sponsored by the Government beginning in July, 1885.

The usefulness of birds was emphasized by the incipient Audubon movement which claimed that ladies and the industry they supported were doing a special disservice:

> To the largest and most important class of our population—the farmers. These are injured in two ways; by the destruction of the birds, whose food consists chiefly of insects injurious to the growing crops, and of that scarcely less important group the Rapaces, which prey upon the small rodents which devour the crop after it has matured.[23]

Gulls and terns, it was pointed out, were aids to mariners and fishermen, while raptors and passerines were helpful to farmers; other groups of birds were useful as guano producers and as scavengers. Some birds controlled disease hosts.[24] It was obvious

21. The initiative for establishing the AOU Bird Protection Committee came from William Brewster, who was elected its first chairman. George Bird Grinnell and William Dutcher were among committee members. In 1885 it was enlarged to 10 members and George Sennett became chairman; see *The Auk* 1 (1884), p. 376, and 3 (1886), p. 143. W. H. Hudson had a complaint similar to Hornaday (1913) about Italian immigrants into Argentina being exterminators of small birds.

22. C. Hart Merriam became head of the Division of Economic Ornithology and Mammalogy on 1 July, 1886. An Act of April, 1896 made it into the Division of Biological Survey which achieved Bureau status in 1905. For details see Jenks Cameron, *The Bureau of Biological Survey* . . . (Baltimore, 1929), pp. 1–2, 22. Hornaday (1913), pp. 213–233, mentions some of the species dealt with by the Biological Survey. A basic bibliography of research into the relations of birds to agriculture was written by Waldo Lee McAtee, "Index to Papers Relating to the Food of Birds by Members of the Biological Survey in Publications of the U.S. Dept. of Agriculture, 1885–1911," *U.S.D.A. Bur. of Biol. Survey Bull.* no. 43. (Washington, D.C., 1913) 69 pp.

23. From the editorial founding the Audubon Society in *Forest and Stream* 26 (11 Feb., 1886).

24. See Sir Harry H. Johnston (Letter to the Editor), *The Times* (London), 24 March, 1920, and reprinted in part in *BNN* 9 (1920), p. 3.

to the opponents of the trade that the value of birds to human welfare far outweighed their employment as ephemeral trimmings by the *haute couture* of Paris and London. Reduced to skins and feathers, birds were items of luxury and conspicuous consumption.

Preservationists did not argue that every bird they wished to protect was useful, nor could they do so. Initially they believed that the heron family, the *cause célèbre* of the plumage dispute, hardly merited the laudits accorded to swallows, bee-eaters and fly-catchers. In fact, many trade sympathizers emphasized that the Ardeidae family were singularly useless. Their statements are best exemplified by the colorful remark of Senator Reed of Missouri, who said in the course of a Congressional debate of the 1913 Tariff Bill:

> I really honestly want to know why there should be any sympathy or sentiment about a long-legged, long-beaked, long-necked bird that lives in swamps and eats tadpoles and fish and crawfish and things of that kind; why we should worry ourselves into a frenzy because some lady adorns her hat with one of its feathers, which appears to be the only use it has.[25]

Increasingly conscious of claims that they were killing ecologically as well as economically beneficial creatures, industry supporters repeatedly expressed their willingness to take precautions against damage to agricultural interests. The numbers and often the kinds of birds to be spared for insect control, however, were impossible to determine. Trade representatives maintained that

25. *Congressional Record* 63 Cong., 1st sess., 16 Aug., 1913, 3426. Senator Reed received his answer in a letter from George Bird Grinnell addressed to Oscar W. Underwood, Chairman of the House Ways and Means Committee, dated 6th Feb., 1913. Arguing against the importation of American birds and their allies into the country, thereby amending Section 438, Schedule N of the Tariff revision bill, Grinnell stated: "Most of the hawks, owls, and herons destroy great numbers of field mice, meadow mice, and other small rodents which injure growing plants and consume grain and other vegetation. In certain portions of the South, some of the herons destroy great numbers of crayfish, often a serious pest to the farmer, while all the smaller herons feed very largely on grasshoppers, cutworms, and other insects." See U.S. Congress, House, Committee on Ways and Means, *Hearings tariff schedule N—Sundries*, 29–30 Jan., 1913, 62 Cong. 3 Session, p. 5344. The Indian Smaller Egret (*E.* or *Mesophoyx intermedia intermedia*) a species intermediate in size between the larger white herons (*C. albus*) and smaller *garzetta* or *thula* species, was guarded jealously for its plumes. It subsisted mainly on insects, especially coleoptera and grasshoppers, E. C. Stuart Baker, *The Fauna of British India including Ceylon and Burma Birds*, vol. 6, 2nd edition (London, 1929), pp. 347–348.

very few insectivorous species were utilized for plumage purposes; they sought pest species or at least "useless" ones.

Pressing this point further, Charles Downham, manager of a reputable London feather firm, insisted that farming itself was inimical to bird life. The spread of urban places and agriculture caused reductions in numbers and the disappearance of many wild birds. He asserted that settlement and habitat change, rather than the plume hunters, were responsible for decreases of herons in Florida. A green parrot of British India, a grain-eating bird he thought of the "worst character," deserved no better end than to supplement the income of the impoverished native who shot it.[26]

India was an early center of dispute about killing insectivorous birds for plumage purposes. A protest against this slaughter was raised in the Madras Presidency in 1881. Controls initiated through the Wild Birds Protection Act (1887) empowered local governments in India to regulate the possession and sale of plumage in the breeding season. Pressure for more stringent regulations finally resulted, in 1902, in the prohibition of the shipment of wild birds from British India for millinery purposes. Trade appeals to have this customs embargo lifted were unsuccessful, however. For many years, considerable quantities of illicit "osprey," kingfisher and other plumage were smuggled out of India and sold openly on the London market. The RSPB published a list of Indian birds taken for their feathers; three-quarters of thirty-two species named were insectivorous and deemed especially worthy of protection.[27]

26. *The Feather Trade: The Case for the Defense* (London, 1911), pp. 20–22. To the Lords Select Committee, 24 June, 1908, Charles Downham pointed out that over 15,000 Indian parrots were sold on the London market in June, 1907, despite the export prohibition. They were smuggled out of the country to France, Germany and England. According to Downham, many of these crop-eating birds were left to rot when killed; thus, the Indian native lost an additional source of income due to an unnecessary law, p. 20.

27. Details of measures taken in India to suppress plumage export, particularly of insectivorous birds, were supplied by the RSPB, *Feathers & Facts* (London, 1911), pp. 13, 61–62; and by Sir Charles Lawson, "India and Her Wild Birds," SPB *Leaflet* no. 36. The list of species captured in southern India for plumage purposes is supplied on page 11. In the *Twelfth Annual Report* (1902), p. 5, the SPB commented upon legislation in India: "It constitutes the first definite action taken by a British Government towards suppressing the trade in birds' feathers. It refers to British India, and is contained in Customs Circular No. 13 of 1902, promulgated at Simla in September. 'In exercise of the power conferred by Section 19 of the Sea Customs Act, 1878, The Governor-General in Council is pleased to prohibit the taking by sea or land out of British India of skins and feathers of all birds, except (a) feathers of ostriches, and (b) skins and feathers exported *bona fide* as specimens illustrative of natural history.' "

At first glance Government action in British India seemed to substantiate claims that the plumage trade was making inroads into populations of useful birds. However, people in the trade said that the 1902 restrictions were imposed arbitrarily with little prior publicity and without public discussion.[28] Sir Herbert Maxwell, M.P., supporting the protectionists, suggested that England would be better served if the millinery industry employed London girls to make hat trimmings of ribbon, lace and artificial flowers rather than having natives half a world away hunt birds, some of which were useful and many attractive. He concluded that rather than wear the wings or heads of owls, in vogue in the 1890's, it would be more flattering if, "assuming it to be necessary for ladies to display the spoils of animated nature in their attire, they should adopt the fashion of wearing the carcases of rats, mice and other furred marauders on their heads." [29]

Utilitarian arguments put forward by the trade to repeal the Indian ban on the export of wild birds' plumage were used again eleven years later in attempts to prevent import restrictions in the United States. Attorneys for New York City feather dealers opposed a provision of the Underwood Tariff Bill (1913) which terminated the trade in foreign wild birds' plumage. They made a special appeal to be permitted to use game birds, whose plumage was held to go to waste when sportsmen dressed quail and waterfowl carcasses for the table. Pestiferous species, such as the English sparrow, crows, hawks, and certain owls, were to be given no quarter, as they damaged crops and barnyard fowl.[30]

William T. Hornaday argued against such proposals because of the transitory meaning of the terms "game" and "pest species." He pointed out that Italians, who cavalierly shot thrushes and warblers under the aegis of sport hunting, differed in their understanding of what was game back home and what was game in America. In fact, Hornaday discovered that many scores of bird species were regarded as game birds at one place or another in

28. Harold Hamel Smith, *Aigrettes & Bird Skins* (London, 1910), p. 25. In the case of India, Hamel Smith supported the establishment of closed seasons for endangered species but not the prohibition of plumage export. Peacocks and parrots formed the bulk of India's plumage exports, therefore, he thought that there was no reason to include them in the 1902 Notification on utilitarian grounds, pp. 47–48.

29. "Fowls of the Air," SPB *Leaflet* no. 23 (1896), pp. 5, 6.

30. Feiner and Maas (Letter to the editor), *New York Times*, 29 May, 1913, p. 10, col. 6. They replied to Hornaday's rebuttal, ibid., 4 June, 1913, p. 10, col. 5.

the world. Not only would import exemptions for game species be unworkable, they would also result in extra pressures on game populations once a species was deemed valuable for plumage as well as meat. "Pest species" was likewise an ambiguous classification likely to be applied on the basis of ignorance or traditional prejudice. Hornaday believed that ongoing research conducted by the Biological Survey into the diet and behavior of birds was discovering that far more were beneficial than deleterious to mankind.[31]

Humanitarian Concerns in the Plumage Dispute

Almost every article, book, report and hearing stressed the issue of cruelty. Continuing diatribes in the correspondence columns of *The Times* (London) and the *New York Times* for a period of more than thirty years testify eloquently to this fact. RSPB and Audubon literature, speeches in Congress and in Parliament addressed the need for curbs upon reckless bird destruction and wantonly cruel methods of plume procurement. The charges were hotly denied or obfuscated by those engaged in the trade.[32] Protectionists believed that although some plume species were not economically useful, they should not be assumed *a priori* to be harmful. Many of these beautiful, innoxious birds, it was held, deserved a better end than as sops to female vanity. Moreover, feather wearing demoralized and degraded womankind and made a travesty of the better instincts of motherhood. An oft repeated remark made by Alfred Newton about a feathered woman was that, "she bears the murderer's brand on her forehead."

The methods used to secure plumes, it was believed, should offend the sensibilities of city ladies accustomed to the Victorian norms of love, thoughtfulness and refinement, which were especially characteristic of the gentler sex. Dead birds on hats were

31. (Letter to the Editor), *New York Times*, 31 May, 1913, p. 10, col. 6. For further comments on the relative meaning of the term pest, see *Our Vanishing Wild Life* (New York, 1913), pp. 223–226, in which the hawk and owl bounty law enacted by Pennsylvania in 1885 apparently resulted in 180,000 scalps being bought in the following two years. "It was estimated that the saving to the farmers in poultry amounted to one dollar for each $1,205 paid out in bounties," p. 223. However, Hornaday conceded that each "bird of prey is a balanced equation." He expressed little sympathy for hawks and falcons.

32. Basic references are listed in note 13, above. *The Times* (London) between 1908 and 1921 gives considerable space to correspondence covering most facets of the dispute, see listings under "Birds, Feathers" in annual indexes.

vulgar and barbaric. What true lady could remain unmoved by a plea to end the needless suffering of winged creatures?

> Ten thousand, thousand little birds
>   In cruel hands a-dying,
> Could you but see the white wings torn
>   From birds alive and bleeding,
> And note their quivering agony,
>   I had no need of pleading.[33]

Trade spokesmen rejected such emotional appeals as products of unstable minds, nourished by female fantasy; but some scientists also used epithets such as wanton, cruel, barbarous, and heartless in their addresses and essays on the subject of feather wearing.

The heron family was selected for special attention as among the longest and most keenly persecuted of plume birds. Ornithologists, travellers and nature writers stepped forward to recount tales of heron slaughter in breeding colonies on all continents. Boyhood experiences in the Florida hummocks left T. Gilbert Pearson (1873–1943) with an indelible impression of bird suffering which he communicated to American and English readers in poignant and colorful language.

> A few miles north of Waldo, in the flat pine region, our party came one day upon a little swamp where we had been told Herons bred in numbers. Upon approaching the place the screams of young birds reached our ears. The cause of this soon became apparent by the buzzing of green-flies and the heaps of dead Herons festering in the sun, with the back of each bird raw and

33. Rev. H. Greene, "As in a Mirror," SPB *Leaflet* no. 2, p. 11. Mrs. Frank E. Lemon read a paper addressed to the International Congress of Women, Westminister, London, 3 July, 1899 entitled "Dress in Relation to Animal Life," (S.P.B. *Leaflet* no. 33). She pointed to the ornithologists' (Howard Saunders, Thomas Southwell and T. Gilbert Pearson) accounts of cruelty in feather procurement. Yet women remained unmoved:

> If an out-and-out worldling declares by her words and her conduct that she will wear feathers procured only at the cost of great suffering, and that she cares nothing for the extermination of lovely species of useful beings, we fear that her heart and conscience must be non-existent; but when good women, who we *know* are in earnest in their desire that right should triumph over wrong, refuse to help our righteous cause, then we feel in despair, and ready to cry. "Let the birds perish! Let them perish! The sooner their sufferings are ended the better, and then, when it is too late, man (and woman) will discover what a poor, worthless, uninhabitable place this world is without the birds" (p. 8).

bleeding. . . . Young Herons had been left by scores in the nests to perish from exposure and starvation.[34]

Vivid photographs of egret killing in New South Wales, Australia, in 1906, caused a stir in England. Submitted by A. H. Mattingley of the Australian Ornithologists' Union to the RSPB, the photographic essay portrayed nesting activities of white egrets terminated by a visit from plume hunters, who left the colony a shambles of dead adults and starving, moribund nestlings.[35] "The Story of the Egret," as the RSPB named the pictures from the Murray Basin, was posted on bill-boards in London and displayed in windows of shops throughout southern England. In the summer of 1911, men with billboards carrying enlargements of the story, patrolled the West End and brought the cruelty behind osprey wearing home to shoppers, businessmen and by-standers. The story was circulated to officials of every large town in England and distributed to interested groups in Paris, Amsterdam, Italy, Spain and Denmark. It received widespread publicity in Australia, and Audubon Societies circulated it in the United States.[36]

The trade response to this kind of attack was varied. Its members branded the RSPB and other protectionist groups as both hypocritical and pharisaical. Their arguments enabled them to thank heaven for being above other men in respect to bird slaughter. Taking a different tact, one trade spokesman, Harold Hamel Smith, pointed to a tenet of the RSPB which declared the Society was neutral about legitimate killing for purposes of sport. "Why should it be legal or less cruel for English men and women to kill birds for pleasure than for the starving or half-starving na-

34. Extracted from a paper read at the World's Congress on Ornithology, Chicago, 1897. The event occurred in 1891 when Pearson was 18 years old. His rendition of Horse Hummock (Fla.) received very wide circulation.

35. The details of slaughter for plumes differed little from those coming from Florida, South America and Europe. However, Mattingly managed to secure photographic documentation of conditions before and after the plume hunters' visits. A. H. E. Mattingley, "A Visit to Heronries," *The Emu* 7 (1907): 65–73. Mattingley made his first visit to Mathoura., Riverina, N.S.W. in November, 1906. There he found *Egretta intermedia* and *Casmerodius albus* breeding. The colony of about 150 birds had already received attention from plume hunters and been reduced from a former count of about 750. On his second visit in December, 1906, he found at least 50 dead adult egrets and at least 200 young birds dead or dying in the nests from starvation.

36. Sir Herbert Maxwell read about this episode in an Australian newspaper and recorded it in the *Pall Mall Gazette*, 25 Feb., 1908. Actions by the RSPB in spreading the story are found in *BNN* 3 (1908), p. 3; (1909), pp. 71–72, 88–89, 94–96; 4 (1910), p. 40; (1911), p. 79; 5 (1913), p. 100; also in *Feathers and Facts*, p. 59.

tives to do so to earn their living?" he asked. Peers active in promoting the Society's goals and image took pleasure in the chase. The cruelty perpetrated from butts on the grouse moors of Yorkshire was conveniently forgotten by the gentlefolk of England who reserved their wrath and consciences for purveyors of bird skins and the auction sales of Mincing Lane. He added that, "the members of the Bird Societies have no more right to dictate what trimming women should wear in their hats than vegetarians have to pass laws to prohibit our taking life in order to eat flesh." His remarks went beyond Britain as he lambasted, quite appropriately, the choice of name made by those bird lovers of the Audubon societies. "Thus Audubon, patron saint, one might say, of American naturalists, glories in the sport of shooting, as do the leaders of those who have stopped the Indian export of birds, and so made the lot of many a poor man or family in India even more desperate than its might otherwise be." [37]

Similarly, Lt. Col. Archer-Shee, member of Parliament for an East London borough, spoke out in the Commons against the Plumage Bill of 1920. He declared that members of the House came to the chambers clad from head to foot in animal produce. Their bodies were clothed in the fleece of sheep, their feet in cattle hide, their heads in rabbit skins and some wore mink coats. What about the cruelty involved in obtaining these pelts? Killing a few birds for female adornment was but a drop in an ocean of cruelty.[38]

These rebuttals raised interesting points. Hamel Smith questioned the distinction between killing for sport and killing for profit (meat, hides and plumage). Cruelty was part of both, whatever the original motives might be. How many hares, bucks and pheasants had stumbled away maimed by the sporting chance afforded them? In comparison, killing for the feather trade, he said, was well planned, swift and efficient. No doubt the small, leisured-class could afford to treat the millinery trade's ends as mundane, buts its methods were less cruel as a premium was placed on quick, efficient killing. Smith questioned the traditional values of the aristocracy, which regarded the hunt as a form of recreation and a

37. Smith, *Aigrettes & Birdskins*, quoted from pp. 60, 26 and 41. His choler towards protectionists sprang from a belief that official committees, especially in England, were prejudiced against the trade. For example, the Lords Committee appointed to investigate Avebury's Bill (1908) was chaired by Avebury himself, sponsor and confidante of bird protection groups. Two of its four peer members were Vice-Presidents and Fellows of the RSPB.

38. *Parliamentary Debates* 5th Series, vol. 128, 30 April, 1920, par. 1667.

symbol of rank and authority. Its medieval context of exclusive-
ness had been challenged by early settlers in America, who threw
off restraints against hunting, and impressed by the abundance of
game, killed animals for pleasure, subsistence and profit. The
sensitivity to wildlife and reaffirmation of the ethics of sportsman-
ship contained in the columns of *Forest and Stream* (first published in 1873) was partly produced by a growing vision of scarcity
and a fear of extermination, as preached by Frank Forester and
others. It was hardly the reflection of any traditional or deep-
seated love of nature, as the protectionist ethos of cruelty im-
plied.[39]

Having contrasted inconsistencies between the beliefs and actions of "bird lovers," commercial spokesmen maintained that
charges of cruelty were groundless for two other reasons. First,
technological improvements, permitted the use of feathers of
domestic fowl, ostrich plumes, and even horsehair and hogs'
bristles in fabricating aigrettes.[40] Second, increasing quantities of
heron and egret plumage came from farms or nesting colonies
where natives collected moulted feathers from the ground and
avoided killing adult birds in breeding condition.

Intended as a response to strident criticism, these stories of
"made-up trimmings," "moulted plumes and egret "farms" served
only to compound the trade's problems. Ornithologists, naturalists
and travellers quickly declared trade claims to be false. They ac-
cused the plumage industry of deceit and generated more publicity
hostile to the trade.

During the energetic, uncomplimentary correspondence about
feather wearing in 1913, an editorial in the *New York Times* (2
June, 1913) stated sardonically:

> Again and again have the [plumage traders] been led—by noth-
> ing worse, doubtless, than over-credulity in the interested re-
> ports of lying agents far away—to misrepresent the facts as to
> bird slaughter and its lamentable effects. Always somebody who

39. Edward H. Graham, *The Land and Wildlife* (New York, 1947), p. 12, passim.
Ernest A. Englebert, "American Policy for Natural Resources: A Historical Survey
to 1862," unpublished Ph.D. thesis Harvard University, 1950); Marvin W. Kranz,
"Pioneering in Conservation: A History of the Conservation Movement in N.Y.
State, 1865–1903," unpublished Ph.D. thesis (Syracuse Univ., 1961).

40. Mr. Matthew Hale, a plumage broker, said: "You have to have a very clever
detective to be able to go round and tell you which were the horsehair and which
were the real egrets. Imitations are made from bristles and horsehair, and it is
done so wonderfully that it is very difficult for anyone but an expert to be able
to tell you which is which." *Lords Select Committee*, 8th July, 1908.

knew has come forward with the truth, more or less horrible,
and now the public is almost as well instructed as to the doings
of the feather hunters in New Guinea or Sumatra as it is about
those of the Florida swamps.[41]

A year later Ernest Ingersoll echoed the fatigue of the public
about the issue in remarking: "the feather men are fighting for
their iniquitious traffic with the same animosity as has so long
animated the slave-traders." [42] The feather industry was then
being curtailed in the United States and was under heavy pressure
in England.

As early as 1896, Sir William Flower, Director of the British
Museum of Natural History, examined hat trimmings of artificial
ospreys. He found them to be genuine heron or egret feathers.
The only artificiality about them was that they had been cut in
half, the lower and upper halves fitted together, in the form of a
brush. A single plume thereby functioned as two.[43] However,
made-up trimmings did exist. Walking through the West End of
London in 1891, Adolph Boucard, naturalist and feather merchant, was surprised to find strings of small birds of "all kinds of
feathers, badly made, some badly dyed, and with the most un-
natural and grotesque appearance." Thinking they were cheap
toys he was chagrined to find they were Parisian trimmings cost-
ing between six and twenty shillings a dozen. They were intended
for ladies with scruples about wearing wild birds.[44] The RSPB
published a *caveat* to lady members about so-called artificial feathers. The Society acknowledged the existence of these trimmings
but believed that genuine ospreys were passed off as fakes, and
bunches of artificial feathers had wild ones set with them.[45]

41. The reference is to the myth of the "dropped plume," and poor starving
people who were dependent upon the trade for their subsistence, p. 6, col. 4–5.
42. Letter to the Editor, *New York Times*, 25 March, 1914, p. 10, col. 6.
43. Letter to the Editor, *The Times* (London), 25 June, 1896, p. 12, and reprinted
as SPB *Leaflet* no. 27. His successor Professor Ray Linkester made a similar statement in the *Daily News*, 16 October, 1903.
44. "What is to be seen everywhere in London," *The Humming Bird* 1 (1891);
1–2 and 9–10. Boucard did his best to impress upon his readers the absurdity of
eschewing plume wearing. He wished to make it known, "especially to the fair sex
of both worlds, to explain that it will make very little difference to the wingy
tribe, if Ladies condemn themselves in not wearing as adorns to their perfections
the most brilliant jewels of Creation . . . which enhances [sic] so harmoniously
with their charms," p. 2.
45. E. Morin, *La Plume des Oiseaux*, p. 65, fig. 18, illustrated butterflies made
from the feathers of cock, goose, and argus pheasant. Aigrettes were made from

Accounts of egret shooting in the breeding season openly contradicted theories about heron farms and moulted plumes. Neither feather dealers nor their opponents denied that aigrettes were mainly dorsal plumage of herons and egrets in breeding condition. The argument between them was over the methods used to procure such plumes.

Egret Farms, Moulted Plumes and Cruelty

The term "farming" in the context of plume gathering had two meanings. In a general sense, farming meant protection. Trade statements emphasized that breeding colonies, or *garceros,* of white Ardeidae were completely protected in South America. Only at the end of the breeding season were natives permitted to enter nesting areas to gather moulted feathers off the ground. Instead of going to waste, these plumes were sorted, bundled and shipped to London, New York, or Paris, where they were properly cleansed and prepared as hat ornaments. The greater the numbers of feathers collected in the *garceros* of Brazil and Venezuela, it was said, the more landowners were able to realize in monetary terms. Therefore, it was incumbent upon the landowners to protect herons so that bird populations remained high. Bird protection was good business. Rather than criticizing dealers and millinery houses for cruelty, it was held that bird groups should congratulate them and lend them support for their intelligent use of a resource. Farming in this sense avoided cruelty, both to individual birds and, in a sense, to species, whose survival depended on a sufficiently large breeding population. In short, trade goals were in concert with those of protectionists.

Informed sources rejected such arguments. Some people scoffed at the tale of collecting moulted feathers in carefully protected *garceros.* The birds involved were mostly *Casmerodius albus* and *Egretta thula.* Both ranged over wide areas of Central and South America, the larger egret (*albus*) reaching into Patagonia and the smaller bird into Chile and northern Argentina. These two species supplied shipments of plumage to Europe and North America.

A total of about 50 kilos of heron plumage was exported from

---

domestic goose quills (figs. 22 and 23, pp. 77, 79) and sweeping bird of paradise feathers were made from cock and rhea plumage (figs. 26–29, pp. 85, 87, 89 and 91).

The RSPB acknowledged the existences of artificial ospreys in *Feathers and Facts,* pp. 16–17, and also in *BNN* (1910), p. 29.

Argentina between 1895 and 1898, increasing to 1,500 kilos from 1899 to 1907 with most of the total going to France and Germany.[46] Between 1901 and 1904, export figures for Brazil listed more than 400 kilos of heron feathers from Amazon ports, some of it bound for the United States.[47] Venezuelan statistics for a nine-year period ending in 1912 revealed that 13,000 kilos of "plumas de garza" were shipped abroad.[48] Was this approximately 15,000 kilos of plumage picked up from the ground? From how many individual birds did it come?

Evidence confirms arguments of protectionist groups that ospreys and aigrettes were obtained largely by killing adult birds during the breeding season. Investigations made by scientists, consular officials, and the testimony of people knowledgeable about methods of collecting heron feathers in South America indicated that the normal way to gather plumes was to shoot herons in or about their roockeries. The little protection afforded to the *garceros* was poorly enforced.[49] Around Belém, from which three firms did good business with Paris fifty years ago, and on nearby Marajó Island, an important source for lower-Amazon egret plumes, herons were killed in large numbers.

Professor Emilio Goeldi (1859–1917) became a pioneer in working for heron protection in Brazil. Naturalist, author, and head of the Natural History Museum in Belém, he wrote two impassioned memorials in 1895 and 1896 to the Governor of the State of Pará.[50] Goeldi argued cogently for a closed season on egrets from July to January, and urged that duties be levied upon the export of wild birds' feathers. He believed that Pará could ill-afford the luxury of plume hunting. In florid prose, precursing William T. Hornaday's grandiloquent style, Goeldi declared indignantly:

46. Argentine Republic, *Anuario de la Dirección General de Estadística* (Buenos Aires, 1896 etc.)

47. Brazil, Serviço de Estatística Economica & Financeira do Tesouro Nacional, *Comércio Exterior do Brasil* (Rio de Janeiro, 1940 *et ante*).

48. Venezuela, Ministerio de Fomento, *Anuario Estadistico de Venezuela* (Caracas, 1912).

49. See Venezuela Department of Fomento, *Law on the Gathering and Exploitation of Heron Feathers of June 26, 1917* (Caracas, 1920), was a translation from the Official Gazette, Caracas, July 12, 1917. The law recognized that as a commercial item feathers must be exported in accordance with law; they could be gathered only at roosts (*garceros*) in moulting time. Killing herons was prohibited and owners of colonies needed written permission from authorities to collect and dispose of their plumes.

50. *Against the Destruction of White Herons and Red Ibises on the Lower Amazon* (Para, 1902) 20 pages; p. 5.

And the Superintendent of the Museum protests in the name of common sense against the barbarous destruction of herons that is being carried on in the Lower Amazon and would rather resign his position than fail to cry out most emphatically against one of the most scandalous crimes that is perpetrated against nature in this beautiful region.[51]

Forty years later aigrettes were still being peddled on the streets of Belém, ostensibly picked up from the ground in nesting areas. Today they are no longer seen in the market place as there is no demand for them. They have been replaced by animal and reptile skins, especially those of predatory cats and alligators.[52]

British and American consular sources in South America provided accounts of egret slaughter and the methods used to procure birds as did travellers and naturalists such as Caspar Whitney, Eugene André and H. J. Mozans. These people reported that sometimes decoys were made of dead or wounded birds and set up in feeding areas to attract unwary neighbors. Hunting from horseback and canoe was said to be common, and on occasion, poisoned fish and shrimp was apparently broadcast over pools frequented by herons.[53]

The purpose was to obtain feathers in their best possible condition. "Live" ones (that is, the unblemished, little-worn, nuptial garb of white herons) were at a premium. The moulted plumes

---

51. Ibid., p. 5.
52. See Arthur H. Fisher, "Marajó—Paradise of Bird Life and Lesson in Protection," *Nature Magazine* 32 (1939): 35–38. Fisher made a visit to Belém and Marajó to investigate the historical and contemporary picture there. Exporters in Belém no longer deal in feathers, but devote their interests exclusively to the skin and live animal trade. A few *Rhea americana* feathers still pass through the port.
53. Different authorities are referred to in RSPB *Feathers and Facts*, pp. 16–18, 42–50. T. Gilbert Pearson, "The White Egrets," *BL* 14 (1912): 62–69, reprinted as National Audubon Society, *Educational Leaflet* no. 54; also William T. Hornaday, *Our Vanishing Wild Life*, pp. 127 ff. Other sources substantiating charges of cruelty were listed by a Plumage Committee of the RSPCA (London) and are found in P.C. Correspondence 7-1-1922. Specific authors mention egret hunting in South America, notably: Leo E. Miller, *In the Wilds of South America* (New York, 1918), p. 148; and Caspar Whitney, *The Flowing Road* (London, 1912), pp. 261–262. The tales of poisoned fish used as bait are referred to by Leo E. Miller, "Destruction of the Rhea, Black-Necked Swan, Herons . . ." *BL* 16 (1914): 259–262; for Aigrette empaillées, see E. R. Wagner, "Chasse à l'Aigrette.," *Revue Franc. d'Ornithol.* 52–53 (1913): 132–35, and F. Geay, "Observations . . . ," *Bulletin Soc. d'Acclim.* 44 (1897), pp. 205–209 for the Orinoco region. Canoe and horseback hunting is mentioned in *Enciclopedia de la América del Sur* tomo III (Buenos Aires, n.d.), pp. 1249–50. However, Menegaux, *Bird Protection and the Feather Trade* (Paris, 1911), rebuts the charges of cruelty, see pp. 8–13.

that came from Venezuela brought but one-fifth to one-sixth the price of live feathers. A "Bird Lover" in a letter to the *New York Times* commented about moulted plumes: "Mucky doesn't half express the sticky condition of the filthy water below their [herons'] homes. Just drop a delicate article like a feather into it, let it lie a day or so, and then view the sorry-looking plume you take out." [54]

The egret-plume hunter's lot was a harsh one. Uncertain, often meager returns left little place for thought about cruelty, gentlemanly conduct or refined instincts. An article from the *San Francisco Call* (3 April, 1898) provides a glimpse of one heron hunter, David W. Bennett of Pomona, California, who operated along the coast of Sinaloa and Nayarit in western Mexico. Bennett had become interested in the feather business in 1873 while prospecting in Yucatan, where he had shot a dozen egrets to supply a gift of feathers to his sisters in New Orleans. Their neighbor was a wholesale milliner who offered Bennett $5 per plume for all that he could procure. Back in Mexico, Bennett cleared more than $4,000 from hunting egrets in two years. Later, he hunted widely in Central America; in 1882, for example, he netted $3,900 for seven months' work in Nicaragua. But returns from the early bonanza years could not be maintained. In the *Call* story Bennett noted that, "everywhere in the regions I have been in and have ever heard about a rapidly growing scarcity of egrets is evident." [55] He said he was well acquainted with the experiences of other plume hunters in Ecuador and Colombia.

Armed with a case of whiskey and sufficient quinine to ward off chills and fever, with canned goods, good guns and plenty of number five shot, Bennett would set out for the sluggish waterways and steaming marshes alone or with helpers. His daily routine included long hours in a rowboat or canoe, careful reconnoitering of bird movements to obtain positions for favorable shots. Campfires on dry land at nightfall relieved the drudgery of the hunting routine by boat, but the motionless hours under a burning sun and mosquito-ridden nights would have tried the patience of Job. A volley of quickly-aimed shots in poor light, followed by rapid sculling to retrieve the dead or wounded waterbirds contrasted with the tensions of stalking. Once Bennett had secured his vic-

54. 28 September, 1913, part IV, p. 6, col. 5.   55. Page 18, cols. 1–7, quote col. 3.

tims, he took extreme precautions to prevent the fine plumes from spoiling or becoming soiled with water or blood. The feathers were carefully cut from each bird and packed into a metal box for safe keeping. Perhaps seven or eight herons in an evening flight fell to the good marksman who generally moved his craft to a new place for the chance to shoot at dawn.

Bennett reported that at first plume merchants purchased stock by the individual plume; however, as millinery interests, particularly in Paris, changed over to buying by weight, bulk purchasing became everywhere the rule. Merchants scrutinized heron plumes closely. The finest ones were looked at under a magnifying glass, and according to Bennett any discoloration or imperfections in them reduced their value up to 50 percent. Agents struck hard bargains. They frequently denigrated the quality of the hunters' spoils, but were adept at cheating their own clients as to the origin, types and quality of feather goods.

A good season's haul for a hunter was 50 ounces or more of plumes and 130 ounces of smaller feathers. Bennett preferred to sell his stock in San Francisco or in New York, where he could get as much as $28 per ounce for high-quality feathers. He was loathe to trust his goods to others to sell for him; he said that in 1884, he had lost his entire take when an unscrupulous middleman had stolen it. His nearest and most convenient market was Mexico City where prices were lower; plumes sold there for only $24 per ounce.

Bennett's measured yet vivid account of egret hunting gives us a glimpse of the solitary life, physical hardships and need for resilience that plume hunting demanded. This life was in many ways similar to that of the market hunter of waterfowl and shore birds on the Atlantic and Mississippi flyways.[56] Returns were undependable and fortunes made in the business were few. A season's haul could be stolen by conniving dealers, whom the heron hunter considered to be one of the chief occupational hazards.

Apparently "Egret" Bennett did well enough by plume hunting. He retired from active work in the field in the late 1890's, having witnessed an increase in wariness and a decline in numbers among

56. Another theme to be explored, one rich in personalities and reminiscences; see David and Jim Kimball, *The Market Hunter* (Minneapolis, 1969), William J. Mackey, *American Bird Decoys* (New York, 1965).

his prey. He believed that pluming had impaired his health, and that it was time for rest and relaxation.[57] Bennett was a person who knew his birds well, their quirks and foibles. He probably had a grudging admiration for his quarry, as some market hunters had for ducks. But his job was to procure good plumes quickly and easily. Shooting was the order of the day, not floundering in the mire hoping to pick up suitable moulted feathers worn out by a season of courtship, and by the incubation of eggs and feeding of fledgling young.

Similar tales provide circumstantial evidence that the bulk of the heron and egret material from tropical America came from birds killed for feathers. How many were killed is difficult to say. The number of birds necessary to provide one kilogram of plumage depended on the particular species and upon estimates of authorities in the business. Between 800-1000 snowy egrets and 200-300 larger birds per kilo appear compromise figures. On this basis, between 12-15 million smaller herons and 3-4.5 million larger ones would have furnished the 15,000 kilos of heron plumage mentioned as being exported from Argentina, Brazil and Venezuela between 1899 and 1912. In the thirty years between 1890 and 1920, scores of millions of herons must have been taken to supply the plumage recorded in export statistics from South American countries, apart from countless hummingbirds and rheas upon which the industry also drew heavily.[58]

In some cases, egrets were reared in enclosures, in which captive birds were induced to nest. Under these conditions their numbers were controlled, their plumage clipped or plucked regularly, and the threat of extermination removed from populations in the wild. The term "farming" seems more appropriate to this practice. In Southeast Asia, particularly Burma, islets or riparian areas reportedly were set aside for egret rearing.[59] Used for fans, fly switches and dusters, heron feathers (together with those of

57. Bennett's story was printed by the RSPB, "An Egret Hunter's Narrative," *Leaflet No. 26.* It was taken from *The Sun,* New York, 7th June, 1896, a slightly different version of the *San Francisco Call* article.

58. Paul Serre, "Aigrettes de l'Orénoque..," *Bulletin Soc. d'Acclim.* 62 (1915): 219–221, states that there were 870 "petites" to one kilo and 215 "grandes." José Candido de Melho Carvalho, "Notas de Viagem aõ Rio Negro," *Public. Avlusas do Museum Nacional No. 9* (Rio de Janeiro, 1952), p. 18, reported that one kilo was made up of 300 large herons (*albus*) or 1,000 *thula.*

59. Jules Forest, "Les Aigrettes: Histoire Naturelle . . . Domestication," *Bull. Soc. d'Acclimatation* 44 (1897): 185–204. He suggested crossing Old and New World varieties of the same species to ensure better quality plumes.

bustards, pheasants and many species of waterfowl) have appeared commonly in Indo-Chinese trade for many centuries, and they continue to do so. Shanghai shipped feathers from all parts of the Chinese empire to Hong Kong and to Europe.[60] Quantities of pelican and other waterbird quills found their way into China from Vietnam and Cambodia.[61] The local demand for plumage necessitated an annual slaughter of waterfowl for skins, meat, feathers and down. The Chinese egret *(Egretta eulophotes)* is a species which has never recovered from the effects of the plumage trade. It is listed as an endangered bird in the I.U.C.N. *Red Data Book.*[62]

During the nineteenth century, the Société d'Acclimatation of Paris became interested in the feasibility of raising egrets for commercial purposes. An enthusiastic proponent of ostrich and pheasant rearing, it hoped to raise white herons on a sustained commercial basis. The first publicized success in this venture came from Tunisia in 1895. Little egrets *(Egretta garzetta)*, captured and placed in a large cage, raised thirty young. Fed cheaply on horsemeat, adult birds were reported to nest twice a year (April and June), and guardians clipped their wing feathers in May and September. The entrepreneur apparently realized a profit from the sale of plumes, and specimens were also sold to tourists and supplied to museums.[63]

Successes in breeding herons in confined conditions were noted

60. U.S. Bureau of Manufacturers, Dept. of Commerce and Labor, *Consular and Trade Reports*, no. 340 (1909) 229–232.

61. Courrier de Saïgon, "Des oiseaux du huyên de Kien-Giang et des eventails fabriques avec leurs plumes," *Bull. Soc. d'Acclimatation* 10 (1873): 289–295. An annual roundup of waterbirds was made in their breeding grounds. They were killed for their meat, feathers and oil; at least 50,000 were said to be taken every year; see Renard, "La chasse aux grands oiseaux," ibid., 4 (1877): 225–234.

62. Volume Two-*Aves* by Jack Vincent, 1966. The egret probably still breeds in parts of China and formerly occurred in Hong Kong (to 1965). It is listed as very rare, believed decreasing, thereby is the cause of considerable anxiety. Vinzenz Ziswiler, *Extinct and Vanishing Animals* (New York, 1967) draws much of his information from Greenway and I.U.C.N. *Bulletins*, and lists only two birds, the Spectacled Cormorant *(Phalacrocorax perspicillatus)* and the Crested Shelduck *(Tadorna cristata)* as becoming extinct due in part to a demand for their skins or feathers. Of the endangered species, the Steller's Albatross *(Diomedea albatrus)* and the Japanese crested ibis *(Nipponia nippon)* are birds endangered due to the feather demand.

63. Ernest Oliver, "Un Parc à Aigrettes en Tunisie," *Bulletin Soc. d'Acclim.* 43 (1896): 302–305; Jules Forest "Domestication des Aigrettes," *Rev. Sci. Naturelles Appliquées* 42 (1895): 740–741; "Les Aigrettes," *Bull. Soc. d'Acclim.* 44 (1897): 185–204; and idem, "La Domestication des Aigrettes," *Revue Scientifique*, 38 (1901): 363–367, 393–398; espec. pp. 394–398.

in Argentina,[64] Brittany,[65] Madagascar [66] and Ceylon.[67] Jules Forest, familiar with the feather trade and an advocate of raising wild birds in captivity, suggested other places suitable for experiments in egret rearing. They included Les Landes in southwestern France, lakes in Morocco, Senegal and the marshlands of the confluence of the Tigris-Euphrates rivers in Mesopotamia. French firms offered a number of prizes to stimulate efforts in heron farming.[68]

The RSPB and Audubon Societies made light of ventures in rearing herons in captivity, as they did of stories of protecting herons in *garceros*. They denounced such stories as "bribed by the trade." Experiences in British India between 1910 and 1920 scarcely warranted the scepticism and disbelief of such "home-keeping sentimentalists." [69] A number of well-documented accounts with information about the captive breeding of egrets for commercial purposes appeared in pages of the *Journal* of the Bombay Natural History Society. Indian Government reports further confirmed that heron rearing was practised on a regular basis.

In 1916, the Indian Government requested information about the extent of egret raising and of cruelty associated with it.[70] This survey was regarded as a necessary first step towards amending legislation covering the export of feathers. A notification from the Finance and Commerce Department of the Indian Government issued in September, 1902, had prohibited the export of feathers

64. L. E. Boutard, "Aigrettes Domestiquées dans la Republique Argentine," *Bull. Soc. d'Acclim.* 44 (1897): 270.

65. A.M. [énégaux], "Un Elevage d'Aigrettes en Bretagne," *Rev. Franc. d'Ornithologie* 80 (1916): 216; also "Etraits des proces-verbaux . . . séance Générale du 24 Décember, 1914," *Bull. Soc. d'Acclim.* 62 (1915), p. 27; and ibid., 68 (1921), p. 10.

66. "Egret and Heron rearing in Madagascar," *Journal Royal Soc. Arts* 63 (1915): 716; also ibid., 64 (1916), p. 103. A.M. [énégaux] "Elevage des Aigrettes à Madagascar," *Rev. Franc. d'Ornithol.* 83 (1916): 248.

67. "Les Oiseaux et la parure," *La Nature* No. 2130 (1914): 273–281, 278. A. Menegaux, "Les Plumes des Oiseaux utilisées pour la Parure," *La Nature* No. 2130 (1914), p. 278.

68. Jules Forest, "La Domestication des Aigrettes," *Rev. Scientifique* 38 (1901): 363–367, 393–398. Also idem, "La domestication des herons-aigrettes," *Bull. Comité de l'Afrique Française* 7 (1897) *Rens. Colon.* no. 3: 75–80. A. Ménégaux, "Les Aigrettes et le Syndicat berlinois," *Rev. Franc. d'Ornithol.* 50 (1913): 119 and ibid., 4 (1916): 216; E. Morin, *La Plume des Oiseaux*, p. 80.

69. C. C. Chevenix Trench, "Egret Farming in India," *Journal Bombay Nat. Hist. Soc.* 28 (1922): 751–752.

70. India office, Commerce Dept., Correspondence to Advisory Committee under Importation of Plumage Act, 1921 (with enclosures). Correspondence submitted by H. S. Marshall to Plumage Act Committee, January 18th, 1922, Custom House Library, London.

of any wild bird from British India. Reports had shown that large quantities of feathers and skins were leaving India at that time for European destinations, particularly London.[71]

The embargo on feathers was partly the result of insistent demands to stop the frivolous waste of insectivorous and decorative species, but the prohibition proved in large part a dead letter. Smuggling became rife. Further legislation enacted to curb the drain of ornamental plumage from the Asian subcontinent was ineffective. A Post Office Notification of February, 1907, gave certain officials the right to open parcels to look for contraband plumes. Recourse was made to a previous Cruelty to Animals Act (XI of 1890) and a Wild Birds and Animals Act (VIII of 1912) further restricted the killing and marketing of wild birds. Despite these measures, large numbers of peacocks, kingfishers and egrets from India continued to be sold in Mincing Lane showrooms in London.

A review of the situation made by the Government in 1916 was prompted by the understanding that if egrets could be raised successfully and humanely in captivity then a cottage industry might be encouraged to provide both revenue for official agencies and for local entrepreneurs. This fact-finding investigation was in part an outcome of an article by George Birch on egret farming in the Sind, published by the Bombay Natural History Society.[72] Birch reported that little egrets (*Egretta garzetta*) were:

> Now being bred and reared with marked success in captivity and on an extensive scale in many parts of Sind and that the Mir-bahars (the generic term by which the fisher-folk of the island waters of the Province are known) are building up a lucrative trade in osprey feather plucked from the plumage of these egrets and that the operation is conducted without injuring the birds, in the same way as feathers are plucked from the Ostrich (Pp. 161–162).

Experiences from a tour of duty in Larkana District led Birch to conclude that no cruelty was apparent in egret farming. Birds

71. P. T. L. Dodsworth, "Protection of Wild Birds in India . . ." *Journal Bombay Nat. Hist. Soc.* 20 (1911): 1103–1114. Dodsworth listed exports of plumage from India between 1895 and 1900 at 11,149,354 lbs. This figure was noted by Douglas Dewar, *Indian Bird Life* (London, 1925), p. 196, as 1,149,346 lbs. of plumage exported between 1895–1910, totalling about 1 million annually. Exactly what Dodsworth's figure indicates is unclear. However, in the same paper he reported that 6,813 lbs. of plumage passed through Bombay Post Office between July 1, 1898, and June 30, 1901; almost all (6,256 lbs.) destined for the United Kingdom, p. 1108.
72. "Egret Farming in Sind," *Journal Bombay Nat. Hist. Soc.* 23 (1914): 161–163.

were housed in "poultry runs" about twenty feet long, eight feet
wide and eight feet high, kept tolerably clean and well-supplied
with fresh fish and water. Nesting took place twice a year and
feathers were plucked by hand. Birch estimated that 1000 birds
were kept in the village of Ber, in the Kamber Taluka, Larkana
District.

Birch's story gained widespread attention and proved contro-
versial. He stuck to it and another report to the same Society
seven years later corroborated his claims.[73] This later essay declared that at least 100 farms existed in Sind, each with about 100
birds. They were "well treated; of this there can be no doubt."
The Collector of Thar and Parkar had personally seen at least
1,700 birds on 19 farms and had not noticed any instance of ill-
treatment, including the blinding of birds to make them more
tractable in confined conditions. Plucking their plumes appeared
no more painful than pulling a few hairs from one's head. The
1921 report concluded:

> It is incontestable that before the inception of the system of
> breeding egrets the birds were ruthlessly slaughtered for their
> plumes and that this barbarous practice has now practically
> ceased as a direct result of the far more economical and lucra-
> tive process of the production of plumes by means of egret
> farms.[74]

73. [Anon.], "Egret Farming in Sind," ibid., 27 (1921): 944–947.
74. Ibid., p. 946. A *Memorandum* from the Commissioner in Sind No. 41 dated
January, 1918, provided background information on egret breeding:

> Prior to the outbreak of the war, the breeding of egrets has assumed very
> extensive proportions in every district of the province wherever were readily
> available the small fish which constitute the natural food of the birds. The
> industry is of recent growth. Some of the breeders report that the system
> found its way into Sind from Bahawalput; others that it originated in Upper
> Sind and was carried thence into the Southern Punjab districts. The syste-
> matic breeding of egret has certainly made great progress in Sind. In the
> first instance the industry was exclusively in the hands of the fishermen on
> the inland waters in these localities; but when the lucrative nature of the in-
> dustry became known, land-holders and banias also participated in it; cultiva-
> tors have been known to sell their lands to be able to devote themselves to
> the occupation. The number of birds on each of the larger farms ran into
> several hundreds. The number of birds in the farms on the Manchar Lake in
> the Larkana district was estimated to exceed ten thousand. Owing to markets
> being restricted after the outbreak of the war, the selling value of egret
> plumes has fallen and the breeding industry has been somewhat checked. But
> it is still a flourishing one, p. 13.

One conclusion drawn from investigations was: "The Commissioner is of opinion
that it has been conclusively established that egrets can be reared in captivity with-

A final detailed and dispassionate article appeared in the *Journal* of the Bombay Natural History Society in 1922.[75] It supported previous statements that egrets in India were no longer cruelly blinded, or used as live decoys. However, when captive birds were moved and required unusual crowding, they might be temporarily blinded: "The lower lid of each eye is pierced by a fine needle and a piece of very fine cotton thread is drawn through. The two pieces of cotton are then tied over the head of the bird, thus causing the lower eyelid to be drawn over the upper eyelid." [76]

After the journey, the thread was cut and sight restored to each bird without apparent ill effects. The passage of the 1921 Plumage Prohibition Act in Great Britain and subsequent refusal of the Plumage Committee to recommend feathers of herons be included in the schedule of permitted species, made the information from India less valuable. This inquiry concluded that egret farming offered a suitable and acceptable compromise between the plumage industry and other parties concerned with the protection of useful and ornamental birds.

In the United States, a unique attempt to restore the number of snowy egrets was made in Louisiana by E. A. (Ned) McIlhenny. In 1892, McIlhenny realized that white egrets were marked for extermination in the bayou country of the Southern Mississippi. He learned about a story of an Indian rajah successfully breeding egrets in the confined quarters of bamboo cages. McIlhenny caught eight young birds in the surrounding swamps and placed them in a large cage where they were fed, protected and allowed to fly about. In the fall of 1892, he liberated the birds, which left the area. However, in March 1893, six snowy egrets returned to their old haunts and fledged young after McIlhenny had carefully protected their nests. In succeeding years, with assiduous protection, numbers of snowy egrets gradually built up and other heron species came into the expanding colony. He successfully "double-cropped" white egrets by placing their eggs in nests of

out cruelty. It would also be possible by control, to prevent the use of cruel methods," India Office, Correspondence to Plumage Act Committee, 1921, makes mention of this.

75. "Egret Farming in Sind," ibid., 28 (1922); 748–750. Salim A. Ali and S. Dillon Ripley, *Handbook of the Birds of India and Pakistan* (London, 1968) Vol. I, pp. 73–74, reported that egret farming was continued in Sind until 1930 and possibly to the present day. Shooting of *alba*, *intermedia* and *garzetta* was intensive.

76. C. E. Benson, "Egret Farming in Sind," *Journal Bombay Nat. Hist. Soc.* 28 (1922): 748–750.

other herons. Ten years after his initial experiment, McIlhenny had 1,000 pairs of egrets nesting on Avery Island. In 1909 he shipped more than 3,000 birds to the Miami area where they were released the following spring. In this novel way, Edward McIlhenny helped bring the snowy egret back from low numbers in Florida where its plumage was literally worth its weight in gold.[77]

Most serious declines in numbers and range were apparent by 1910 when wardens patrolled nesting places in the South to ward off plume hunters able to sell aigrettes for as much as $80 an ounce in New York City.

Scientists Against the Feather Trade

From the 1870's, natural scientists in the United States expressed anxiety about the trend towards extinction of many plume birds. Beginning with Joel A. Allen,[78] many interested persons believed that gulls, terns and herons were doomed. Hunters waged war upon seabirds along the Atlantic coast and upon herons in the Gulf states and in Florida. The literature on the subject between 1880 and 1920 is voluminous.

The seriousness of declines in certain species and well-publicized accounts of hunting methods touched the hearts and minds of writers and scientists, many of whom communicated their concern to the American public. In England a similar concern was expressed over the survival of birds of paradise, herons and Asian pheasants. However, London depended mainly upon imported plumes, and the full poignancy of the situation never made itself felt in England as it did in America. Lord Lilford commented on this point in a letter to Frank Lemon, secretary of the RSPB: "I believe that many plumiferous ladies would shrink from wearing robins', swallows' and other common British birds' skins or feathers, who would never give a thought to wearing bright plumage of birds with which they have no personal acquaintance." [79]

In the United States, such well-known journals as *Living Age*,

77. Edward Avery McIlhenny, *Bird City* (Boston, 1934); idem, *The Autobiography of an Egret* (New York, 1939).

78. "Decrease of Birds in Massachusetts," *Bull. Nuttall Ornithol. Club* 1 (1876): 53–60; idem, "On the Decrease of Birds in the United States," *The Penn Monthly* 7 (1876): 931–944.

79. Trevor-Battye (ed.), *Lord Lilford on Birds* (London, 1903), p. 265. Letter of July, 1885.

Independent, Harper's Magazine, and *Scientific American* condemned the practice of killing native birds for their ornamental feathers and expressed a concern for the future of a number of species. *The Auk,* the organ of the AOU, and *Bird-Lore,* the publication of the Association of Audubon Societies, listed numerous startling examples of bird slaughter. The sportsman's journal *Forest and Stream* in September, 1873, noted that the Seminole Indians were selling plumes of the snowy egret for a good price. Audubon had been aware of the custom of wearing aigrettes early in the 1830's.

> The long plumes of this bird [American Egret] being in request for ornamental purposes, they are shot in great numbers while sitting on their eggs, or soon after the appearance of their young. I know a person who, on offering a doubled-barrelled gun to a gentlemen [sic] near Charleston, for one hundred White Herons freshly killed, received that number and more the next day.[80]

He mentioned that John Bachman visited a heron colony some 40 miles from Charleston to shoot specimens, "as the ladies were anxious to procure many of their primary feathers for the purpose of making fans." This documentation of heron destruction became a primary concern expanding in detail, scope and volume as the century progressed. The American public was treated to a plethora of lurid accounts of bloody egret slaughters.

Among the first detailed descriptions of an egret slaughter in Florida was one penned by W. E. D. Scott (1852–1910). Scott sailed southwards from Tarpon Springs at the end of April, 1886, and recorded only about a dozen breeding herons near Anclote Keys, where in 1880 "there were literally thousands of them." [81] A herony near Clearwater Harbor was deserted. In Charlotte Harbor, where a few years ago "it would be difficult to exaggerate in regard to their numbers," the plume hunters had done their work well. Scott was able to quote prices for many types of waterbirds, such as the roseate spoonbill (*Ajaia ajaja*), which sold for between two and five dollars a flat skin.[82] He saw a freshly slaughtered colony of over 200 reddish egrets (*Dichromanassa rufescens*),

80. *Ornithological Biography,* Vol. 4, pp. 603–604.
81. "The Present Condition of Some of the Bird Rookeries of the Gulf Coast of Florida," *The Auk* 4 (1887): 135–144, quote 136, 213–222, 273–284.
82. Ibid., p. 143 Charlotte Harbor quote p. 140.

American egrets, Louisiana herons (*Hydranassa tricolor*) and little blue herons. Their dorsal plumes had been cut away and some birds had lost their wings. He summarized his feelings:

> It would be difficult for me to find words adequate to express, not only my amazement, but also the increasing horror that grew on me day after day as I sailed southward. . . . The great Maximo rookery at the mouth of Tampa Bay was no longer a rookery; it was a deserted mangrove island.[83]

Scott's account was amplified by later essays in the same and other journals.[84] Plume hunters had become so active in Florida that by 1890 Scott made the claim that "there are absolutely *no Heron rookeries* on the salt water bayous or on the outlying keys of the Gulf Coast of Florida from Anclote Keys to Cape Sable." [85]

This description of plume hunting in Florida exemplifies conditions in the 1880's as perceived by ornithologists and natural scientists not overly given to hysterical remonstrations. In addition to Allen and Scott, Frank Chapman, William Dutcher, Witmer Stone and T. Gilbert Pearson likewise expressed the gravest concern over the future of herons in Florida.

William T. Hornaday, from his earliest association with the New York Zoological Society, put the plumage issue squarely in the context of bird destruction by attempting to measure trends in bird numbers over the United States. From a questionnaire sent out to state officials and other persons, he concluded that there had been a 46 percent decline in bird numbers in 28 states, the District of Columbia and Indian Territory, during the period 1883–1898. Four distinct activities were held responsible for this drop in numbers—sports hunting, market killing, boys' mischief, and millinery demands. Obviously, many of the people whom Hornaday polled believed that the plume business was a major

83. *The Story of a Bird Lover* (New York, 1903), pp. 256–257. The book is written in a simple, engaging style from which one catches the atmosphere of Scott's times. Especially commendable are Scott's vignettes of Florida and its birds.

84. See also "A Summary of Observations . . . Gulf Coast," *The Auk* 5–7 (1888–1890), and *Forest and Stream* 30 (1888), p. 316; 32 (1889), p. 355 and 509; 33 (1890), p. 485.

85. "An Account of Flamingoes . . . in the vicinity of Cape Sable, Florida," *The Auk* 7 (1890): 221–226; 221. H. K. Jamison in the *The Auk* 8 (1891), p. 233, reported at least 2 heron nesting areas from Little Sarasota Bay to Ten Thousand Islands in May, 1890. Scott replied that he was aware of these few nests but compared with the mid-1870's and the rookeries of Tampa Bay, Sarasota Bay, Charlotte Harbor and Thousand Islands, these herons were but pitiful remnants of "countless myriads," see *The Auk* 8 (1891): 318–319.

Kittiwakes provided an early focus for protective measures in the United Kingdom. These breeding birds offered tempting targets to marksmen and their wings were used to decorate ladies' hats.

The bird on the hat is a tern, one of many kinds of seabirds greatly reduced in numbers along the Atlantic shore of the United States by millinery demands. Courtesy *The Millinery Trade Review* 26 (1901), p. 29 (left).

Feathered brooches, costume and hat pins in various shapes and colors which were made in France and sold in the United States. Courtesy *The Millinery Trade Review* 28 (1903), p. 107 (right).

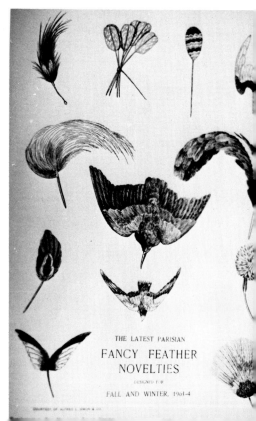

THE LATEST PARISIAN

FANCY FEATHER
NOVELTIES

DESIGNED FOR

FALL AND WINTER, 1903-4

George F. Watts' "The Wounded Heron," celebrated for its sympathy for wild creatures' suffering from human cruelty. Courtesy The Trustees, Watts Gallery, Compton, Guildford, England.

George F. Watts' "A Dedication," acclaimed by the RSPB for its sensitivity to the loss of birdlife and their cruel end as millinery oddments. Courtesy The Trustees, Watts Gallery, Compton, Guildford, England.

Fashionable hat trimming of whole bird from *The Millinery Trade Review* 26:11 (Nov., 1901), p. 43 (left).

Go, Lovely Bird

Go, lovely bird,
Speed from my lady warily.
   For she hath heard
That finches dainty decking be,
And her sweet charms mean death
      to thee!

   For at the sight
Of ruffled breast and stiffened
      limb
   Her eyes grow bright.
A wreath of death will bravely
      trim
The circlet of my lady's brim.'
      (*Punch*, 28 October, 1903)

The plume hunter's spoils as "The Tribute to Vanity." (*Pearson's Magazine*) (right).

A BIRD OF PREY.

Linley Sambourne's cartoon in support of the SPB, published in *Punch* May, 1892 (left).

A gesture of reconciliation between plumage interests and the Audubon Society appeared in *The Millinery Trade Review* 28 (1903), p. 42. It was noted that "there is an abundance of birds and plumage in the market that can be sold safely and at a fair profit without recourse to law breaking" (right).

HANG THIS PLACARD UP IN A CONSPICUOU
PLACE IN YOUR STORE

We Do Not Sell Bir

...OR...

Bird Plumage

That are in violation of Law
Public Sentiment. All our go
are sold in conformity with
agreement between

The Audubon Societ

...AND...

The Millinery Merchant
Protective Association

The advertisement in *The Millinery Trade Review* 29 (1904), p. 16, reflected the position of several firms selling aigrettes. They assured tradesfolk and members of the public that it was legal to deal in imported millinery (left).

Linley Sambourne's rendition of the vain, heartless lady without mercy for the sufferings of white herons and egrets (*Punch* Sept., 1899) (right).

A KILLING HAT.

*" The dealers declare that the demand for birds of every description will this year be greate
than ever."*—FASHION PAPER.]

Caricature in *The Westminster Gazette* (July, 1901), reprinted by
the RSPB at 2d. per dozen. The lady wears an assortment of
ornamental plumage. A rhyme accompanying the cartoon ended:

> I have found out a gift for my fair—
> A pair of stork legs—think of that!
> If they do look absurd
> That's the fault of the bird,
> Not to grow legs more fit for a hat.

factor contributing to the decimation of bird life throughout the nation.[86]

Hornaday was a blunt man with an unusual capacity to irritate people. He was a self-appointed prophet of doom for plume birds and for game birds and mammals. His fulminations against unsportsmanlike conduct (jacklighting, spring hunting, repeating rifles), market hunting, and even hunting by foreigners, resulted from his conviction that extermination was imminent and inevitable for many species. He was to play an important role in promoting the passage of the 1913 tariff bill.

The disappearance of herons from the southern states in the 1880's had its parallel in the eclipse of gulls and terns from breeding grounds along the Atlantic coast. Collectors of carved, wooden bird decoys have uncovered heron and gull "stools" devised for coast gunners. Along the New Jersey coastline and Long Island Sound, passing gulls and herons were attracted by these handmade replicas conspicuously set out on the marshes or in lagoons. Placed among a rig of duck or goose decoys, a wooden heron decoy was also intended to give confidence to passing waterfowl so that they would settle in range of a hunter's blind or punt-gun.[87]

86. "The Destruction of Our Birds and Mammals . . . ," *New York Zoological Soc.*, Second Annual Report (1898): 77–107. Edward H. Forbush made similar investigations in Massachusetts, see *Decrease of Certain Birds, and its Causes with Suggestion for Bird Protection* (Special Report on), 2nd edit., revised, (Boston, 1908). Milliner's hunters came 7th on a list of 14 man-made factors of extermination in the States, p. 54.

87. Paul Woodburn Parmalee and Forrest D. Loomis, *Decoys and Decoy Carvers of Illinois* (DeKalb, 1969), p. 91. In discussing confidence decoys the authors include species, body size, position and format; this is a broader definition than Mackey's (1965), who believed that gull decoys were the only true stool type decoys. Adele Earnest (1965) included plume bird species as fulfilling both true decoy purposes (for plumage) plus confidence purposes (for market hunting). Kingdom B. Hemming and Hal Sorenson, "Hats, Bonnets and Decoys," *Decoy Collector's Guide* 2 (1964), give some useful insights into decoys and millinery: "And this is where *decoys* enter the hat and bonnet picture, for they were frequently used to lure birds to the gun, not for meat or sport, but for the feathers they provided. Shooting certain species for this purpose was a profitable side-line for many of the market hunters who supplied ducks and shore-birds for the big city restaurants.

"One such feather hunter was Don McKeeman, of Freeport, Long Island.

"Back around 1900, when the main street of Freeport was paved with clam and oyster shell, Don McKeeman was engaged in the profession of market hunting. When wild-fowling was slow, Don would—with the aid of sea gull decoys—take to the water and proceed to bag a mess of gulls.

"These he took to New York City where he sold the wings to Macy's department store for eleven cents a pair. The remainder of the gull skins were sold to professional fly tiers who used them in making trout and salmon flys [sic] . . . As the 'wild' bird feathers disappeared from sight, so did the decoys used to gun the birds for market. Today, decoys for the gull, tern and heron are among the rarest to be found," pp. 12–13.

Examples of tern destruction along the eastern seaboard are provided in Table 5. These statistics paint in sombre colors the picture of seabird destruction along the Atlantic coast. One area in particular, Cobb's Island, Virginia, appears to have been especially utilized by plume hunters and egg collectors during the 1880's. Situated about twenty miles north of Cape Charles, Virginia, the small dune island was the scene of intensive seabird shooting and later became one of the focal points for protecting breeding gulls and terns along the east coast. W. E. D. Scott had visited the island in 1881 to collect a series of eggs and skin for Princeton University. He was impressed with the busy flocks of gulls and terns. "Here vast colonies of them found a breeding ground. It is difficult to say which kind were more numerous; there were myriads of all." Twenty years later he complained that egging and pluming "had achieved the usual result." [88]

An extract from the *Baltimore Sun* published in the *Forest and Stream* (7 August, 1884) throws light on events on the island. A New York woman had agreed with a Parisian millinery firm to deliver 40,000 or more bird skins in the summer of 1884. She had hired gunners to go out to Cobb's Island to kill as many terns as possible at ten cents a skin. The havoc of Long Island's tern shooting was extended to Virginia.

Protective measures instituted by the Audubon movement in 1900 under the auspices of Abbott H. Thayer provided funds for wardens and gave respite to the seabirds of Cobb's Island. At that time about 100 pairs of common terns (*Sterna hirundo*) were present with larger numbers of black skimmers (*Rynchops nigra*) and laughing gulls (*Larus atricilla*). Least terns (*Sterna albifrons*) and royal terns (*Thalasseus maximus*) had been completely shot out.[89]

Hunting to obtain ornamental feathers was by no means confined to the Atlantic seaboard. A number of stories from the Midwest and California appeared in bird journals. In the Tule Lake and Lower Klamath basin of Northern California, forster's terns (*Sterna forsteri*), western grebes, (*Aechmophorus occidentalis*) and white pelicans (*Pelecanus erythrorhynchos*) were shot for their plumage. For example, 50 pelican skins were shipped from Cali-

88. *Story of A Bird Lover,* pp. 180, 183.
89. "The Destruction of Small Birds," *Forest and Stream* 23 (1884): 24; also Frank M. Chapman, "The Bird-Life of Cobb's Island," *BL* 5 (1903): 109–114.

TABLE 5

Tern Shooting on the Atlantic Coast, 1870–1900

Numbers	Place	Date	Source
Hundreds	Muskeget Island, Mass.	1870's	W. Brewster, 1879 p. 17.
10,000 in one year	Muskeget Island, Mass.	Probably	E. H. Forbush, 1908, p. 29.
500 per week	Beach Haven, N.J.	1882	W. Dutcher, 1886, p. 198.
40,000	Cape Cod region	c. 1883	T. S. Palmer, 1899, p. 273.
3,000	Seaford, N.Y.	1883	W. Dutcher, 1886, p. 198.
Considerably decreased	New England	1880's	W. Brewster, 1889, p. 67.
Two piles knee high	Near Cape May, N.J. for New York dealers	1884	W. Stone, 1896, p. 24.
Practically exterminated	South side of Long Island, N.Y.	1886	W. Dutcher, 1897, p. 23.
not one in a hundred left	Cape Hatteras	1896	T. G. Pearson, 1937, p. 51.
1,400 in one day	Cobb's Island, Virginia	Before 1903	Chapman, 1903, p. 110.

fornia to New York, where they supposedly fetched one dollar each in 1901. Grebe shooting occurred in Northern California from about 1886 and persisted for at least 15 years.[90]

A much publicized case of seabird destruction took place in the North Pacific. W. A. Bryan of Honolulu (who later became an Audubon representative) in a letter to President Roosevelt dated 31 October, 1904, called attention to the practice of poaching albatross and tern skins on United States' atolls. Marcus Island, Midway, and Lisiansky had all been heavily plundered before 1904. Bryan made a plea for regular patrols by revenue cutter.

90. W. L. Finley in "Report of Audubon Societies for 1905," *BL* 7 (1905), pp. 336–342. Ibid., 10 (1908), pp. 291–295. In the 1908 Report, Finley mentioned indictments for plume hunting on Lake Malheur, Oregon. Pluming from the 1870's, one hunter reported making 500 dollars a day in 1898. The same person said that he had helped shoot out Tulare, California, between 1886 and 1889.

An estimate of 300,000 birds taken on Lisiansky was matched by an equal number taken on Laysan five years later.[91]

In England the fear of extermination was expressed repeatedly by SPB members and ornithologists in the final decades of the nineteenth century. Alfred Newton, W. H. Hudson and others believed that bi-monthly auction sales in Mincing Lane spelled the end for several species, particularly of birds of paradise.

The RSPB gave considerable publicity to Walter Goodfellow's first-hand account of conditions in Dutch New Guinea in 1910. Having traveled in the area for several years, Goodfellow expressed dismay "at the wholesale slaughter of these wonderful birds." [92] He believed that the extermination of birds of paradise was imminent because many species had specialized ranges, and shooters had begun to penetrate deeper into the interior for four stock birds, *Paradisea apoda, minor, rubra,* and *raggiana.*[93] The literature covering the life histories of birds of paradise is comprehensive. A recent text by Thomas Gilliard summarizes the importance of plume hunting on New Guinea. Gilliard noted that the traffic in bird skins became commercially lucrative from the 1880's to 1924. Natives and Europeans were able to derive a steady income by shipping eight or more species to European markets. Ernst Mayr, a world authority on birdlife of New Guinea, is reported to have discounted claims of permanent harm to birds of paradise, because of the vast rainforest hinterland and the official practice of shooting well-plumaged males permitting sub-adults to mate with drab-colored females.[94]

The threat of extinction posed by the commercial inroads into heron, gull, tern and bird of paradise populations led to other problems. Extermination would truncate basic research into plume birds, as it had done for the Labrador duck (*Camptorhynchus labradorius*), but ornithology was becoming in this post-Bairdian period (to use Coues' term [95]) a study of life histories and community relationships. Serious declines in bird popula-

91. William Dutcher, "Annual Report of . . . Audubon Societies for 1904," *BL* 7 (1905), pp. 58–74; espec. pp. 69–70; ibid., 14 (1912): 279–83. An overview is provided by C. A. Ely and Roger Clapp "Natural History of Laysan Island . . ," *Atoll Research Bull.*, No. 171 (1973).

92. *Feathers and Facts*, p. 65. Also RSPB, *Proc.: Annual Meeting* 1911, pp. 19–21.
93. Charles F. Downham, *The Feather Trade*, pp. 46–55.
94. *Birds of Paradise and Bower Birds* (London, 1969), pp. 30–34.
95. *Key to North American Birds*, 3rd edition (Boston, 1887), historical preface, p. xxv.

tions through direct human agency helped to finally explode the myth of super-abundance of natural resources. Such massacres of wildlife contradicted vague notions of duck and snipe factories beyond the north wind, or unlimited stocks of herons somewhere in Florida south of the Everglades.

Work undertaken by the U.S. Bureau of Biological Survey into the economic value of wild birds, particularly insectivorous ones, shed new light on the distinction between pest and non-pest species. By killing off an unwanted species or introducing a new one for beneficial purposes, new problems could be created almost overnight. The English sparrow [96] was an example to scientists to tread carefully before manipulating wildlife to get rid of a "bad" species or to shelter a "good" one. Gulls, terns, herons and others needed study it was claimed, before they could be dismissed as ecologically unimportant to man.

It is curious that in the body of literature devoted to endangered species, little space was given to the discussion of extinction itself. In popular articles and in serious essays, facts and figures of declines in particular species were argued about incessantly without the inevitability or even necessity of extinction being discussed. Was not extinction, some asked, concomitant with progress?

Charles Downham remarked that civilization and progress inevitably led to the withdrawal and disappearance of several birds. However, he never stated that extinction was to be welcomed. The trade went to great lengths to deny the reputed precarious status of many hard-hit birds, but it rarely argued that a heron could have no finer end than to improve, in some small degree, the human condition. Hamel Smith did touch upon this theme, but limited his arguments to the importance of giving employment for needy girls, or providing indigent natives with income. Senator James A. Reed came nearest the mark in denouncing with tongue in cheek the maudlin sympathy of the supporters of the plumage amendment. As he put it:

> The swamp herons' afflictions are doubtless solaced by the thought that it is only a miserable, homely creature, of no use

96. A whole volume could be written about the change of attitudes to birds exemplified by *P. domesticus*. J. R. Collette in, "House Sparrow," *American Naturalist* 4 (1870): 54–55, provides a favorable picture of the English Sparrow; the Division of Economic Ornithology and Mammalogy, which suggested various ways of eradicating this pest, provides a more critical one.

on earth except for one feather, and that its departing agonies must be alleviated by the knowledge that that feather will soon go to glorify and adorn my lady's bonnet.[97]

Tradesfolk hesitated to dismiss extinction as unimportant. No doubt part of the reason was that evolutionary thought had brought into relief the interdependence of life forms and the web-of-life concept represented by Charles Darwin. Modern arguments on behalf of endangered species stress the utility of a wild gene pool for future contingencies, but this is a later development. The durability of the natural ecosystem is today recognized by many as a function of its diversity. Natural variety is seen to be antithetical to instability. The retention of wild places and wild animals provides us and our progeny with a rough yardstick with which to measure how far we have traveled from our past.[98]

Seventy-five years ago, however, the the argument was still being cast in terms of religious and natural "laws."

> These laws are part of nature's economy, and man's title to interfere with them can only be justified by an appeal to the higher law of his own welfare—subject even in that case to the supreme law of humanity, which forbids wanton cruelty to the meanest of living things—and not by the less worthy motives of feminine vanity or masculine greed.

This statement from an article in *The Times* (page 7, col. 5) 25 December, 1897, provides a convenient point of departure for a discussion of the various historical attitudes towards man's place in nature. Typical of one late nineteenth-century school of thought on this issue, *The Times'* quote bears traces of the eighteenth century physico-theology of Leibniz, Herder and others. According to this view, man was placed at the apex of creation, transcending the brutes by his essential rationality. Made in God's image, he enjoyed the natural privileges spelled out in the first chapter of *Genesis,* having dominion over all creatures.

The idea of a divinely designed world has been investigated by Clarence J. Glacken, who has traced it in Western thought to

97. U.S. Congress, Senate, 16 Aug., 1913. *Cong. Record,* 63 Cong., 1 session, 3433.
98. The kind of thought current about man and nature is drawn together by Joseph L. Fisher, "New Perspectives on Conservation," *Biological Conservation* 1 (1969): 111–116.

the close of the eighteenth century. His treatment of the idea of design in the world and especially its historical dimensions, has a special significance for the philosophical questions raised by the plumage controversy.[99] Referring to our Christian heritage, Lynn White [100] has condemned theology and dogma as inimical to nature and basic to our current environmental crisis. The singular exception in this warfare on nature, according to White, was St. Francis of Assisi. Glacken, however, indicates that there were several divergent views about the environment within Christian ideology. One school, according to Glacken, argued that love of God is achieved through love of man and respect and admiration for creation and its creatures.

While Glacken's disagreement with White is rather more implicit than otherwise, René Dubos' recent statement that Christianity holds man responsible for his treatment of the environment and wildlife is openly hostile to White's thesis. Dubos finds it difficult to believe that the Judeo-Christian tradition has been as influential as White thinks in promoting environmental destruction. In any case, Dubos points to the second chapter of *Genesis,* where man is instructed to care for the land, and concludes that "to dress and keep the land means that man must be concerned with what happens to it." [101] Although made in the image of God, man must answer to his Creator and render account of his stewardship, a concept close to the "supreme law of humanity" alluded to in the *The Times*' piece.

From the standpoint of the Thomistic synthesis, each order within nature tends to its own intrinsic perfection and fulfillment. Each inferior chain of being may be subsumed by a higher one, justifying the human use of creatures for material and spiritual ends. However, it can be argued that the universe was not made with only man in mind but was created for the greater glory of its Creator. Thus, each component in nature mirrors some attribute of God and tends towards the perfection of the while universe. Additionally, the creatures provide man with a knowledge of God and, by analogy, His divine nature. On a metaphysical plane, extinction detracts from the perfection of the uni-

---

99. Clarence J. Glacken, *Traces on the Rhodian Shore* (Berkeley and Los Angeles, 1967).
100. "The Historical Roots of Our Ecologic Crisis," *Science* 155 (1967): 1203–1207.
101. "A Theology of the Earth," Lecture delivered 2 October, 1969, Smithsonian Institution, Washington, D.C.

verse. The divine command was not only to subdue and multiply but to name and answer for every creature, for the creation is essentially good.[102]

The term "nature's economy" in the *Times* article indicates an awareness of the interdependence of life forms in nature. In 1858, Wilson Flagg expressed similar thoughts in his remarks about insectivorous birds:

> It is a vain hope that leads one to believe while he is engaged in exterminating a certain species of small birds, that their places can be supplied and their services performed by other species which are allowed to multiply to excess. The preservation of every species of indigenous birds is the only means that can prevent the over-multiplication of injurious insects.[103]

Twenty years later the same author alluded to biblical sources describing order, harmony and beauty in nature, all created "to assist the great work of progression." Flagg noted, too, that birds "are important in the general economy of Nature, without which the operation of her laws would be disturbed, and the parts in the general harmony would be incomplete." [104] As more was learned about the life histories of birds, their importance in the balance of nature became increasingly obvious. Moreover, J. A. Allen had remarked that once birds were exterminated it was beyond the power of man to reconstitute their species or their numbers. Human actions on the land were not beneficial *per se* nor were human endeavors without considerable repercussions. By the turn of the present century the power of man as an agent of environmental change was indisputable and the cause of the gravest concern.

A final argument "for posterity" was commonly leveled against plume hunting. People stressed that unborn generations should have the opportunity to see and hear the birds before they were eliminated by the trade. James Buckland put it succinctly by saying that as a trustee of birds of the present and future, he was

102. The religious theme of man and nature has been treated in depth by Joseph M. Marling, *The Order of Nature in the Philosophy of St. Thomas Aquinas* (Washington, D.C., 1934); C. F. D. Moule, *Man and Nature in the New Testament* (Philadelphia, 1967) and Joseph Sittler, "Theology for Earth," *The Christian Scholar* 37 (1954): 367–374.
103. "The Birds of the Pasture and Forest," *Atlantic Monthly* 2 (1858): 863–875, p. 871.
104. *Birds and Seasons of New England* (Boston, 1875), pp. 159–160.

duty bound to seek avian protection, and if people wished to call him a sentimentalist then that was their right. He could not sit idly by and see the most beautiful creatures in nature destroyed for so unworthy a cause.[105]

In America, the argument had more force. Wildlife diminution provided an example of the effects of the "highly organized industrial and commercial system that has superseded the individualistic system of a few decades ago," as Henry Oldys put it.[106] Here the exuberance, variety and beauties of nature had been celebrated by the Bartrams and had been used by Franklin, Jefferson and Adams to refute Buffon's claim that nature was weaker in the New World. In the nineteenth century, America's natural assets were being rapidly sacrificed on the altar of expediency and material gain.

This conspectus of the arguments surrounding the plumage dispute demonstrates that birds were understood as economically, aesthetically and even philosophically important creatures to many people, especially children. Birds were seen as necessary links in the great chain of life which man was seeking to understand and upon which his survival depended. These sentiments occupied the protection literature for thirty years from the 1880's. Other arguments have been forwarded since on behalf of conserving and preserving wild bird species. Such nature philosophers as Aldo Leopold and Joseph Wood Krutch have revamped and made more cogent the older themes, but the literature of the plume dispute represents the beginnings of the roots of these later writers and of the modern ecology movement itself.

105. Pros and Cons of the Plumage Bill (London, 1911), pp. 15–16. He remarked: "Birds are an inheritance which it is our duty to safeguard in order to give posterity what is honestly its own," see "Value of Birds to Man," *Journ. Royal Soc. Arts* 63 (1915): 701–711.

106. "Audubon Societies in Relation to the Farmer," U.S.D.A. *Yearbook* (1902): 205–218, 207.

3

Movement Against the Feather Trade

In the final twenty years of the nineteenth century, British and American crusaders for bird protection, spurred by enthusiasm and a sense of impatience, began efforts to render illegal the killing, possession, sale and importation of plume birds and ornamental feathers. For a long time their efforts met stiff resistance.

In England, the RSPB commented bitterly: "bird protectors must continue to press for this one plain, straightforward measure, in spite of all the parleyings and equivocations of plume-dealers and politicians." [1] This remark was made in 1918, ten years after efforts had been initiated to push a plumage bill through Parliament. Members of the AOU and the incipient Audubon movement suffered similar fits of melancholy. An AOU Committee drafted a law for the protection of non-game birds which some state legislatures acted upon and about which many others procrastinated. Some states restricted the sale of ornamental plumage after arduous lobbying by Audubon Society members and persons of like mind. Other states took an interest in the plumage issue then allowed it to lapse.

Motion towards banning the use, sale and importation of ornamental feather trim was hesitant and slow. Some people thought this was because only international agreements could solve the issue. Several speakers at ornithological conferences drew attention to the worldwide impact of plume hunters. They called upon all countries to restrict bird killing within their confines and to limit shipments of bird skins and feathers beyond their frontiers. To this end, the United Kingdom called for a conference to be

1. RSPB, *Twenty-seventh Annual Report* (1917), p. 13.

held in London to seek an end to bird killing. Nothing came of the request because certain nations with an interest in the plumage trade declined to participate.

Anti-plumage Groups in England and in the United States

A precedent already existed for the drive for effective bird protection, which intensified in the final years of the nineteenth century on both sides of the Atlantic. In England, The Sea Birds Preservation Act (1869) had attended to the parlous conditions of certain seafowl. A bird protection association had worked at the county level for the original bill. After its passage, this body (known as the Association for the Protection of British Birds and led by Rev. F. O. Morris) continued to concern itself with the protection of plume and other birds. In 1885, Morris and his group offered grassroots support to an anti-plumage league which in turn acted as an active reservoir of goodwill for the Society for the Protection of Birds (SPB), founded in 1889. Aided and abetted by natural history societies and other local organizations, the SPB began to spearhead moves against the British plumage industry.

The English plumage story began in 1869 when Christopher Sykes introduced a bill to control the slaughter of seabirds for millinery purposes along the Flamborough cliffs in Yorkshire. His measure received sympathetic attention from both Houses of Parliament. The Lords' Committee to which the bill was referred underestimated the persistence of the feather wearing habit. The Archbishop of York noted that gulls were suffering because "their feathers adorned the hats of the fairer sex." However, the Duke of Richmond believed that fashions were by nature ephemeral and feather trimmings would become unpopular.[2] With the measure safely through Parliament, Professor Alfred Newton's 1868 lament about seabird destruction had been acted upon. A seabird association had pushed successfully for the Act. At Bridlington near Flamborough, Canon Barnes-Lawrence wrote in his diary on 10 July, 1869: "Mr. Tasker, of Sheffield, shot 28 birds after reading the Act in order to try the Law."[3] Tasker was prosecuted and convicted in accordance with it, and the Canon continued: "our biggest concern now is to stop the horrible dumping of

2. *Parliamentary Debates* 196, 4 May, 1869, par. 78–81.
3. "The Preservation of Seabirds," *BNN* 14 (1931), p. 137.

waste oil on sea and shore." [4] However, the provision in the Act for a closed season on 33 species of waterfowl proved unenforceable and of little consequence to the plumage trade. The legislative fight was only an early skirmish between the movement for bird protection and the feather trade.

In the 1870's and '80's, further action was taken to improve bird protection in Britain but the laws were characterized by low penalties, incomplete or inoperative schedules, and ineffective closed seasons. It appeared to some landowners that predatory birds were created expressly to grace gamekeeper's gibbets. Rarer birds were shot by taxidermists as collector's specimens and as skin series. Their eggs lined zoologists' cabinets. Many birds fared badly. Professional bird catchers, equipped with traps, nets and glutenous lime, ranged field and hedgerow to obtain larks, buntings and finches as table delicacies or as songsters. Plume hunting, then, was only one of a number of reasons for the decimation of bird populations in the British Isles.

The 1880 and 1881 bird protection bills, supported by Sir John Lubbock (who as Lord Avebury was destined to take an important role in British plumage legislation) were attempts to provide help for a number of birds. They were incomplete, however, and not very systematic:

> Nearly all the land-birds which became included were added to the list by the Lords. To Lord Selborne we owe the inclusion of Nightjar and Woodpecker; to the Duke of Somerset the Cuckoo; to Lord Lilford the Owl (strongly supported by the Duke of Buccleuch and Lord Kimberley) . . . to Lord Walsingham the Goldfinch, Nightingale, Hoopoe, Roller, Bee-eater, Bittern, and American Quail; to Lord Aberdeen the Kingfisher. The 'Ariole' (sic) was also placed on the list.[5]

4. Ibid., p. 138. Not only had the plumage question been left unresolved but destruction of seabirds actually continued. A letter from the Rev. F. O. Morris, Nunburnholme Rectory, Hayton, Yorks., to *The Times* (London) 17 August, 1885, p. 6, col. 5, lamented the shortness of the closed season under the 1869 Act. He enclosed letters from correspondents who recalled a quarter of a ton of seabirds shot in one day about the Flamborough cliffs in the 1850's. In 1885, as soon as the closed season terminated, gunners took a terrible toll of adult and juvenile birds on the same cliffs. As late as 1900, London milliners advertised for supplies of thousands of gulls and terns. See Ralph Chislett, "A Century of Ornithology in Yorkshire," *The Naturalist* 879 (1961): 139–144, and Charles Wilson, "A Hundred Years of Bird Protection," *BNN* (1969): 267–270.

5. "The Story of Bird Protection," Part II, *BNN* 4 (1910), p. 15. Reference is made to Mr. Dillwyn's bill to amend the bird act (1872) by providing a closed season for all species not previously covered.

An outcry from poulterers against the 1880 Act led to charges in 1881 permitting a variety of small birds and waders to continue to be offered for sale. Amendments played into the exploiters' hands. Birds hunted for their feathers fared little better and occasioned additional action.

The Reverend Francis O. Morris, an indefatigable worker for the 1869 Seabird Act, promoted an anti-plumage league in 1885. Moves to found the league began with a letter to *The Times* (London) in August, in which George A. Musgrave reported that at least 400,000 West Indian and Brazilian birds, and more than 350,000 from the Orient, had been sold in London during the first quarter. He concluded:

> Is there no society willing to care for the beauty of the world? If ancient monuments can be, thanks to the energetic Sir John Lubbock, protected from Stonehenge to Nikko, surely some plan can be devised for making a general work of destruction at least unfashionable.[6]

The Times expressed sympathy with Musgrave's sentiments. In an editorial comment it was noted that although feather wearing was not as conspicuous as it had been, the mawkish trade for stuffed birds and animals, to set off clothing and furniture, persisted. The newspaper suggested that the Royal Society for the Prevention of Cruelty to Animals (RSPCA) should redouble its educational efforts in industrial towns, especially among children, to increase interest in "animated" nature.

Within six months of Musgrave's appeal for an organization to champion the cause of birds of bright plumage, the Reverend Morris, an aging John Ruskin and several others founded an anti-plumage group.[7] George Musgrave lent the movement his

6. 17 August, 1885, p. 6, col. 4. *The Times* continued to keep its readers abreast of millinery activities, printing comments from Alfred Newton on 28 January, 1876, and others from Baroness Burdett-Coutts. *Punch* gave support to the plumage issue on 19 February, 1876; See *BNN* 4 (1910), p. 37.

Details of the British bird protection movement are taken from "The Story of Bird Protection," *BNN* 4 (1910): 1–3, 14–15, 26–27, 37–39; (1911): 49–50, 61–63; also see "History of the Society," *BNN* 1 (1903): 1–2. Ties between the SPB and RSPCA are referred to by Edward G. Fairholme, *A Century of Work for Animals* (London, 1934).

7. *BNN* 4 (1910), p. 38. The League was founded through the offices of Lord and Lady Mount-Temple at their home in Broadlands, Hants. See also F. O. Morris' letter, "A Plumage League," *The Times* (London), 18 December, 1885, p. 14, col. 1, in which he described Lady Mount-Temple as "a devoted friend to the cause of

wholehearted support and agreed to merge it in 1886 with a sister organization that he had promoted called the Selborne League. This league, kindred in spirit to the Folk-lore Society and the Society for the Preservation of Ancient Monuments, was devoted to nature protection in its broadest sense. Renamed the Selborne Society, its members taught others to love and defend nature, and a knowledge of natural history. The true Selborne Society member displayed catholic interests in the physical and cultural landscape, and was a person: "who loves every stone of the old abbey, beautiful even in its ruins, and reverently garners the legends of its ancient fame, will strive to preserve also the trees and flowers that gather round its walls, and the birds that have in its desecrated altars 'a nest where they may lay their young.' " [8]

The Selborne Society differed from the SPB (which was to get underway three years later) in its attitude toward feather wearing. The Selborne Society's officers argued for a practical, or what they termed a "reasonable," approach to the issue of feather wearing. It approved the wearing of ornamental feathers of game birds and of species harmful to farmers, for example. The SPB, by contrast, never approved using plumage of noxious birds.

What is now called the Royal Society for the Protection of Birds dates from February, 1889, when Mrs. Robert W. Williamson of Didsbury, Manchester, formed a group of ladies into a "Society for the Protection of Birds" (SPB). From the outset, this anti-plumage organization enjoyed the good will of the Selborne Society and the RSPCA. When the Society moved to the London area in 1891, Mrs. Edward Phillips, of Croydon and Mrs. Frank E. Lemon of Redhill, both active in campaigns against cruelty to animals, became involved in its development. Shortly thereafter, formal committee meetings were held in the RSPCA's offices in Jermyn Street. After four years, the SPB's membership had risen to 9,000, and Winifred Dallas-Yorke, the Duchess of Portland, had become its president, a position she held for 63 years until her death in 1954.[9]

---

humanity towards all and every of our dumb fellow-creatures, both in fur and feather." The league appeared a loosely-knit group of people intent upon changing "this shameful destruction to meet the tasteless fashion of covering ladies' bonnets, hats and ball gowns with lovely specimens."

8. Selborne Society, *Nature Notes* 1 (1890), p. 2.

9. James Fisher has thrown light on early ladies' groups interested in bird protection. He attributed the start of the plumage campaign to Alfred Newton (referring to his letter of denunciation to *The Times*, 28 January, 1876) and

The Society existed "in the hope of inducing a considerable number of women, of all ranks and ages, to unite in discouraging the enormous destruction of bird life exacted by milliners and others for purely decorative purposes." [10] The Society's rules were:

1. That members shall discourage the wanton destruction of birds, and interest themselves generally in their protection.
2. That Lady-Members shall refrain from wearing the feathers of any birds not killed for purposes of food, the ostrich only excepted.
3. That each Local Secretary shall subscribe one shilling a year. . . .[11]

The SPB urged local secretaries to persuade ladies to make a pledge to its second rule. Upon payment of twopence and an agreement to forego feathers each lady was sent a membership card.

The press gave the SPB considerable publicity and encouragement. In its *First Annual Report* (1891) the group expressed thanks to 60 parish magazines, local newspapers, ladies' home journals, and especially to *The Times* (London), for helpful comments about its objectives. It prospered, increasing fivefold in membership and tenfold in income during 1892. *Punch* had occasion to lampoon the feather fad in a picture "A Bird of Prey" (14 May, 1892), and cartoonist Linley Sambourne, abhorring feather trimmings, became an SPB stalwart.[12]

In the United States, laws protecting non-game birds, including plume species, existed in several states before the inception of the Audubon Society in 1886. This Society was to work hard to make bird laws effective, to broaden their scope and to introduce

emphasized the importance of three "formidable women," Eliza Elder (Mrs. George Brightwen), 1830–1906; Margaretta Louisa Smith (Mrs. Frank Lemon), 1860–1953; and Winifred Dallas-Yorke (Duchess of Portland), President of the RSPB from 1891–1954. The "Manchester Group," headed by the Duchess of Portland, appears to have joined in with a "Fur, Fin and Feather," body. This group was organized by Mrs. Edward Phillips in the London area. See *The Shell Bird Book* (London, 1966), pp. 136–139.

10. SPB *First Annual Report* (1891), p. 7.
11. Ibid., pp. 7–8.
12. A useful series of essays on the RSPB written by Mrs. Frank E. Lemon appeared as "The Story of the R.S.P.B.," *BNN* 20 (1943): 67–68 84–87, 100–102, 116–118. Sambourne's activities for the Society are referred to in an orbituary, "Mr. Linley Sambourne . . . ," *BNN* 4 (1910): 25.

new ones in states without them. Broader in social base than the SPB in England, large numbers of women and children supported the Audubon Society. In liaison with the AOU's Committee on Bird Protection, it worked to make feather fashions unpopular among American ladies. Nevertheless, Audubon officials, unable to cope with administrative and financial problems and somewhat disillusioned about the practical impact of the society in fashion circles, allowed the Society to lapse after three years. In the mid 1890's, when ornithologists and nature lovers renewed protective efforts for plume species the Society was reborn.

The second Audubon movement achieved major growth after 1900; in 1902, a National Committee was formed to coordinate activities in nature study and in bird preservation carried on by state and local groups; and in 1905, the National Association incorporated. When T. Gilbert Pearson, secretary of the National Association, testified before Congressional committees in support of ending ornamental plumage imports in 1913, he was able to claim a following of 100,000 members—a sizable force for the interests of birdlife.

The first Audubon Society, founded by George Bird Grinnell, reflected concerns for bird protection which were similar to, but more specific than the concerns of its sister society in England. The following suggestion appeared in the sportsman's journal, *Forest and Stream,* on 11 February, 1886:

> We propose the formation of an association for the protection of wild birds and their eggs, which shall be called the Audubon Society. Its membership is to be free to everyone who is willing to lend a helping hand in forwarding the objects for which it is formed. These objects shall be to prevent, so far as possible (1), the killing of any wild birds not used for food; (2) the destruction of nests or eggs of any wild bird, and (3) the wearing of feathers as ornaments or trimming for dress. . . .
>
> The work to be done by the Audubon Society is auxiliary to that undertaken by the Committee of the American Ornithologists' Union; and will further the efforts of the A.O.U. committee, doing detail duties to which they cannot attend. Those who desire to join the Audubon Society, established on the basis and for the purpose above set forth, should send their names at once to the FOREST AND STREAM, 40 Park Row, New York.[13]

13. "The Audubon Society," *Forest and Stream* 26 (11 February, 1886): 41. See also J. A. Allen, "An Ornithologist's Plea," (letter) *New York Times,* 25 November, 1897, p. 6, col. 6.

The habitual reader took the proposal in stride, being familiar with numerous accounts of wildlife destruction published in the journal. In *Forest and Stream*'s first issue (September, 1873), Charles Hallock, its editor, had printed extracts from *Chambers' Journal* entitled "Man the Destroyer" and "The Balance of Nature." In other issues he drew attention to the growing scarcity of wildlife, as exemplified by the bison. Ten years before the formation of the Audubon Society, in an article called "Spare the Birds" (25 March, 1875), Hallock had also acquainted American readers with particulars of the London feather trade and presaged a dim future for America's "gay plumaged birds." He had spoken out against the craze for fancy feathers: "Every bird whose gift of glorious plumage makes him a mark for the adornment of a lady's hat, is eagerly sought for in the market, and the coming fashion of ornamenting dresses also, is increasing the demand and correspondingg slaughter," (page 104).

George Bird Grinnell (1849–1938), traveller, author, naturalist and expert on American Indian affairs, became editor of *Forest and Stream* in 1876, and urged sportsmen to limit their bags of game. He, too, expressed a strong distaste for market and plume hunting. An editorial comment in 1884 proved particularly pungent: "The destruction of American wild birds for millinery purposes has assumed stupendous proportions," Grinnell said. The creatures that make up the "musical, joyous, beautiful feathered life of our own yards and orchards" were being killed, from Florida to Maine, by a system of trapping and shooting of almost diabolical perfection. *Forest and Stream* would in the future combat the league of killers by providing readers with details of bird destruction.[14]

14. "The Sacrifice of Song Birds," *Forest and Stream* 23 (7 August, 1884): 21; William Dutcher, "History of the Audubon Movement," *BL* 7 (1905): 45–57, lists a number of articles pertaining to bird destruction published in the *Forest and Stream*. However, he does not exhaust the material to be found in early volumes, some of which goes back to before 1883.

Isaac McLellan, Spare the Swallows," 21 (20 September, 1883): 143, composed a poem apropos to an editorial on swallow destruction. It concluded:

Ah, pity 'tis these plenteous wing'd guests
That please our hearts and rid life of its pests,
That charm the blithesome air with chirping sweet,
And fill the merry sound each calm retreat
Should die that Youth should win another grace
To nod above the witchery of her face!
Ah! she forgets that to enhance her bloom,
A sweet bird dies to yield its purple plume.

Grinnell's idea of an Audubon Society was appropriate for another reason. As co-founder of the AOU bird protection committee, he had taken an interest in learning about bird destruction and about millinery demands for feathers. A year after its formation in 1884, and two years before Grinnell's Audubon Society, the AOU committee of six (which included William Dutcher who later became first President of the National Association of Audubon Societies) was enlarged. One group collected millinery statistics, another sought to further legislation for plume and non-game bird species. The Audubon Society helped publicize the aims of the AOU committee. A growing membership promised to be a force for political action and by their example thousands of lady members showed disdain for "vulgar" feather trimmings. George Sennett, chairman of the AOU committee, congratulated *Forest and Stream* for its help in creating and sustaining the Audubon Society.[15]

A year after Grinnell had founded the Audubon movement, open free of charge to anyone willing "to cooperate in any degree for bird protection," the Forest and Stream Publishing Company (of which Grinnell was president) began to publish *The Audubon Magazine*. Each copy cost six cents and members were asked to contribute fifty cents a year to help offset printing costs. The journal was designed "to create a rational interest in birds," and to highlight the economic importance of wildlife to human welfare, especially agriculture. It was intended to be a family monthly with a stress on children's nature stories. It was to be the medium by which local chapter officers throughout the nation communicated their concern for birds.

In 1888, the Audubon Society began to offer prizes to persons collecting ten or more subscriptions. Terms of membership were set down in a pledge to be signed and forwarded by each prospective member. He or she agreed to prevent:

1. The killing of any wild bird not used for food.
2. The taking or destroying of the eggs or nest of any wild birds.

The topic of electrocuting migrating swallows in the South of France was given considerable attention by protection groups. Issues of *Forest and Stream* in the 1880's covered a wide range of topics from whooping crane hunting to seafowl destruction. In most instances new laws or better enforcement of existing ones were thought necessary.

15. *Forest and Stream* 26 (11 March, 1886), p. 124. "By a resolution of the A.O.U. Committee for the Protection of Birds, I am authorized to communicate to the

3. The wearing of the feathers of wild birds. Ostrich feathers, whether from wild or tame birds, and those of domestic fowls, are specially exempted.

The great aim of the Society is the protection of American non-game birds.[16]

Every month from 1887 to 1889, the magazine's episodic descriptions of the past activities of John James Audubon and Alexander Wilson entered more and more homes. Essays about "Woman's Heartlessness" or "The Wounded Redstart" were designed to make readers think carefully about the consequences of using and abusing birdlife. The magazine contained tales for the young. Bird enthusiasts entered into the lives of feathered creatures of town and country. They were helped with bird identification and were informed about happenings in the world of wildlife protection by newsworthy entries in the "Audubon Note Book."

Under George Bird Grinnell's direction the Audubon movement enjoyed popular support, and included 50 honorary vice-presidents. Like most of its members, these persons came mainly from eastern states, particularly New York, Massachusetts and Pennsylvania. A few lived in Canada, others were scattered in such places as Des Moines, Chicago and San Francisco. Even, with circulation of almost 50,000 however, the journal was not self-supporting; and it came as a shock to the reader to learn that the magazine was to be discontinued. An editorial in the last issue (January, 1889) declared that the publication was "not essential to the progress of the movement, and as its preparation calls for a great deal more labor than our busy staff can well devote to it, we have decided to discontinue it."

Grinnell had been prescient in founding, promoting, and sustaining the Audubon Society and had done so out of affection for birdlife fostered in him, at least in part, by Lucy Audubon, school

---

AUDUBON SOCIETY our approval of its plan and the sanction of our authority in the work it undertakes."

16. *Audubon Magazine* 1 (1887), p. 20. Miss A. C. Knight began *The Bird Call*, a publication of the Pennsylvania Audubon Society founded in April, 1886. The wording of the Audubon pledge varied. The form to be filled out stated in pledge no. 3 that: "I pledge myself not to make use of the feathers of any wild birds as ornaments of dress or household furniture, and by every means in my power to discourage the use of feathers for decorative purposes." George Sennett, Report, November, 1886, MS—Addendum, Smithsonian Institution, (Washington, D.C., 1886).

TABLE 6
Membership of the Audubon Society
January 1887–December 1888

Months	1887	1888
January	19,830	43,683
February	22,397	44,308
March	26,751	45,154
April	29,956	45,651
May	32,570	46,484
June	36,024	47,095
July	37,453	47,415
August	38,981	47,644
September	39,750	47,841
October	40,783	48,046
November	42,246	48,518
December	42,897	48,862

teacher, and the widow of the great bird artist. Membership figures listed in table 6 mark his success. During the first year of the magazine, membership had more than doubled. However, growth had tapered off to less than 350 new pledges in December, 1888, compared with over 3,350 in the same month of 1887. Membership had risen by only 5,000 in 1888, as against 20,000 in 1887.

The reasons for this slowed pace of growth are unclear. Robert Welker [17] had the impression that the Audubon Society failed because it did not enlist citizens of note who were to step forward during the Society's revival at the state and local level ten years later. Honorary members of the Society were identified only once, in the first issue of February, 1887. Later copies, however, did contain letters from such eminent figures as John Greenleaf Whittier, Henry Ward Beecher, John Burroughs and General F. E. Spinner, "Watch Dog of the Treasury," who endorsed the Society and its mission.

Of particular interest is the suggestion that the magazine was not essential to the progress of the movement. In an article entitled "Reintroduction of Feather Millinery," [18] the reader learned that the "Parisian mondaines or demi-mondaines," had decided that feathers were in vogue again. It was wondered whether the

17. *Birds and Men*, p. 207.   18. *Audubon Magazine* 2 (1888): 207–208.

Selborne or Audubon groups had aroused their ire and caused them to demonstrate their contempt for anti-plumage groups, or whether, as was more probable, they had simply never heard of bird protection groups. The essay stated candidly: "The suggestion that the Audubon Society or the moral idea it represents could influence the women of America to reject the Paris fashion . . . would do no more than provoke an amused smile," (p. 207). The return of feather millinery was proof that ladies of fashion were either not taking the anti-plumage campaign seriously or believed it was confined to a faddist minority: "Phenomenal as has been the growth of the Audubon Society, its fifty thousand members constitute less than one in a thousand of our population; and widely although we have advertised the movement, the Society . . . is probably not known to one in a hundred of the people of the United States," (p. 208).

Such soul-searching about the role of the Audubon Society indicated that those in charge of the magazine recognized that they might be losing the plumage battle. If fashion depended on a small coterie of American women, numbering at most a few hundred, then members of that elite band did not belong to the Audubon Society, and presumably had little time for its tenets. In England, on the other hand, influential people had begun to make efforts to interest their peers, and ultimately the Royal family, in the SPB and its message about the consequences of feather wearing. They were to succeed where the Audubon movement initially failed. However, organized resistance from British business interests largely offset support from upper classes. Paris, of course, remained aloof and impregnable.

The Audubon Society's work for American bird protection was complemented by the AOU's Committee on the Protection of North American Birds. This committee had been formed at ornithologist William Brewster's (1851–1919) behest at the second annual meeting of the Union in 1884. Considered humanitarian rather than scientific in its work, the group under George B. Sennett, Witmer Stone and later William Dutcher, cooperated with humane societies, state Audubon chapters and the press, to inform and educate people in the mid 1880's about bird slaughter for millinery ornament. Reporting in 1886, after twenty meetings of the ten-man committee, George B. Sennett (1840-1900) expressed satisfaction about favorable newspaper coverage given to the AOU group. He believed that the AOU was interesting the public in literature on bird protection but should guard against intemperate fanaticism, or lukewarm philanthropy.[19] The AOU Committee guided by Sennett became less active after 1888 and eventually ceased to report to the annual meeting of the Union. It was shaken up in 1895, however, and William Dutcher became its new chairman.

William Dutcher (1846–1920), a man of single-minded devotion to bird preservation, held joint chairmanship of this AOU Committee and another constituted later by the National Association of Audubon Societies. He was Treasurer of the AOU from 1887 to 1903 but began to devote most of his time to the new National Association of State Audubon Societies when what he termed the "second cycle" of bird protection commenced in the mid 1890's with the organization of an Audubon Society in Massachusetts.

Frank M. Chapman, author and ornithologist in the American Museum of Natural History, also served on the AOU bird protection committee. He founded, owned and edited *Bird-Lore,* the periodical of the Association of Audubon Societies, first published in 1899 and similar in format to the original *Audubon Magazine.* Without becoming engrossed in the personalities active in the AOU and Audubon movements in the 1890's and later, mention must be made of legislative efforts promoted by these leading figures.[20]

Model Laws and Millinery Agreements

The AOU bird protection committee formulated a proposal for a "Model Law" for non-game bird protection and published it

19. Joel A. Allen, *The American Ornithologists' Union A Seven Years' Retrospect* (New York, 1891), pp. 10–11, Sennett, "Report of AOU Committee on the Protection of North American Birds," November, 1886, Ms. Smithsonian Institution (Washington, D.C., 1886), declared that several thousand copies of *The Science—supplement* on bird destruction were sent to the press, superintendents of schools and legislators. The New York *Evening Post,* 9 February, 1886, carried a note on fashion and bird destruction by one of the Committee, E. P. Bicknell; J. B. Holder contributed another on 20 February, 1886. George Musgrave of the English Selborne Society offered his fullest cooperation with the AOU bird protection committee, and Montagu Chamberlain, another member from New Brunswick, was spreading "the word" in Canada; see pp. 3–6, 12.

20. I am indebted to suggestions made by Dr. Fred Evenden of the Wildlife Society who has recently completed research upon the history of the AOU. See also Carl W. Buchheister and Frank Graham, "From the Swamps and Back: A Concise and Candid History of the Audubon Movement," *BL* 75 (1973): 4–45.

as a supplement in *Science* on 26 February, 1886. Novel in its clarity, it had been preceded by other laws covering plume birds in the United States (table 7 deals with the nature of earlier state laws relating to various insectivorous, song or small birds). Florida enacted a provision against bird destruction for millinery purposes as early as 1877. A subsequent Texas Act (1891) "for the protection of certain birds and their eggs," included in it "any seagull, tern, shearwater, egret, heron or pelican," and drew attention to the fact that many persons were engaged in killing birds for their plumage.[21]

As T. Gilbert Pearson discovered, however, many of the 19 state laws covering birds before the formation of the AOU in 1883 were dead letters. The AOU bird protection committee, maintained that prior to 1901 only five states had passed laws that met the group's high standards.[22] Many state laws had no funding provisions, incomplete closed seasons, or were ineffective or inapplicable in certain regions or counties.

The AOU law defined game birds as Anatidae, Rallidae, Limicolae and Gallinae. The remainder were non-game birds whose possession, purchase and sale was to be prohibited, the English Sparrow excepted. Three months after this Model Law appeared in *Science,* the New York State Legislature passed a bill similar in scope and intent to the AOU formulation:

> Section 1. No person in any of the counties of this State, shall kill, wound, trap, net, snare, catch, with bird lime, or with any similar substance, poison or drug, any bird of song or any linnet, blue bird, yellow hammer, yellow bird, thrush, woodpecker, cat bird, pewee, swallow, martin, bluejay, oriole, kildee, snow bird, grass bird, gross beak, bobolink, phoebe bird, hummingbird, wren, robin, meadow lark or starling, or any wild bird, other than a game bird. Nor shall any person purchase, or have in possession, or expose for sale any such song or wild bird, or any part thereof, after the same has been killed. For the purposes of this act the following only shall be considered game birds: the Anatidae, commonly known as swans, geese, brant, and river

21. Texas, *General Laws,* 22nd Legislature (Austin, 1891). The bill passed the House 79–6 and the Senate 22–2.
22. William Dutcher, "Results of Special Protection to Gulls and Terns . . . ," *The Auk* 19 (1902), p. 36. The States were: Indiana, statute dated March 5, 1891; Vermont, statute dated November 22, 1892; Arkansas, statute dated March 15, 1897; Illinois, statute dated April 24, 1899; Rhode Island, statute dated May 4, 1900

TABLE 7

State Legislation for the Protection
of Non-Game Birds, 1818–1887

1818	Massachusetts	Closed season for several species including larks and robins.
1846	Rhode Island	Similar to Massachusetts.
1849	Minnesota	Sunday hunting prohibited.
1850	Connecticut	Year round protection to insectivorous birds.
1850	New Jersey	Protection to small and "harmless" birds.
1851	Vermont	Year round protection, plus nests and eggs.
1855	Massachusetts	All year protection to warblers, woodpeckers, and others and forbidding sale or possession of them.
1855	Iowa	Sunday hunting prohibited.
1857	Ohio	First game law including flicker in a closed season plus some non-game birds all the year.
1858	Maine	First protection for lark, robin, woodpecker and sparrows in spring.
1859	Pennsylvania	Protection to insectivorous birds.
1861	Kentucky	First local game laws aided birds smaller than quails.
1861	Nevada	First game law with certain non-game birds protected.
1862	New York	Non-game bird protection.
1865	Michigan	First protection for any small non-game bird except blackbirds.
1869	West Virginia	All year protection for any birds, except some predators, woodpeckers, and blackbirds.

Similar measures were adopted for non-game or insectivorous birds in South Carolina (1872), Indiana (1872) and Kansas (1876), and the District of Columbia (1878).

Millinery provisions began to be mentioned from 1870–1890.

1877	Florida	Sea and plume bird law, 2 March. (strengthened 1891 and 1901).

TABLE 7 (*continued*)
State Legislation for the Protection
of Non-Game Birds, 1818–1887

| 1885 | New Jersey | Against the killing, possession and sale of gulls, terns, shorebirds, herons, insectivorous and song birds, 20 April. |
| 1887 | Wisconsin | An Act to prevent the killing of birds for millinery purposes, included the robin, thrush, swallow and 27 others, but no water-birds, 11 April. |

SOURCES: T. S. Palmer 1902 and 1912, and selected *Reports of State Laws.*

and sea ducks; the Rallidae, commonly known as rails, coots, mud-hens and gallinules; the Limicolae, commonly known as shore birds, plovers, surfbirds, snipe, woodcock, sand pipers, tatlers, and curlews; the Gallinae, commonly known as wild turkeys, grouse, prairie-chickens, pheasants, partridges, and quails.[23]

The Model Law aimed at orthodoxy and unanimity among the states in defining game and non-game birds, and afforded protection to species sought for their plumage. Before 1900, eight states had passed versions of the AOU law, or possessed paragraphs protecting non-game birds, as table 8 indicates. Some of these, such as the New York law, were repealed or emasculated. In the next decade, another 34 states followed provisions of the Model Law, but, constant vigilance was needed to prevent repeals or local exemptions. In 1902, Theodore S. Palmer (1868–1955), of the U.S. Biological Survey, reported that 12 states had non-game bird laws. He stated that "nearly all of the States east of the Mississippi and north of the Ohio and Potomac rivers now have effective modern laws." [24] At that time a revision of the Model Law, approved by William Dutcher, stated "that no part of the plumage, skin, or body of any bird protected by this section will be sold or had in possession for sale." [25]

23. See "Chapter 427, For the Preservation of Song and Wild Birds," *Audubon Magazine* 1 (1887) p. 21.
24. T. S. Palmer, "Legislation for the Protection of Birds Other than Game Birds," U.S.D.A., *Biol. Survey Bull.* No. 12, revised edition (Washington, D.C., 1902).
25. Ibid., p. 56.

TABLE 8
AOU Model Law: Date of First State Passage

1886	New York *, Massachusetts *
1889	Pennsylvania *
1891	Indiana *
1892	Vermont *
1896	Maryland *
1897	Arkansas *
1899	Illinois *, Utah *
1900	Rhode Island *
1901	Wisconsin *, New Hampshire *, Florida *, Maine, Connecticut *, New Jersey *, Delaware *, District of Columbia *, Wyoming *, Nevada *
1902	Kentucky, Alaska, Ohio
1903	Tennessee, Texas *, Virginia *, North Carolina, Georgia, Colorado, Oregon *, Washington, Minnesota *
1904	Louisiana, Mississippi
1905	Missouri, California *, Michigan *, South Carolina
1907	Alabama, West Virginia, Iowa, South Dakota
1909	North Dakota, Oklahoma

(Many states amended or repealed legislation once lobbying became effective, others were slow to enforce legislation once it was on their books.)

SOURCES: After William Dutcher, *The Auk* 19 (Jan., 1902) p. 36, the same *BL* (1905) p. 47, T. S. Palmer 1902, pp. 34-35, and 1912, p. 13.
* Certain plumes birds provided for by 1902. See *Appendix* II (Palmer, 1902, pp. 34-35).

This plumage provision was important because many plume birds were not covered under the game or insectivorous provisions of the Model Law. Palmer named seven states in 1900 (Arkansas, Illinois, Indiana, Massachusetts, New York, Rhode Island, Vermont, with Canada's Manitoba and Ontario) with provisions against birds taken for ornamental purposes. Sixteen years later in a letter to Ernest Ingersoll of the National Association of Audubon Societies, T. S. Palmer, legal expert on wildlife laws, asserted that "about three-fourths of the States prohibit the sale of heron aigrettes." He said that state laws covering the plumage issue fell into three groups: First, statutes like those of New York, New Jersey, Pennsylvania and Vermont, which covered not only native bird plumage but also foreign species of the same families. Second, laws like those of Massachusetts, Rhode Island and Michigan giving special protection to herons. Third, laws like the AOU formulation prohibiting the possession and sale of all wild birds or their plumage. In some states, however, these AOU laws did not prohibit the sale of plumage.[26]

The improved situation for birds Palmer described in 1916 had come about through an uphill struggle in state and federal chambers. An important beginning for state bird laws was provided by a federal bill introduced by John F. Lacey (1841–1913) of Iowa on 1 July, 1897. Revisions, amendments and repeated introductions of this measure, finally signed into law on 25 May, 1900, enlarged its original scope.[27] The Lacey Act made bird protection a concern of the U.S. Department of Agriculture, and prohibited interstate traffic in birds killed in violation of state laws. The shipper of game for the market and the millinery agent could continue his work only where local laws did not prohibit killing. Laws in the state of destination also had to be obeyed or confiscation and fines were imposed. The Lacey Act did not stop the importation of foreign bird skins for millinery purposes (unless they entered as live wild species, which in many cases required permits from the Department of Agriculture) but it did circumscribe millinery activities in states which had laws similar to the AOU prototype.

One of the first enforcements of the Lacey Act was the seizure of 2,600 gulls in a millinery establishment in Baltimore, Maryland. Theodore S. Palmer who was party to the seizure reported the broader consequences of the case. He noted that:

> One of the largest wholesale millinery firms in Baltimore requested an official inspection of their stock and agreed to abandon the sale not only of gulls and terns but also of grebes, pelicans, herons and other birds protected by State or Federal law. I interviewed practically all the wholesale milliners in the city and without exception they took the same ground and promptly

26 See *The Evening Star* (Washington, D.C.), 15 October, 1900, cited in Palmer, Personal Papers, Library of Congress, Ms. Division, and Palmer to Ingersoll, 29 July, 1916, Bureau of Biol. Survey, National Archives.

27. 31 Stat. L., 187, see Jenks Cameron, *The Bureau of Biological Survey* . . . (Baltimore, 1929), pp. 65ff; and U.S.D.A., *Biol. Survey, Circular* No. 29 and 30. See Theodore W. Cart, "The Lacey Act: America's First Nationwide Wildlife Statute," *Forest History* 17 (1973): 4–13.

withdrew these birds from sale. Judging by the action of these dealers, I believe that the wholesale trade in native plume birds in Baltimore has practically ceased for the time being, and a beginning had been made for similar action in other States.[28]

The gulls in question had been shipped from Morgan City, Louisiana, to Maryland, where a law forbade the killing and sale of more than twenty birds, including swallows, hummingbirds and gulls. This case of interstate transfer of plumage in violation of the Lacey Act resulted in a $100 fine to the party involved and in the withdrawal of plumage from other wholesale millinery houses. It was an example to firms in Boston, New York and Philadelphia to familiarize themselves with their own state bird laws, and to be prepared for inspection of stocks for illegal plumage. It appears to have caused a drop in sales, particularly of seabird plumage, which only the previous year had totalled some two million birds.[29]

In addition to pushing for state and national laws to curb bird destruction, the AOU and Audubon Societies took positive steps to protect dwindling gull, tern and heron colonies along the eastern seaboard. By the efforts of the AOU protection committee, wardens were hired to protect the terns of Muskeget, Massachusetts, and Gull Island, New York in the early 1890's. Expansion and coordination of these efforts began in 1900 when Abbot H. Thayer, artist and bird enthusiast, contacted Witmer Stone (1866–1939), Chairman of the AOU Committee, about steps to protect breeding seabirds from millinery agents. Stone conferred with William Dutcher who took a keen interest in Thayer's suggestion. Through Thayer's efforts, funds were collected for wardens to patrol certain bird dunes and islets from Maine to Florida in spring and summer. Table 9 gives a breakdown of warden services during Dutcher and Thayer's successful campaign for seabird protection, which the National Association of Audubon Societies took

28. *The Auk* 18 (1901), p. 72, the quote of Palmer is in the Report.
29. *The Evening Times* (Washington, D.C.), 10 and 19 October, 1900; *The Baltimore World*, 18 October, 1900; and Theodore S. Palmer, "The Lacey Act," *Forest and Stream* 58 (25 January, 1902): 61, 68–69. The first Federal Court case under the Lacey Act was a small shipment of gulls and terns from Brownsville, Texas, to New York in which fines were imposed. *The Evening Times* (Washington, D.C.), 20 June, 1902, reported 80,000 shorebird plumes intended for out-of-state millinery purposes were seized in North Carolina. Contained in Palmer, Personal Papers, Game Laws, Box 67, Ms. Division, Library of Congress, Washington, D.C.

TABLE 9

Bird Protection Under the Thayer Fund

Date	Financial support ($)	Wardens	Number of states covered	States
1900	over 1400	At least 4	6	Virginia, Maryland, New Jersey, Connecticut, New York, Maine
1901	1680	27	6	Louisiana, Massachusetts
1902	1945	c.26	7	Florida
1903	3603	33	8	North Carolina, Michigan
1904	4070	34	10	Oregon, Texas

SOURCE: *The Auk* Vols. 18–21 (1901–1904), *BL* 7 (1905), p. 58, National Association of Audubon Societies, Miscellaneous Subjects Correspondence, 1900–1931, item no. 172, and AOU, Correspondence 1900–1903, item no. 166. New York Public Library, Ms. Division.

over in 1905. Looking back on the effort, T. S. Palmer remarked, "What Alfred Newton did for sea-bird protection in England half a century ago, Thayer later accomplished on a larger scale for the birds of our Atlantic coast." [30]

Bird preservation work brought both conspicuous success and tragedy to the Audubon movement. Tragedy struck in Florida in July, 1905, when Guy Bradley, a warden of the National Association, was shot and killed while arresting plume hunters on Oyster Key, near Flamingo. Bradley had been appointed a warden in remote Monroe County in 1902, was also a County Game Warden. He had previously run afoul of Walter Smith, his alleged killer, and associates, while protecting waterbirds. Charged with homicide, Smith was jailed, then released on $5,000 bond, but was never convicted.

The National Audubon headquarters set up a fund to support Bradley's widow and children, and the Florida society erected a plaque marking his grave near East Cape Sable where his boat had drifted for a day before its gruesome cargo was discovered. Bradley was the first martyr of the plume dispute but not its last. Three years later Warden Columbus McLeod was killed near

30. T. S. Palmer, "Abbott H. Thayer's Contribution to Bird Protection," *BL* 23 (1921): 227–228, quote p. 227.

Charlotte Harbor, Florida, and other wardens were threatened or assaulted.[31]

Seabird populations responded to protection. In addition to giving the decimated least tern and gulls a chance to recover their numbers, protection of breeding grounds on the east coast led logically to the idea of preserves and sanctuaries. The first federal involvement in such a project was at Pelican Island, Indian River, east of Orlando, Florida. Frank Chapman had visited the island in 1898 and noted that plume hunters were seeking waterbirds. He insisted that a guard be placed on the island to stem depredations. As the island was government property, a member of the General Land Office suggested that it be declared a bird preserve. In an Executive Order of 14 March, 1903, President Roosevelt, who had given longstanding encouragement to the Audubon movement, acceded to the requests of the AOU and Bureau of Biological Survey, and declared it a Federal Bird Reserve. In the beginning, the AOU provided warden service for Pelican Island. However, as it came under the jurisdiction of the U.S. Department of Agriculture, the Secretary soon appointed Paul Kroegl as warden to the island, reportedly the second game warden ever appointed by federal agencies. In setting aside public areas as bird preserves, the U.S. Government set a precedent for a network of refuges from coast to coast, spread over approximately 30 million acres, as the century has progressed.[32]

Millinery agencies and bird protection groups attempted to reach compromise agreements over the plumage issue. The first

31. The event appears in *BL* 7–9 (1905–1907), and in *The Auk* 22 (1905): 443–444. Recent attention to the killing comes from Charles M. Brookfield, "The Guy Bradley Story," *BL* 57 (1955): 170–174, and from Frank Graham, *Man's Dominion* (New York, 1971). A report of the murder of L. P. Reeves, employee of the South Carolina Audubon Society, possibly at the hands of "fish-pirates," can be found in *BL* 11 (1909): 50–52. On 3 May, 1911, Jake Ward an Audubon warden in South Carolina, together with his assistants, exchanged shots with plume hunters on the South Santee River. The poachers had fired at law officers on two other occasions, and had repeatedly shot up an egret rookery at Secessionville, near Charleston; *BL* 13 (1911): 277–278.

32. T. Gilbert Pearson, *Adventures in Bird Protection* (New York, 1937), pp. 236–257, esp. 236–237. Dutcher, "Report . . . ," *The Auk* 21 (1904), pp. 121–124. Particulars of the move to set aside Pelican Island as a reserve are contained in correspondence files of the Biological Survey, especially William Dutcher to James Wilson, 26 February, 1903, Bureau of Biological Survey, Reports. Reservation—Pelican Island, RG 22, National Archives. Dutcher's letter specifically mentioned pelicans exterminated by tourists and plume hunters. Considerable inroads into the bird population had been made there in the winter of 1885–1886. A concise treatment of the refuge movement is given by Robert P. Allen, "The Wild-life Sanctuary Movement in the United States," *BL* 36 (1934): 80–84.

such attempt in the United States stemmed from millinery activities in Delaware in 1900, where Witmer Stone and others noted that crows and blackbirds were killed for the trade. The illegality of shooting protected birds was pointed out to Delaware residents. Stone helped organize a state Audubon Society and enlisted the cooperation of the governor. Charles Farmer of the Millinery Merchants' Protective Association of New York contacted Stone about press reports he considered exaggerated and unfavorable to millinery firms. After lengthy correspondence, a compromise was proposed whereby the AOU and Audubon Societies would pledge themselves to prevent the passage of laws detrimental to the trade. In return members of the Millinery Association would:

> Pledge themselves not to kill or buy any more North American birds. . . . However, we shall continue to manufacture, sell and dispose of all such North American birds and their plumage, as we now have in our stocks. . . . This does not refer to plumage or skins of barnyard fowl, edible birds or game birds killed in their season, nor to the birds or plumage of foreign countries *not* of the species of North American birds.[33]

Witmer Stone considered the wording of the agreement unfortunate. However, with J. A. Allen and William Dutcher, he believed that the proposal was a practical step towards controlling millinery activities. Frank Chapman's editorial in *Bird-Lore* about the pledge suggests also the extent of his willingness to compromise:

> We cannot hope to abolish the trade in feathers, but if, by a concession, we can so control it that our native birds shall be exempt from its demands, we shall have afforded them a measure of protection we had not expected to secure in this generation nor the next.[34]

Mabel Osgood Wright, editor of the Auddudon Department of *Bird-Lore,* strongly opposed the proposed agreement as did William Brewster, AOU member, Curator of the Museum of Comparative Zoology at Harvard and first President of the Massachusetts Audubon Society (founded in 1896). The majority of the

33. Wright, BL 2 (1900), p. 98.   34. Ibid., p. 93.

22 active Audubon Societies took Brewster's position. With this opposition, the agreement never became operative.[35]

A second compromise was made in April, 1903, by the same millinery group and the Audubon Society of New York. The societies in Pennsylvania, Wisconsin and elsewhere, supported it. The pledge was for milliners:

> To abstain from the importation, manufacture, purchase or sale of Gulls, Terns, Grebes, Hummingbirds and song birds . . . and after January 1, 1904, the importation, manufacture, purchase or sale of the plumage of Egrets or Herons, and of American Pelicans of any species, shall cease. . . .[36]

It was agreed that restrictions on gulls, terns, grebes, herons, and hummingbirds should apply to these birds irrespective of their country of origin. For its part, the Audubon Society of New York State pledged to:

> Prevent all illegal interference on the part of game wardens with the millinery trade; to refrain from aiding the passage of any legislation that has for its object restrictions against the importation, manufacture or sale of fancy feathers obtained from domesticated fowls or . . . of foreign birds, other than those specifically mentioned above.[37]

This agreement was signed by Millinery Associations, by a dozen Audubon Societies and by William Dutcher on behalf of the AOU. It was extended (in 1906) when members of the Millinery Jobber's Association of Chicago condemned the use of aigrettes and agreed not to sell them or other birds mentioned in the earlier agreement. In the midwest, Audubonists believed that a spirit of cooperation prevailed, whereas in the east by that time aigrettes were back in fashion. The position of many milliners was reflected in an article printed in *The Millinery Trade Review* (January, 1906) entitled, "The Audubon Society Against the Fancy Feather Trade." The trade journal had previously made restrained comment about the agreement in 1903 and had emphasized the responsibility of millinery firms to adhere to it. An entry

35. See Witmer Stone, "Report of the Committee on the Protection of . . . Birds . . . ," *The Auk* 18 (1901), pp. 68–76; see Chapman, *BL* 2 (1900), p. 127, and also pp. 128–130.
36. *BL* 5 (1903), pp. 104–105.   37. Ibid., p. 105.

in *Bird-Lore* in 1906, however, was understood to belittle all wearing of feathers, except ostrich, and angered the trade. In reaction the *Review* protested that: "There is no alternative but for the importer and manufacturer to take up the gauntlet and meet these [Audubon] people in a battle royal. . . . It is absolute folly for the trade to keep silent on this matter to avoid agitation for fear of hurting the sale of the goods. . . . Give these people an inch and they will take an ell." [38]

Accords between millinery and bird protection groups were partial and short-lived. The one in 1900 sought cooperation from all bird protection factions; however, most Audubon Societies refused to take part in it. The agreement with the New York Society and others in 1903 was far more comprehensive from the bird protection standpoint, because it promised to exclude importation of key plume species. Nevertheless, the reluctance of most Audubon groups to sign the 1903 pledge was understandable, for by it they were bound to refrain from promoting both state and federal moves against the entry of foreign birds, except species named by milliners. Birds of paradise, pheasants, peafowl and kingfishers, doves, paroquets, bee-eaters, bustards, and vultures could continue to be shipped into the United States for millinery purposes. Chapman's earlier bleak comment indicated that he thought the first millinery agreement was a godsend. In rejecting all compromise, his co-workers soldiered on to eliminate altogether foreign and American wild birds from millinery parlors. Chapman went with his colleagues.

Legislation in the United Kingdom: First Attempts

Initiatives to cripple the plumage trade in England differed from similar moves in America. The SPB began by interesting the Royal family in the issue of plume wearing. On the floor of the Commons, in June 1898, Sir John Lubbock (later Lord Avebury) asked the Under-Secretary of State whether he was aware that ospreys (in the millinery, not the ornithological sense) worn by certain regiments were stripped from birds in the breeding seasons. Mr. St. John Broderick, recognizing the issue of cruelty in the question, replied that orders had already been given to find substitutes for such plumes, but that substitutes were difficult to

38. Wright and Dutcher, *BL* 8 (1906), pp. 37–38; *The Millinery Trade Review* 28 (1903), pp. 13, 42; and 31 (1906), pp. 54, 57.

locate.[39] The question was solved satisfactorily in an order confirmed by Queen Victoria the following year, whereby officers of
the Hussars, Queens Royal Rifles, Rifle Brigade and Royal Horse
Artillery ceased to wear ospreys on 1 January, 1902.

The mission and name of the SPB received a considerable fillip
in 1904 when Edward VII granted the Society permission to use
the prefix "Royal" in its title.[40] On 16 February, 1906, the Council of the RSPB presented a Memorial to Queen Alexandra about
feather wearing. The Council pointed out that "great barbarity"
and even extermination threatened white herons and birds of
paradise. "If it were once known that your Majesty disapproved
of a fashion in itself so indefensively cruel, and involving such
bad consequences, that fashion would, we are convinced, speedily
die out." The reply came in barely a month:

> The Queen desires me to say in answer to your letter that she
> gives you [Winifred Portland] as President full permission to use
> her name in any way you think best to conduce to the protection
> of Birds. You know well how kind and humane the Queen is to
> all living creatures, and I am desired to add that Her Majesty
> never wears osprey feathers herself, and will certainly do all in
> her power to discourage the cruelty practised on these beautiful
> birds.[41]

The RSPB and sympathizers were jubilant. High society on
both sides of the Atlantic could hardly relegate the Queen to the
supposedly faddist minority and scoff at her comments. In America, William Dutcher forwarded a copy of the Queen's letter to
President and Mrs. Theodore Roosevelt, looking on them to
urge American ladies to think hard about donning aigrettes. English society journals such as *Vanity Fair, The World* and *Truth,*
together with such illustrated weeklies as *The Sphere* and *The
Graphic,* and fashion periodicals such as *The Queen* and *The*

39. *Parliamentary Debates-Commons,* Vol. 59, 23 June, 1898, par. 1209–1210.
40. In granting the name of "Royal Society" to the Society for the Protection of
Birds, it was noted that one of the objects and powers of the Society was: "To discourage the wanton destruction of birds and the wearing of feathers of any bird
not killed for the purposes of food, other than the ostrich, but to take no part in
the question of the killing of game birds and legitimate sport of that character."
This was the article to which Harold Hamel Smith took exception in accusing
the RSPB of a double standard in humanitarian arguments about the plumage
issue, RSPB, *Fourteenth Annual Report* (1904), pp. 18–22.
41. RSPB, *Fifteenth Annual Report* (1905) Appendix IV, pp. 56–58; quote p. 58.

Lady, expressed satisfaction on learning of Queen Alexandra's remarks about bird-trimmed millinery. *The Birmingham Post* (21 March, 1906) summed up the plume question: "The few words: 'The Queen never wears osprey feathers,' will probably be more influential than a hundred reports or speeches innumerable. In any event, we fervently hope that such may be the case." [42]

With the support of their Majesties and increasing public attention, the time was deemed ripe for Parliamentary action on behalf of plume species. The push for effective bird laws was long, arduous, but finally rewarding. Table 10 provides details of the plumage campaign in Parliament.

On 5 May, 1908, Lord Avebury introduced into the House of Lords a bill to prohibit the importation of plumage into the United Kingdom. This measure provoked important discussion in the Select Committee to which it was referred before finally being killed in the Commons. After amendments in Committee, the principal clause stated:

> 1. Any person who, after the commencement of this Act, shall have in his possession for the purposes of sale or exchange the plumage, skin, or body, of any dead or wild bird imported. . . into the United Kingdom . . . which is not included in the schedule to this Act, or otherwise exempted from the operation of this Act, shall be guilty of an offence. . . .[43]

This bill was similar to the one which King George V assented to thirteen years later. It gave the Board of Trade permission to grant licenses for feathers to enter the country for scientific purposes. It specifically exempted from seizure that plumage on wearing apparel worn by travellers entering the country. Ostriches and eider ducks (*Somateria mollissima*) appeared on a list of species permitted free entry, as did other wild birds ordinarily used as articles of diet. On one critical point the first and last bills differed. The 1908 bill prohibited the sale of plumage whereas the 1921 Act proscribed only its importation, not its possession for sale.

The Board of Trade was cool towards the 1908 bill; outright

---

42. Similar comments appeared in the *Liverpool Courier* 28 March, 1906; the *Dublin Express* 21 March, 1906; and *Eastern Daily Express* 22 March, 1906. See *BNN* 2 (1906), pp. 19–20; *Birmingham Post* is cited p. 20.
43. *BNN* 3 (1908), p. 27.

TABLE 10
Important Events in Plumage Legislation
of the United Kingdom

31 October, 1903	Lord Medway called for a bill to prohibit the sale of any plumage but excluded the ostrich and game birds. (*The Times* [London], p. 13, col. 3).
5 December, 1903	*The Times* (London) reported that The Humanitation League has prepared a bill proscribing the possession and sale of species contained in a schedule. No MP took it up.
5 May, 1908	Lord Avebury introduced a bill into the House of Lords to prohibit importation of the plumage and skins of wild birds. The bill passed The House of Lords on 21 July.
22 July, 1908	Avebury's bill introduced into the House of Commons by Lord Robert Cecil; it did not pass.
31 March, 1909	Sir William Anson introduced a Plumage (Prohibition of Sale and Exchange of) Certain Wild Birds bill into the Commons.
17 June, 1909	Mr. Ramsey Macdonald introduced a second similar bill.
1909	The British Government approached various countries for an international conference on the traffic in plumes, but received unfavorable replies from France, Germany, Italy and elsewhere.
15 March, 1910	Mr. Percy Alden introduced a Plumage (Prohibition of Sale or Exchange of) bill.
25 May, 1910	First meeting of an Inter-Departmental Conference on the Destruction of Plumage Birds.
19 July, 1910	Alden introduced a second plumage bill.
22 February, 1911	Mr. Percy Alden introduced a bill "to prohibit the sale, hire or exchange of the plumage and skins of certain wild birds."
28 February, 1912	Mr. Percy Alden's bill "to prohibit the sale, hire or exchange of the plumage of skins of certain wild birds."

TABLE 10 (*continued*)
Important Events in Plumage Legislation
of the United Kingdom

25 June, 1912	Final Report of Inter-Departmental Committee on the Destruction of Plumage Birds was unfavorable to the millinery trade.
27 June, 1912	Alden's "Plumage (no. 2) Bill" to prohibit the sale, hire or exchange of the plumage and skins of wild birds from British Colonies and Dependencies.
August, 1912	A second effort was made to elicit international co-operation in the traffic of plumage; the conference was never held.
13 March, 1913	Mr. Page Croft's bill "to prohibit the sale, hire, or exchange of the plumage and skins of wild birds from British Colonies and Dependencies."
4 August, 1913	Mr. Charles E. Hobhouse presented an "Importation of Plumage (Prohibition) Bill" and gained government support for it; however, it did not pass. The plumage issue was raised on the floor of the Commons seven times between 10 March and 15 August.
13 February, 1914	Hobhouse's bill to prohibit the importation of the Plumage and Skins of Wild Birds. Prime Minister Asquith favored its passage but it was dropped on the outbreak of war. Questions about plumage importation were brought up eighteen times in 1914 session.
April, 1916	223 MP's sign petition presented to President of the Board of Trade to prohibit the importation of wild birds' plumage as a luxury unbecoming a wartime economy.
23 February, 1917	A Board of Trade Prohibition of Importation (no. 14) Proclamation included ornamental plumage.
24 August, 1917	Anglo-French accord permitting the import of ornamental plumage except for seven species.
17 November, 1919	The President of Board of Trade revealed that prohibitions against imports of plumage had been relaxed.

TABLE 10 (*continued*)
Important Events in Plumage Legislation
of the United Kingdom

13 February, 1920	Col. Charles Yate, supported by Viscountess Astor, introduced a bill "to prohibit the importation of the plumage of wild birds and the sale or possession of plumage illegally imported."
9 March, 1920	The Marquess of Aberdeen introduced a bill similar to the Yate measure into the House of Lords; and on 29 March, the bill passed the Lords.
14 May, 1920	The Yate bill was sent to standing Committee C, but was never reported back.
18 February, 1921	Two bills introduced by Mr. Galbraith and Capt. Brown.
9 March, 1921	Mr. Trevelyan Thomson (supported by Viscountess Astor and 10 others) introduced an Importation of Plumage (Prohibition) bill no. 3.
10 June, 1921	The Thomson bill was amended and passed its third reading.
1 July, 1921	Royal assent given to "An Act to Prohibit the Importation of Plumage," (11 and 12 Geo. 5).
1 April, 1922	The Importation of Plumage (Prohibition) Act, 1921, became operative.

opposition to it was expressed in a *Resolution* of the Textile Trade Section of the London Chamber of Commerce and presented to the Lords' Committee by Eugene Henneguy, Managing Director of a long-established firm dealing in feathers. This *Resolution* pointed out that the bill, if passed, would destroy a legitimate branch of British trade and divert feather produce to continental markets. Plumage interests claimed that it would deprive a large number (upwards of 5,000) of workers from gainful employment. Moreover, feather brokers believed that the bill would not save the birds it was designed to protect. Only international agreements could effect this. Rare birds had never been part of the plumage trade and the species utilized as ornament were in no danger of extermination.

The *Report* of the five-member Select Committee, considered biased by the trade, acknowledged these objections to Avebury's bill and answered them point by point. About injury to domestic and export trade the report stated that: "Any reduction, therefore, in the importation of feathers of birds protected by the Bill, would in the opinion of the Committee, be counterbalanced or so far as employment in this country is concerned more than counterbalanced, by the use of other feathers or of artificial flowers," (p. iii).

The Committee asserted boldly that bird populations were declining because of demands for feathers. Particulars of London auction sales, placed before the House of Lords Committee from the outset of the hearings, were constantly referred to in discussions with trade representatives. The statistics were alarming: "The Committee have carefully considered the facts submitted to them, and they are satisfied that while many birds are being greatly reduced in number, others are in danger of being actually exterminated," (p. iii).

Taking trade suggestions to heart, the peers expressed a wish that the British government should act to secure international cooperation to protect birds. However they supported Avebury's bill, realizing that export interdiction, particularly in India, was being neutralized by active markets in London, New York and on the continent. The Lord's report concluded: "The Committee believed, therefore, that the Bill would not only be of general advantage, but would also render more effective the legislation of India, of Australia and of the United States," (p. iv).

In communicating their proceedings and recommendations to the House of Lords, Avebury and his Select Committee encapsulated the pros and cons of the plumage dispute for the first time and rendered a rational, restrained account of facts about the trade.

The news media took an interest in the bill and a score or more newspapers and journals made favorable comments about its operatives. *The Nation* (23 May, 1908) contained a note about public attitudes to feather-wearing:

> This surely is a question on which any Government may dare to be bold. Public opinion is divided about vivisection; it is not even absolutely unanimous about some of the practices covered by the Spurious Sports Bill. But this use of murdered beauty for adornment has no articulate defender. There is hardly a fash-

ioned paper base enough to advocate it outside its advertising columns [*BNN* 3(1908):22].

This enthusiastic comment over-estimated the matter of government daring and under-estimated the number of articulate defenders of the trade (of whom there were many). Despite the generally favorable press, no other feather bill, except the Hobhouse measure sponsored by the Government in August, 1913, came as close to passage as Avebury's bill (which cleared the House of Lords, but foundered in the Commons). The trade proved to have competent and powerful supporters who worked hard in subsequent years to stall action on successive proposals.

   Failure could not always be laid at the door of trade spokesmen. Several plumage bills, suspected of loopholes, were introduced into Parliament without RSPB support. Sir William Anson's bill of 1909 would have excluded possession for sale or exchange of skins and plumage of certain species, mainly ones covered by laws in British colonies and in foreign countries. The RSPB, believing that this measure was unwieldy and open to fraud, withheld its support.[44] Percy Alden's efforts in 1910 drew a lukewarm response from the same group, which deemed proposals similar to Avebury's more desirable.[45]

   A concerted effort was made in August, 1913, and February, 1914, to pass a plumage law in the United Kingdom. Backed by E. S. Montagu, Under-Secretary for India, and Mr. Sydney Buxton, President of the Board of Trade, Henry Hobhouse introduced a bill into the Commons similar to that which had failed in 1908. This Government-sponsored bill prohibited the importation, possession and sale of birds' plumage, except species named in an official imported-under-license list. Both Houses supported Hobhouse's measure when it was introduced at the opening of the 1914 session. As might be expected, British and French feather dealers were deeply disturbed by it.[46]

   Several members of Standing Committee B, to which the bill was referred, made repeated assaults on the proposal, negating

44. See RSPB, *Nineteenth Annual Report* (1909), p. 2.
45. RSPB, *Twenty-Second Annual Report* (1912), p. 15.
46. Edmond Morin of the French Association of Feather Merchants and Manufacturers urged repeal of plumage sections of the U.S. Tariff Act, and opposed impending Canadian and British legislation. An International Congress of Plume Dealers met in Paris in June, 1914, and expressed similar distate for British and American moves; see *New York Times,* 10 June, 1914, p. 4, col. 6.

favorable reactions from the Trustees of the British Museum, British Ornithologists' Union, Our Dumb Friends League and others. From as far away as Australia came letters and petitions in favor of the plumage bill. Ten weeks after its second reading, it was reported to the House of Commons with 42 amendments and new clauses. Six pages of modification similar to ones thrashed out in committee were submitted for the consideration of the whole Commons. The Prime Minister declared that: "I should very much regret . . . if the time and energy which have been devoted to the discussion of the measure almost from the first night of Session should be altogether wasted." [47] His fears proved well-founded, for the bill faltered and foundered in committee. A small group of Members had managed to stall action for ten weeks; with war clouds looming, the subject of bird protection was lost in graver concerns and anxieties.

Before the World War I, two important events in the anti-plumage movement occurred which deserve special mention. In January, 1910, Lord Crewe, Secretary of State for the Colonies, suggested that representatives of the Colonial Office, the India Office, the British Museum of Natural History and the Board of Trade gather in an inter-departmental forum to discuss ways to lessen the destruction of plume species. The ten meetings over a two year period rehashed material dealt with by Avebury's Select Committee.[48] The same spokesmen appeared before the inter-departmental group to argue for embargoes on the plumage trade, and reiterated claims or accusations similar to ones made in 1908. The focus of this conference, however, was upon the need for international cooperation to diminish bird destruction.

Many interesting facts came to light during committee hearings. James Buckland, an energetic figure for bird protection in Britain, assured members that the continent was a major purchaser of feathers. He claimed that hundreds of thousands of albatrosses, killed in the Pacific, went directly from Yokohama, Japan, to

47. *Parliamentary Debates, Commons*, Vol. 64, 17 July, 1914, par. 2280. In the Second Reading of the Bill on 9 March, considerable opposition was voiced to it from Sir Edwin Cornwall, of the Port of London Authority. The Standing Committee met twelve times before their revisions were presented to the House.

48. See Colonial Office, *Report and Hearings*. Dr. S. F. Harmer, FRS, Mr. C. E. Fagen, Mr. W. R. Ogilvie-Grant represented the Natural History Museum; Messers. G. W. Johnson, H. J. Read, R. E. Stubbs, the Colonial Office, Hon. E. S. Montagu M. P. represented the India Office; and Mr. P. H. Illingworth, the Board of Trade Ten meetings were held between 25 May, 1910 and 25 June, 1912.

Paris. Great numbers of magpies, owls and other birds from Siberia came to Paris from Perm, a conveniently located city which drew also from the Caspian lowlands and Ural mountains. Subtract ostriches, birds of paradise and egret feathers from the London market and little else remained.[49] Buckland affirmed that heron plumes from upper Senegal and Niger never passed through London warehouses but went directly to Paris or perhaps Germany. The large quantities of plumage sold on markets other than London were attested to some years later by T. Gilbert Pearson, who discovered from French customs records that 50,300 tons of plumage had entered France between 1890 and 1929.[50] The need for international agreement in the matter of ornamental plumage was as apparent to the Inter-Departmental Conference in 1912 as it became to Pearson twenty years later.

In June of that year, the Committee recommended:

> a) That it is eminently desirable that all practicable measures should be taken for the suppression of the traffic in the feathers of those species of birds which are now destroyed merely for the sake of their plumage;
>
> b) that the only thoroughly satisfactory method of attaining this end is to secure an international agreement by which the importation of such feathers will be prohibited by all civilized countries, except when they are introduced for *bona fide* scientific purposes. . . .
>
> 8. In the event of its being found impossible to summon an international Conference . . . we urge that His Majesty's Government should set an example to other nations by independently and at once introducing legislation on the lines indicated in section (a) and (b) in the preceding paragraph. . . .[51]

Although not unanimous in its recommendations, the report did set the stage for the British government to initiate moves for a world conference about plume birds. Before the War, the Government made at least two attempts to gain wider discussion of the plumage question. On both occasions the French and others saw in such a meeting a threat to domestic millinery industries and interests and refused to participate. Accordingly, high level meet-

49. Colonial Office, *Hearings,* Miscellaneous. No. 263, co. 885/21, 1911 (Public Record Office).
50. *Adventures in Bird Protection*, p. 272.
51. Colonial Office, *Report*, pp. 2–3.

ings were never held, despite requests on the floor of the House of Commons to keep the matter under discussion.

A second significant event in this brief conspectus of British plumage legislation was an attempt to bring together millinery and scientific interests. In 1912, a Committee for the Economic Preservation of Birds began discussions about birds of plumage. Members of the Textile Section of the London Chamber of Commerce, the Zoological Society and the Selborne group sat on the panel, a British equivalent of earlier millinery rapprochements undertaken by certain state Audubon Societies in the United States. The RSPB would have nothing to do with the committee, which applauded efforts to raise species in captivity and which sought to reassure concerned citizens about the propriety of wearing feathers of game and noxious species.

In America, William T. Hornaday denounced the committee in the *New York Times* as a "cheap stalking horse for the London feather trade." [52] The Selborne Society, which supported the use of the feathers of game and pest species, had three of its members on the Economic Bird Preservation Committee and lent it support. This rather strange assortment of bedfellows sought to silence dissent from bird protectionists by labeling as 'purist' groups like the RSPB, which condemned most types of plumage trimmings.

Government Sanctions in the United States

In the United States, three federal laws, enacted before World War I, had a bearing on the plumage issue. The first consisted of a group of amendments to the Underwood Tariff bill of 1913, which curtailed the entry of foreign wild birds' feathers into the United States. The other two laws, the Lacey Act of 1900, already referred to, and the Migratory Bird Act of 1913 and subsequent Treaty with Great Britain (1916), limited in a general way millinery activities and bird species available to the trade in the continental United States and Canada. The Lacey Act and Migratory Bird Treaty Act have received considerable attention from his-

52. See *New York Times*, 30 September, 1913, p. 12, col. 6; Hornaday cited two pledges made by members of the Committee for the Economic Preservation of Birds: "That the committee will as far as possible discourage irresponsible attacks upon the trade in feathers, and will publicly deny those charges . . . which this committee may find in the course of its investigations to be untrue or unfounded."

torians of the wildlife protection movement.[53] The Tariff Act is less well known, and it created a flurry of argument over plume birds in the chambers of Congress. Initial moves by bird protection groups caught trade interests napping. They recovered quickly, however, and almost succeeded in nullifying House amendments to the Act of 1913, which proscribed most importations of plumage.

A battle royal over the feather issue took place at the end of the 62nd Congress and during the first session of the 63rd in 1913. Onithologists and others argued their case for terminating the "nefarious" trade in foreign bird feathers before House and Senate committees. In the Senate, the going became especially rough when Senator Hoke Smith of Georgia led a counterattack for millinery interests. On the Senate floor, George McLean of Connecticut made a long, well-documented and impassioned plea on behalf of anti-plumage legislation. He succeeded in having the measure recommitted to the Finance Committee which had modified the original House amendment that was unfavorable to the trade. In a vehement debate on 2 September, 1913, Senators Chamberlain and Lane of Oregon led a revolt against committee recommendations and managed to defeat the trade lobby. The House provisions of the plumage section of the Underwood Tariff bill were restored and the United States became the first major importing country in the world to outlaw shipments of foreign wild birds' plumage.

William T. Hornaday [54] and T. Gilbert Pearson [55] played im-

53. A detailed chronology of Federal Migratory Bird legislation is in John C. Phillips, "Migratory Bird Protection in North America," *Special Public. of American Committee for International Wild Life Prot.* 1 (1934), pp. 33–36. Phillips attributed the idea of unifying State laws to Charles Hallock, sportsman and writer. Rep. George Shiras from Pennsylvania introduced "a bill to protect the migrating game birds of the United States" into Congress on 5 December, 1904. His effort was unsuccessful, but maintained subject's visibility. Rep. Weeks of Massachusetts and Senator George P. McLean of Connecticut took up the cudgels for migratory birds in 1908 and 1911, respectively; and finally, in 1913, the so-called Weeks-McLean Bill became law. The first Migratory Bird Law placed such birds within the custody of the U.S. Government. The U.S.D.A. was permitted to set up hunting regulations which put a stop to spring shooting and reduced the marketing of song and other migratory species. The ratification of the Migratory Bird Treaty with Great Britain (8 December, 1916) an Enabling Act (3 July, 1918, 40 Stat. 755, 16 USC 703–711) and the first regulations under it (31 July, 1918), preempted the 1913 law, which had been declared unconstitutional in a test case (U.S. vs. Shauver 214 Fed., 154 [1914]) before an Arkansas District Court.
54. See Hornaday, 1913, 1915 and 1931.
55. Pearson, *Adventures in Bird Protection;* and, by the same author, "The Passing of the Feather Trade," *The Craftsman* 24 (1913): 303–308; "The White Egrets and the Millinery Trade," ibid., 22 (June, 1912): 417–424.

portant roles in shaping the plumage provisions of the 1913 Tariff Bill. Both wrote accounts of their activities before Government committees and drummed up support for their positions among conservation groups. Early in 1913, Pearson claimed to have received a letter from Henry Oldys (1859–1925), AOU associate and co-founder of the D.C. Audubon Society, recalling the efforts of Senator George F. Hoar of Massachusetts to interest Congress in bird protection back in 1898. Senator Hoar had introduced a bill for the protection of song birds into Congress. It was intended to stop the importation, interstate commerce and sale of birds or ornamental feathers in much of the United States; but, in fact, it pleased no one. Millinery firms were angered by it; and protection groups feared that a demand for native birds would result if Hoar's bill became law. Accordingly, it eventually foundered after passing the Senate with amendments on 24 March, 1898.[56]

During the next fifteen years a great deal of public attention became focused on attempts to preserve wild birds. More than 30 state Audubon Societies were active all over the country and were building up impressive memberships. Sanctuaries had been set aside for birds. Hundreds of books and articles on wildlife, and nature protection, and on birds as friends, neighbors, guests or partners of man, had been disseminated throughout the nation. In 1910, a plan was developed to organize Junior Audubon Clubs in schools as adjuncts to "Bird Day," which had become popular in several states.

On this groundswell of support, Oldys' proposal to insert a plumage amendment in the Underwood Tariff bill appeared opportune and attractive to Pearson. Accordingly, he contacted R. A. Doughton, a Congressman from North Carolina, where Pearson had founded an Audubon Society and was well-known in conservation circles. The Congressman encouraged him to speak before the House Committee considering Schedule N of the Tariff Bill. Initially rebuffed by Underwood, Pearson urged Audubon members to support his request by writing to the Committee. The ploy worked. He was accepted to testify on Schedule N and contacted William Hornaday about campaign strategy. Two weeks before the hearings of the House Committee on Ways and Means, Hornaday published and distributed to every member of

56. T. S. Palmer, Personal Papers, Game Laws, Box 66, Ms. Division, Library of Congress, Washington, D.C.

Congress, a copy of his *Our Vanishing Wild Life*. Written with bombast, verve and with much pugnacity, Hornaday intended to "soften up" his opposition, and to stir apathetic politicians into doing something about what he considered were the calamitous conditions of American wildlife, in this case plume birds.[57]

Hornaday and Pearson appeared before the Committee on Ways and Means, on 30 January, 1913. Hornaday argued for a total ban on the importation of wild birds' feathers into the United States. He claimed that there were at least 100 species of the most beautiful and most interesting birds in the world actually being exterminated by the trade.[58] Overstaying his time, Hornaday succeeded in showing bird millinery to members of the House Committee and deposited with them a lengthy brief extracted in large part from his new book. Next, Pearson took the stand as a representative of the National Association of Audubon Societies. He proposed a change under Schedule N, Section 437 of the Tariff Bill to read: *"Provided,* That the importation of plumage of American birds or of plumage indistinguishable from that of American birds, including aigrettes, crude or manufactured, is hereby prohibited, except for scientific purposes."[59]

Pearson argued that the amendment was necessary because some birds were becoming extinct. He claimed that American birds were of great economic value; that traffic in their plumage was already illegal in many states; that the trade was destructive, barbarous, and unnecessary; and that the loss of import revenues could be made up from other quarters. Pearson documented and explained each of his charges. Snowy egrets and Louisiana herons benefited farmers in the insects and rodents that they consumed. Of the tens of thousands of egrets that once bred in the southern states, he reported that only 5,000 had been located in 1912; a remnant population whose loss to millinery depredations had already moved state legislatures to help protect them. Revenue from imported aigrettes was insignificant according to Pearson, as the greatest volume of ornamental plumage entered the United

57. Hornaday decided to write the book in the winter of 1912 after amassing a great many facts about wildlife extermination in the United States. He sent 6,500 copies to federal officials, with the New York Zoological Society carrying much of the financial burden. It appeared in time to be read by congressional members involved in both the Weeks-McLean migratory bird bill and the tariff measure.

58. U.S. Congress, House. Committee on Ways and Means, Tariff Schedules, *Hearing . . . On Schedule N—Sundries,* (Washington, D.C., 1913), p. 5308.

59. Ibid., p. 5327.

States in a raw state: "Assuming that the importations for any one year amounted to half a ton or a thousand pounds, the duty at $3 an ounce would be $48,000 and at $4 per ounce, $64,000." [60]

In his pleas for native birds, Pearson admitted that he preferred Hornaday's "whole loaf" extending to foreign birds, rather than his compromise option covering native American species and others similar to them. Henry Oldys' brief deposited with the same House Committee equalled Pearson's in its articulation and vehemence. The spirit of the age, according to Oldys, was marked by ignorance, cupidity and supineness, all of which combined

> To exterminate the whale, the seal, the manatee, the alligator, the American antelope, the moose, the caribou, the elk, and hosts of fur-bearing animals, besides many valuable, beautiful, and interesting birds and swarms of valuable food fishes. History will not listen to the plea, "It was not my business." I[t] will answer: "You were there and could have prevented it; therefore, it was your business. You failed to do your duty. The only explanation is that you were corrupt, ignorant, or weak." [61]

Hornaday's strong personality and command of detail, Pearson's organized, succinct appraisal of the *status quo,* Oldys' plea for greater sensitivity to American wildlife, appears to have favorably disposed members of the House Committee on Ways and Means to plume-bird protection. The deck had been stacked, however, as no tradesmen were prepared to respond to the ornithologists' attacks. They charged later that they had received no fore-knowledge of the plumage amendment and they proceeded to wage a vigorous battle in the Senate to answer charges levelled at their livelihoods by the faddist bird lovers.

After the January hearings, Congressman Francis B. Harrison appears to have requested Hornaday to draft a restrictive plumage clause for the Tariff Bill. When the measure went to the House in April 1913, it included Hornaday's recommendations.

A Senate amendment, however, legitimized imports of game, food and harmful birds' plumage, and further work upon the clause in the Finance Committee and its sub-committee (composed of Charles F. Johnson of Maine, Hoke Smith of Georgia and

60. Ibid., p. 5329.   61. Ibid., p. 5348.

William Hughes of New Jersey) proceeded to overturn the House's version.[62] Reflecting on the occasion, Pearson was sure that the Senate sub-committee on Finance had decided, before its May hearings, that the House provision should be abandoned. New York importers and manufacturers of foreign bird plumage argued against Hornaday's amendment, which cut off supplies of raw or processed wild birds' plumes, except feathers of ostriches and domestic fowl. They would accept, they said, only international agreements. Restrictions on plumage imports would not dampen the demand for ornamental feathers if London and Paris continued to accept them; killing birds for sport and meat but not for plumage was poor business and made little sense.[63]

The sub-committee reported favorably to millinery lobbyists. The House amendment was changed drastically to exempt "the feathers or plumes of birds commonly recognized as edible or pestiferous" from import restrictions. This meant that robins, blackbirds, nighthawks and others, eaten in the Southern states, and scores of other birds regarded as table delicacies in foreign countries, could be imported into America. In July, the Democratic majority of the Senate Finance Committee revised Schedule N again and struck out the entire House clause, except for aigrettes. Pearson's and Hornaday's work appeared negated.

When Hornaday learned of the Senate Committee's commitment to plumage interests, he drafted a circular, entitled "The Steam Roller of the Feather Trade in the United States Senate," in which he castigated politicians opposed to his own bird protection interests. Hoke Smith brought up the matter of Hornaday's pugnacity to the Senate floor. About the latter's circular Smith declared: "I want to say for myself that, if he [Hornaday] is no more truthful in his other publications than he was in that, the

62. An amendment by Senator Clapp of Minnesota in April, 1913, permitted feathers of game birds, pest species and others used as food to be employed for millinery purposes. This was the first effort to dilute the House measure favoring bird protection groups. The Senate Finance Committee further weakened House restrictions, much to the chagrin of the National Audubon Society which urged its members to communicate their wishes to Senate Committee members. Petitions, mainly to Jacob Gallinger of New Hampshire, are on file in the National Archives, Sen. 63A–J23 (Schedule N 63rd Congress, 1st session) 2 bundles. The Society argued that admission of edible species exposed an assortment of game and non-game birds, and would endanger them in the breeding season when their plumage was at its finest.

63. U.S. Congress, Senate. Committee on Finance, *Tariff Schedules*, Vol. III, Schedules M & N par. 357, 1580–1589 (Washington, D.C., 1913).

article was so utterly false, I would not care to read anything he wrote." [64] Senator McLean, who favored protectionists, was forced to assuage the Senator's feelings with the lame reply, "they are zealous men, these ornithologists;" a token response to what Smith had taken as a personal attack.

The evening of 2 September, 1913, proved decisive. The Democratic caucus took up the provision now unfavorable to bird interests. Senators Chamberlain and Lane of Oregon led a five-hour battle to reinstate House amendments deleted by the Finance Committee. They successfully prevailed in this endeavor, and in the following month President Woodrow Wilson signed into law paragraph 347 of the Tariff Act.

> *Provided* That the importation of aigrettes, egret plumes or so-called osprey plumes, and the feathers, quills, heads, wings, tails, skins, or parts of skins, of wild birds, either raw or manufactured, and not for scientific or educational purposes, is hereby prohibited; but this provision shall not apply to the feathers or plumes of ostriches, or to the feathers or plumes of domestic fowls of any kind.[65]

President Wilson supported the bird movement in the United States, to the displeasure of the millinery fraternity. Herbert Syrett penned a letter to the *New York Times* on behalf of the trade which received short shrift from press and public alike. He was vexed with President Wilson's youngest daughter, Eleanor, for her part in a theatrical performance dedicated to bird protection.

Barely a week after the momentous Senate parley over plumage importation, President and Mrs. Wilson attended a performance of "Sanctuary—A Bird Masque," by George Mackaye. Miss Eleanor Wilson played Ornia, a bird spirit, and her sister Margaret sang "The Hermit Thrush" offstage. Performed in the sanctuary of the Meriden, New Hampshire, Bird Club, the graceful allegory in an open-air setting before a well-to-do audience, charmed the eye and ear. The masque was a poetic plea for bird preservation. Ornia persuaded the surly plume hunter to cast aside

---

64. *Congressional Record*, Senate, 16 August, 1913, p. 3431.
65. 38 Stat. page 148, par. 347. For the caucus fight see *The Washington Post*, 3 September, 1913, p. 2, col. 5; and Hornaday, *Statement Wild Life Fund: 1913–1914* (New York, 1915), p. 67.

his gun and become a bird lover, much to the joy of a cast of costumed feathered friends.[66]

Social and public recognition of this nature helps explain how the Audubon movement, well supported by womens' groups, ornithologists', sportsmen's and humane associations, managed to translate deeply-felt sentiment into legislative action. For Pearson and Hornaday it was a moment of hard-won satisfaction. Hornaday received a gold medal from the French Société d'Acclimatation and another one from the RSPB for his part in bird protection.[67]

The public, however, was not completely pleased with federal regulations of millinery items. Passengers returning to the United States ran the risk of losing their ornamental feather trim on disembarking at east and west coast ports. In January, 1914, for example, one lady returning from Bermuda was relieved of five hats valued at $500 because of their ornamental plumage.[68] Customs officials had much difficulty in distinguishing legal from illegal plumes among crowds of passengers and visitors on New York harbor piers. When the *Lusitania* docked, another woman was followed to her downtown hotel where her feather millinery was seized. In June, 1914, Miss Bonita, a noted vaudeville dancer landing from Liverpool, had her plumes confiscated. Other well-publicized confiscations of ornamental feather millinery angered many travelers and inconvenienced a multitude of others.[69]

Amendments to the plumage clause of a New Tariff Act (67th Congress, second session, 1922) added birds of paradise to the original provision but permitted plumage on personal effects to go untouched.

> *Provided further,* That birds of paradise and the feathers, quills, heads, wings, tails, skins . . . [of aigrettes and wild birds] . . . which may be found in the United States, on or after the passage of this Act, except as to such plumage or parts of birds in actual use for personal adornment . . . shall be presumed for the purpose of seizure to have been imported unlawfully after October 3, 1913, and the collector of customs shall seize the same unless the possessor thereof shall establish, to the satisfaction of

66. *New York Times*, 13 September, 1913, p. 10, col. 7, and p. 11, col. 1–2.
67. Madison Grant, *Statement Permanent Wild Life Protection Fund: 1913–1914* (New York, 1915), pp. 89–92.
68. "Hold Up of Five Hats," *New York Times*, 9 January, 1914, p. 1, col. 7.
69. Ibid., 10 January, 1914, p. 2, col. 3; 20 June, 1914, p. 3, col. 2; 18 April, 1914, p. 1 col. 7.

the collector that the same were imported into the United States prior to October 3, 1913. . . .[70]

Inbound travellers were inconvenienced no more by officials plucking feathers from their hats, fans or boas. Feathers, found in the country on or after the Act, however, could be deemed contraband unless satisfactory documentation of their entry before October, 1913, was provided. Later in England, officials had to prove millinery had been illegally imported. In America there appears to have been an assumption of "guilty unless proved innocent." Restrictions on plumage in United States' Tariff Acts of 1913 and 1922, and later 1930, made exceptions for artificial fishing flies.[71]

An Act of 17 July, 1952, changed laws covering plumage. During the 1940's, the National Audubon Society reported that quantities of feathers were entering the country under the guise of educational, scientific or fly-fishing articles. Affidavits had sufficed as evidence that the plumage was to be used for fly-tying, and some interests, it appeared, had abused this "honor" system. The Audubon Society, fishing-tackle firms, and a millinery association agreed to meet and suggest quotas on the numbers and types of birds to be imported. In 1952, a Congressional amendment of the Tariff Act reflected the understanding that:

> The importation of the feathers or skin of any bird is hereby prohibited. Such prohibition shall apply to the feathers or skin of any bird—
>
> (1) whether raw or processed;
>
> (2) whether the whole plumage or skin or any part of either;
>
> (3) whether or not attached to a whole bird or any part thereof; and
>
> (4) whether or not forming part of another article . . . this paragraph shall not apply—
>
> (1) in respect of any of the following birds (other than any such bird which, whether or not raised in captivity, is a wild bird): chickens (including hens and roosters), turkeys, guinea fowl, geese, ducks, pigeons, ostriches, rheas, English ring-necked pheasants, and pea fowl. . . .[72]

70. 42 Stat. pp. 915–916 par. 1419.

71. See 38 Stat. p. 127, par. 136, 3 October, 1913. 42 Stat. p. 881, par. 344, 21 September, 1922. 46 Stat. p. 668, par 1535, 17 June, 1930.

72. 66 Stat. 755; 19 U.S.C., sec. 1001, par. 1518, reprinted by U.S.D.I. Bureau of Sport Fisheries and Wildlife, Branch of Management and Enforcement, February,

Annual imports not exceeding 5,000 skins of grey jungle fowl (*Gallus sonnerati*) and 1,000 mandarin ducks (*Dendronessa galericulata*) or a total of 45,000 pheasants of six species could be imported into the United States under license.[73] The Department of Interior could change quotas and make restrictions if birds were deemed to be endangered. Thus, the grey jungle fowl was withdrawn from entry into the United States in 1969 because of diminishing numbers in the wild, as reported by the Indian government. Any endangered bird, formerly exempt, is now excluded entry under the 1969 Endangered Species Preservation Act.[74]

The United Kingdom's Plumage Act

After the First World War, the RSPB urged the British Government to continue Board of Trade wartime limitations upon imports of wild bird plumage. However, ornamental plumage had continued to be shipped into the United Kingdom after a ban in February, 1917, because exemptions were made for millinery already *en route* and for advance orders and payments. The President of the Board of Trade admitted under questioning in the Commons that thousands of pounds of feathers were still entering the country (almost 2 million pounds of non-ostrich material from the outbreak of the war to 1917), and that an Anglo-French Agreement (of August, 1917) had been made to allow ornamental plumage, with certain exceptions, to continue to be unloaded in London.

A delegation of the RSPB met with the President of the Board of Trade in July, 1919, to seek prompt support for legislation to end all wild-bird feather imports. They presented a *Memorial* addressed to Prime Minister Lloyd George that concluded: "We

1962, p. 1. See also the "Tariff Classification Act of 1962," Schedule I, pt. 15D, Headnote 2. Title 19 U.S.C., section 1202, which the Branch follows currently.

73. These pheasants are: Lady Amherst, golden, silver, Reeves, blue-eared, and brown-eared.

74. Details of moves to protect the grey jungle fowl are located with the ICBP, "Presidential Correspondence," 13 February, 1969, and 22 July, 1969, in the Mus. Nat. Hist., Smithsonian Institution. Mention is also made in ICBP *Asian Section News* 1 (1968), and ICBP, *President's Letter* no. 17 (1969): 1–2. A national mail order firm was indicted on six counts of smuggling neck feathers of G. *sonnerati* into the United States in 1970 for purposes of making fishing flies. The bird had been prohibited from export from India after 1967. See *Minneapolis Tribune*, 3 December, 1970, and *St. Paul Dispatch*, 3 December, 1970, p. 34. The "Tariff Classification Act of 1962" (19 U.S.C., Section 1202) is an up-to-date ruling on feathers and skins of wild birds utilized by the Branch of Management and Enforcement of the Bureau of Sport Fisheries and Wildlife.

desire to prevent the slaughter of *all* birds for the sake of the plumasier. We therefore demand that a Bill prohibiting the importation of wild birds' skins and feathers, similar to that which passed its second reading in 1914, be brought before the House of Commons immediately such action is possible." [75] Hardened campaigners in the bird movement, such as W. H. Hudson, signed the petition with over a hundred others, including Sir Arthur Conan Doyle, Lord Tennyson, G. K. Chesterton and Bertrand Russell.

The Government did nothing, so Colonel Charles Yate introduced a plumage bill into the Commons in February, 1920. Trade sympathizers greeted it with a barrage of amendments (over 100 were presented in Standing Committee), and had a hand in creating quorum difficulties in Committee. About the ensuing unsuccessful struggle, the RSPB commented dryly:

> The coincidence of other Committee meetings, the lure of Ascot, and other events told considerably; but . . . Members not over-keen on spending their mornings in the House, probably felt still less inclined to do so merely to listen to the round of arguments gone through, after the manner of circus horses in the ring, by Mr. Bartley Denniss, Major Archer-Shee, and Lieut.-Commander C. Williams.[76]

The defeat of the Yate bill disappointed many people including Trustees of the British Museum, Harold J. Massingham's Parliamentary Plumage Group and the Women's National Liberation Federation. Its failure engendered ill-feeling among MPs, especially those in favor of plumage restrictions. They had become impatient over constant haggling in committee chambers when a majority of the Commons had repeatedly expressed a wish to end the plumage dispute.

Early in 1921, three more plumage bills were placed before Parliament. One presented by W. Trevelyan Thomson omitted a clause which had been present in earlier bills prohibiting "the sale or possession of plumage illegally imported" into the United Kingdom. This weaker bill, after being read into Committee, at first met with the familiar delays, but finally emerged with amendments acceptable to both trade and bird groups. It cleared the

75. RSPB Correspondence Files 28 July, 1919, reprinted in *BNN* 8 (1919): 53–56.
76. RSPB, *Thirtieth Annual Report* (1920), p. 4.

Commons, passed through the Lords unopposed, and received King George V's assent on 1 July, 1921.[77]

The impasse to legislation was finally breached by an agreement to form a committee under the Board of Trade empowered to recommend exemptions to the law's import prohibitions. In the interval between the loss of the 1920 bill and the success of the 1921 version, Sir Bartley Denniss, M. P. for Oldham and sympathetic to the trade, contacted Sir Sidney Harmer of the British Museum of Natural History about possible ways of agreeing on the plumage issue. In a series of meetings at the Museum, its representatives and trades' people drew up a list of eighteen birds, including egrets, for which a *prima facie* case could be made for exemption under a plumage law. These fruitful conferences appeared to have dissuaded the trade from further objections to a plumage bill, in particular to Mr. Trevelyan Thomson's bill.[78]

In its final form "An Act to Prohibit the Importation of Plumage," contained four important sections:

1. (1) Subject to the provisions of this Act a person shall not import into the United Kingdom the plumage of any bird. . . .
2. (1) The plumage of the following birds, namely—
   (a) birds for the time being included in the Schedule to this Act;
   (b) birds imported alive;
   (c) birds ordinarily used in the United Kingdom as articles of diet;
   is excepted from the prohibition on importation imposed by this Act.

   (2) The prohibition on importation imposed by this Act shall not apply to any plumage imported as part of the wearing apparel of a passenger if, in the opinion of the Commissioners of Customs and Excise, that plumage is bona fide intended and is reasonably required for the personal use of the passenger.

   (3) Where an application is made to the Board of Trade for the addition to or removal from the Schedule of this Act of the name of any bird, the Board may, after taking into consideration the recommendation made in the matter by the advisory committee to be appointed under this Act, by order add to the said Schedule or remove therefrom, as the case may be, the name of that bird.

77. 11 & 12 Geo. 5, *Importation of Plumage (Prohibition) Act*, 1921. Chapter 16.
78. P.C., Correspondence, Letter to Marshall from Sidney F. Harmer, 2 January, 1922, (Brit. Mus. Nat. Hist.) 5008/21; also referred to by Denniss in *Parl. Debates, Commons*, 13 April, 1921, par. 1238.

An order made under this provision shall specify the name of the species and of the order, if any, to which the bird mentioned in the Order belongs.

(4) The Board of Trade may grant to any person a license subject to such conditions and regulations as they may think fit authorizing the importation of plumage for any natural history or other museum, or for the purpose of scientific research, or for any other special purpose . . . .

3. Within four months of the passing of this Act, the Board of Trade shall appoint an advisory committee consisting of—

(a) An independent chairman,

(b) Two experts in ornithology,

(c) Three experts in the feather trade,

(d) Four other members.

All applications for additions to or removal from the Schedule to this Act shall be made to the Board of Trade, which shall refer such applications to the advisory committee, which shall, after due inquiry, submit a recommendation to the Board of Trade in regard thereto.

4. (1) In this Act the expression "plumage" includes the skin or body of a bird with the plumage on it.[79]

The RSPB expressed concern about the composition of the committee appointed under the plumage act. They were relieved to discover, however, that Edward G. Fairholme, Secretary of the RSPCA; Harold J. Massingham and Mrs. Pamela McKenna, of a Parliamentary Plumage Group working for legislation; and Lord Buxton, Hon. Treasurer of the RSPB, were the "four other members" designated in the Act's section three. With Lord Crewe as chairman, the Committee of ten was evenly weighted with Messers Downham, Dunstall and Joseph speaking for trade interests and Dr. Eagle Clarke and Mr. Stuart Baker as expert ornithologists.

The members of the Advisory Committee questioned Museum spokesmen at length about their previous liaison with millinery interests. These spokesmen were embarrassed to learn that their role had been misunderstood by all parties. Trade groups had compiled a list of birds with the assistance of Museum experts and had expected the list to be approved more or less intact by the Advisory Committee. When it wasn't, the tradesmen became suspicious of the Museum's role. Bird interests, too, were wary of

79. 1 & 12 Geo. 5, op. cit.

Museum officials who had supported previous plumage bills and had, it appeared, compromised their position to gain passage of the 1921 act.[80]

Committee discussions, as reflected in minutes and correspondence (both of which remain unpublished), were generally lively. Most meetings indicate a broad range of opinions, and a desire to determine facts on which considered judgements could be based. For instance, the group took a long, hard look at the desirability of exempting common birds such as starlings, magpies and jays, exotic Indian parrots and Australian shearwaters from protection. It sought the opinion of experts about "domesticating" and "farming" egrets. It debated theories of "moulted" plumes and "pest" species, and familiarized itself with the status of birds reported to be endangered.

Later, under the direction of Lord Buxton, the Committee tackled problems of smuggling and was sympathetic to customs agents' difficulties in enforcing provisions of the 1921 Act. In seventeen meetings between November, 1921, and November, 1925, with a final one in 1937, this advisory group of various viewpoints performed its task with distinction and dispatch, considering the data available and the pressures for rulings on millinery trade requests. The detailed problems facing the Committee deserve further elaboration.

There are at present, twelve kinds of birds allowed into the United Kingdom without special permit from the Board of Trade. Two of them, the ostrich [81] and the eider duck, were contained in the original schedule of the 1921 Plumage (Prohibition) Act and did not fall under the purview of the Plumage Committee. The ten remaining birds were added between 1922 and 1925, upon recommendation of that Advisory Committee, and are shown in table 11. These ten birds were a fraction of the sum that millinery firms asked to be exempted under the 1921 ban on plumage. Beginning in December, 1921 (before the Act even became operative), the London Chamber of Commerce began to seek additions to the schedule of exempt birds. The Chamber forwarded a list of birds that it sought to have included with those that had been drawn up in conference with members of the British Museum of

80. P.C., Minutes, second meeting, 13 December, 1921.

81. In the Schedule of the original Act, the term is "African ostriches." This becomes simply "Ostriches" in later references.

TABLE 11

Board of Trade Exemptions under the Plumage
(Prohibition) Importation Act 1921

Name of bird	Date of addition to schedule
Rhea Rothschildi (common rhea, *R. americana*)	25th March, 1922
Common jay (*Garrulus glandarius*)	12th June, 1922
Common magpie (*Pica pica*)	"
Common starling (*Sturnus vulgaris*)	"
Java sparrow (*Munia oryzivora*)	"
West african ring-necked parrakeet (*Palaeornis docilis*)	"
Chinese bustard (*Otis tarda dybowskii*)	"
[a] Green (or Japanese) pheasant (*Phasianus versicolor*)	"
[a] Copper pheasant (*Phasianus soemmerringi*)	"
Golden pheasant (*Chrysolophus pictus*)	"
[b] Common or mute swan (*Cygnus olor*)	30th June, 1923
Common cormorant (*Phalacrocorax carbo*)	10th December, 1925
Common shag (*Phalacrocorax aristotelis*)	"

[a] Birds removed from the Schedule on the recommendation of the Advisory Committee on 5 December, 1923.[82]
[b] Removed from the Schedule 29 July, 1924.

Natural History earlier that year. The list appeared in Plumage Committee Correspondence as:

> EGRETS, farmed and moulted feathers.
> HERONS, farmed and moulted feathers.
> RHEAS, farmed feathers.
> PHEASANTS, Golden, Green (versicolor), Copper, Silver, Numidie (crossoptilon)—Farmed feathers.
> PARROTS, Indian Ringneck (including green) and Rose head,

82. RSPCA, Plumage Files, London.

African Ringneck, or Green, South American, certain species,
particularly CONURUS CACTORUM.
MACAWS
KINGFISHER (Halcyon smyrnensis).
JAY, European.
MAGPIES, Russian.
PEACOCKS, Moulted or farmed feathers.
PTARMIGAN
EMUS, farmed or legalized.
BUSTARDS, Chinese. PELICANS, moulted feathers.
COMMON STARLING.
JAVA SPARROWS, farmed.
BENGALIS, farmed.
STORKS, Indian and African Marabou, farmed.
SWANS, cygnus olor, farmed.
TANAGERS.[83]

The Chamber of Commerce's tally of birds posed certain problems to the Committee. The use of the terms "farmed or moulted
feathers" after several entries caused the Committee to seek clari-
fication of its powers to admit species on the basis of a clearly defined geographical origin and on the basis of the method of
plumage procurement. Legal counsel offered by the Board of
Trade ruled that such farmed or moulted birds could not be included in the schedule. Accordingly, much to the displeasure of
Downham and other millinery-trade members, the Plumage Committee refused to give formal consideration to the Chamber's list.
Undaunted, the London trade group resubmitted a revised version dropping the phrase "farmed and moulted" and leaving out
herons and egrets which the Committee had already decided not
to exempt.

After prolonged discussion, in March, 1922, the Plumage Committee recommended that six birds (mentioned in table 11) should
be included in the schedule of exempt species. In June of the same
year, certain pheasants were added on a trial basis but were subse-
quently withdrawn when Charles Downham pointed out that no
demand existed for the copper (P. *soemmerringi*) or green pheasants (P. *versicolor*). Similarly, the mute swan was withdrawn when
Dr. Eagle Clarke argued that if swan plumage were permitted

83. Letter from Marshall to the Board of Trade, 16 May, 1922, P.C., Correspondence.

to be imported the birds would probably be shot in the breeding season. Moreover, customs officers had trouble separating swan feathers from other ornamental feathers.

Final additions to the schedule were made in 1925 when the Plumage Committee recommended that two fish-eating birds, the cormorant (*Phalacrocorax carbo*) and shag (P. *aristotelis*) should be permitted into the United Kingdom because they were "voracious and destructive" to commercial fishing interests, and were employed in Norway as coat and dress trimmings. There appears to have been little or no demand for them in the United Kingdom; but despite the reservations of ornithologists, both species were allowed to appear on the schedule of birds exempted by the 1921 Act.[84]

Invariably, Mr. Massingham and Mrs. McKenna, with the interests of bird protection at heart, voted against additions to the plumage schedule. After a discussion of additions to the list, in a minority report submitted to Lord Crewe, they stated that the Committee was negating the spirit and purpose of the original plumage law by encouraging the killing of foreign wild birds for their feathers. In the future, they argued, the Committee should consider for the schedule only birds whose plumage could be gathered without injury or cruelty, such as ostriches, eider ducks and perhaps rheas.[85]

Downham pointed out the distinction between cruelty to birds and serious declines in their numbers to which the Act was directly opposed. He urged that farmed feathers should be permitted free entry into the United Kingdom.[86] Lord Crewe, the chairman, agreed that the Massingham statement was too narrow in its interpretation of the 1921 Act. It paid no attention to killing pest species for their feathers and appeared inconsistent in condemning killing for feathers but not killing for flesh. He also asserted that Downham's opinions had been ruled on by legal attorneys of the Board of Trade. They had said that farmed feathers could enter only through Parliamentary modification of the Act. Such an amendment was unlikely to occur because it would increase the

---

84. M. G. Mecham, personal communication 23 June, 1970. The list of birds currently exempted is provided by the Board of Trade, Summary of Import Licensing Regulations, Notice to Importers No. 1180, Schedule 1, p. 6.

85. P. C., Minutes, tenth meeting, 10 May, 1922, letter to Lord Crewe (insert after p. 46).

86. Ibid. (insert after p. 46).

workload of customs agents and necessitate courses in bird and feather identification.[87]

Smuggling on Both Sides of the Atlantic

The plumage dispute in Britain was not settled by the 1921 Plumage Law or the formation of the Advisory Committee. Until well into the 1930's, bird protection groups continued to push actively for restrictions on the possession and sale of wild birds' feathers, and not just an end to the importation of plumes. The protectionists argued that import restrictions and quotas would always be evaded until ornamental plumage ceased to be displayed in shop windows and worn by film stars and fashion models. On the other hand, feather tradesmen believed that the Board of Trade's refusal to permit egret and bird of paradise skins into the United Kingdom was unreasonable because procuring these birds was neither cruel nor detrimental to overall numbers.

Caught in the middle, customs authorities had the difficult task of enforcing regulations on feathers. Identification of exempted species presented agents, who had been given no additional training in bird identification, with serious problems. Clipping, dyeing and techniques of mounting made illegal feathers and skins extremely difficult to distinguish from legal ones. Single or loose bundles of plumes could enter the country and agents, lacking special knowledge, had only vague notions of the species from which they came.[88]

In the early 1920's, customs officers made very large plumage confiscations, because considerable quantities of illegal plumage clearly were entering the country in spite of the 1921 law.[89] Figures on seizures of stock millinery birds, such as herons, pheasants and birds of paradise, taken in the decade following the 1921 Act, are set forth in table 12. Prosecutions, however, seldom took

87. Ibid. (insert after p. 46).
88. P. C., Minutes. On 14 June, 1923, A. S. Lupton, an Assistant Secretary to the Commission of Customs and Excise, appeared before the Committee to describe the major difficulties of administering the 1921 Act, and to answer questions posed by members. A transcript of the discussion was placed with Committee's Minutes, another copy with Committee Correspondence.
89. Ibid., transcript p. 37. Lupton estimated that 300 seizures had been made in nine months following the enforcement of the Act. Asked by Viscount Ullswater about its effectiveness, Lupton replied: "My statistics are exceedingly incomplete, but so far as they go, they show that it has not stopped the bulk of the importation of millinery articles and so on." Nor had it reduced them, pp. 48–49.

TABLE 12

British Seizures of Prohibited Millinery, 1923–1932 [a]

Items	1923	1924	1925	1926	1927	1928	1929	1930	1931	1932
Herons and egrets	52	47	1118	3205	352	476	311	244	133	0
Birds of paradise	22	7	49	34	7	1	1	4	300	1
Kingfishers	2	4	42	99	97	3	84	60	149	10
Prohibited pheasants	15		846	302	255	2	4	30	407	69
Pea fowl	57		978	841	595	96	50	244	174	33

SOURCE: Plumage Advisory Committee Correspondence (Customs Archives); and Plumage Group Correspondence (RSPCA Archives), London.
[a] Plumage seized was in bundles, millinery mounts, brooches, single feathers and in assorted manufactured articles.

place. Guilt was readily explained away as a mistake made by a foreign agent, or as a gratuitous, unsolicited consignment sent to the United Kingdom by dealers beyond the arm of British law. In fact, table 13, supplied by the Board of Trade, reveals that in the nine years between 1922 and 1936, only fourteen prosecutions took place. One of the cases, in 1923, involved two Frenchmen charged with willfully concealing in egg boxes birds of paradise skins valued at £7,500. The case was dismissed on grounds of insufficient evidence. Omitted from the table 13 is a 1924 case in which 135,956 grebe skins (of three species) were seized. It coincided with renewed displays of these fine "furs," as they were called, in London fashions.[90]

Members of Parliament introduced bills to outlaw the possession and sale of plumage throughout the United Kingdom on no less than seven occasions between 1922 and 1940. All of these attempts failed. One bill by Lord Danesfort received favorable comment in the House of Lords in 1928 but was defeated in the

90. See *BNN* 11 (1924), p. 73 which was quoted from *The Times* (London) 20 November, 1924. In April, 1925, RSPCA inspectors turned up quantities of grebe skins in the markets of Smithfield and Leadenhall. On 10 February, 1925, Col. Clifton Brown was told in the House of Commons that 14 seizures had been made (of grebe plumage) since April, 1922; in *Parl. Debates, Commons,* oral answers, par. 9–10. Customs statistics in the RSPCA Files reveal that 12 consignments of grebe skins were taken in the final six months of 1924; 52 skins seized with 26 trimmings from January–March, 1925, and 207 skins (from Germany) between April and June of that same year. An instance of smuggled bird of paradise plumage (in egg boxes) was reported in *BNN* 10 (1923), pp. 70–71, and by Lupton before the Advisory Committee on 14 June, 1923, pp. 5–6.

TABLE 13
List of Cases in which Legal Proceedings Were Instituted
Against Importers of Plumage

Date of prosecution	Quantity and description of plumage	Penalty imposed
20th February, 1923	119 kingfisher skins	£20 fine plus £31 10s. costs. Fine and costs paid.
13th March, 1923	Five boxes birds of paradise skins concealed	Case dismissed. Evidence insufficient against consignees in this country.
20th March, 1923	One fan, Lady Amherst pheasant	No conviction recorded. Defendants ordered to pay £21 costs. Costs paid.
10th April, 1923	30 millinery mounts, peacock, reeves pheasant, falcated teal	£10 fine and £21 costs. Fine costs paid.
1st May, 1923	One mechanical peacock (made of peacock feathers) 12 bandeaux (heron feathers) Two mechanical peacocks (made of peacock feathers) One hat trimmed with golden pheasant and kingfisher plumage	£5 plus £7 7s. costs in respect of each of the four importations. £49 8s. in all. The fines and costs were paid.
3rd October, 1923	12 bundles of four different unknown kinds of egret feathers	Fines £20 and £2 2s. costs. Fine and costs paid.
18th December, 1923	An assortment of hat mounts, bandeaux and loose feathers for the most part prohibited (including bird of paradise, heron, etc.)	Fined £1 1s. and £4 4s. costs. Fine and costs paid.
18th December, 1923	An assortment of feather hat mounts including plumage of the chinese greenfinch, chinese tit, etc.	Fined £1 1s. and £4 4s. costs. Fine and costs paid.
25th February, 1925	325 bundles of egret plumage	Fined £50; fine paid.
8th October, 1925	One egret wing; 10 bundles marabou stork plumage. One bundle egret plumage	Fined £5; fine paid.
25th May, 1927	50 egret feathers	Fined £5 and £2 2s. costs. Fine and costs paid.
24th April, 1930 to 1st May, 1930	239 bundles of egret feathers	£375 plus £25 costs. Fine and costs paid.

TABLE 13 *(continued)*
List of Cases in which Legal Proceedings Were Instituted Against Importers of Plumage

Date of prosecution	Quantity and description of plumage	Penalty imposed
30th October, 1930	66 bundles of aigrettes	£100 including costs or three months imprisonment. Fine paid.
16th January, 1931	Bird of paradise and egret plumage	£100 or six weeks imprisonment. Fine paid.

SOURCE: United Kingdom, *Parliamentary Debates, Commons,* 310, 2 April, 1936, 2160–2162.

Commons.[91] Danesfort's bill was aimed at preventing the sale of plumage illegally imported in violation of the 1921 law. The bill's opponents stated that, if it passed, innocent dealers would have to clear themselves of guilt before selling their wares. The Marquess of Salisbury argued that, "if you are going to alter the law, the burden of proof is on you and not on the innocent trade. . . ."[92] From this viewpoint, it remained relatively simple for firms to claim that their feather stocks predated the 1921 Act and therefore could be legally sold. As late as 1936 when Mr. Mathers introduced a non-plumage sale bill, supported by the RSPCA, dealers still claimed the feather stocks they sold were old ones. Despite numerous indications of smuggling, Mathers' efforts came no nearer success than others before him.[93]

Plumage Confiscations in America

In the autumn of 1913, lady voyagers returning to New York and other American ports from sojourns abroad were politely but firmly requested to relinquish ornamental-feather trim on hats

91. A concise summary of legislative actions, and arguments for amendments to this and other bills, is found in an unpublished brief of Mathers, of the Plumage Act Group, dating back to the 1930's and housed in RSPCA Files. The important test came on 22 March, 1928 (*Parl. Debates, Lords,* 70: par. 569–593) and the bill was finally defeated on 9 May, 1928. Other measures were proposed on 5 February, 1926; 7 April, 1927; 19 December, 1929, and 25 March, 1936.

92. *Parl. Debates, Lords,* 70:22 March, 1928, par. 591.

93. *Parl. Debates,* 310: 25 March, 1936, par. 1237–1241, "The Importation of Plumage (Prohibition) Act (1921) Amendment." H. G. Williams commented: "This Bill is prompted by societies which exist for the collection of subscriptions from people whose sympathy is excited by stories of past horrors which do not exist to-day," (1240–1241). Other bills were introduced by Mr. Mathers on 23 November, 1936; 23 June, 1938; 22 December, 1938. Viscountess Astor supported all of them as she had done bills leading to the 1921 Act. Trade sympathizers had to reckon with her ascerbic comments when they took the floor.

and clothing. Pearson found these months stirring times, and derived much satisfaction from reports of "hundreds and even thousands . . . relieved of their decorations so proudly borne aloft as evidence of recent visits to London or Paris millinery-houses." [94] Customs officers also confiscated illegal plumage at West Coast ports. By March, 1914, personnel in San Francisco had made 26 seizures. Most were of pheasant, with some egret, pelican and bird of paradise material, and were taken from crewmen on Pacific vessels.[95]

As there were no federal restrictions against selling feathers in 1913, a brisk smuggling business sprang up and hard-to-get plumes became extremely valuable. New York was the main port for contraband plumage, although T. Gilbert Pearson recalled that two men were apprehended crossing the Rio Grande near Laredo in 1916 carrying 527 male bird of paradise skins.[96] As secretary of the National Audubon Society, he became alarmed at considerable smuggling and, in 1915, requested authorities to investigate aigrette shipments by parcel post. He believed that an abundance of plumage worn by New York City ladies had been obtained, in part, through the mail from Florida.[97]

By the end of 1915, quantities of plumage were regularly being seized in New York. State conservation officers acted 20 times in December, for instance, to prevent illegal trim entering or being sold in New York City. One feather importing firm reported losing $95,000 on aigrettes it could not sell. Its managing director was fined $5,000 and sentenced to jail for fraud.[98]

A remarkable case of smuggling was detected the following year when a crewman from the liner *Kroonland* was found wearing a belt of 150 birds of paradise plumes. Jailed for eleven months, he admitted to being part of a feather-smuggling ring based in England. He implicated others and further investigations netted $100,000 worth of contraband plumage from a feather company.[99]

94. *Adventures in Bird Protection*, p. 267.
95. University of California, Mus. Vert. Zoology, Correspondence Files, Accession No. 801. Customs officials sent confiscated plumage to the museum. Most of it, except examples of P. *minor* and *raggiana*, was discarded in 1950. By December, 1914, enough plumage had been turned over to the University to warrant a request from Tracy Storer, Curator of Birds, for selectivity in submissions.
96. *Adventures in Bird Protection*, p. 268.
97. *New York Times*, 26 July, 1915, p. 11, col. 4.
98. *New York Times*, 19 December, 1915, VI, p. 12, col. 4; 16 December, 1915, p. 7, col. 6; and 21 December, 1915 p. 14, col. 3.
99. Pearson *Adventures in Bird Protection*, p. 268. Stanley P. Young to R. H. King, 1 October, 1934, believed that efforts to break up traffic in aigrettes and bird heads

Pearson lost no time in pressing for legislation against the possession and sale of plumage. A revision of the Tariff Law in 1922 stated that ornamental plumage, other than of ostriches and domestic fowls, found in the United States, could be assumed to have been illegally imported unless it was in actual use as personal adornment or intended for educational or scientific purposes. Unless the possessor could prove that such plumage had entered the country prior to October, 1913, officers were permitted to confiscate ornamental material.

These regulations were aimed at making plumage less accessible to the general public. Trends in dress, particularly the decreasing use of hats and trimmings, hastened a decline in ornamental feather use in the 1920's and 1930's. A resurgence of this trim did take place, however, during World War II.

In late 1939 and early 1940, investigators of the National Audubon Society discovered that New York and Philadelphia millinery firms were selling large quantities of wild-bird feathers. Long "Robin Hood" type quills were considered stylish at that time and no less than 24 firms were discovered selling feathers of foreign birds of prey. Others offered plumage of native eagles (*Aquila chrysaetos, Haliaeetus leucocephalus*) shot and trapped in western states, and the list of foreign bird plumage being sold illegally covered 20 other species.[100] Believing that birdlife, both American and world-wide, faced "its worst threat in the last three decades," [101] the Audubon Society urged tighter controls on loopholes in plumage laws.

The Society considered the original 1913 Tariff Act deficient in three areas. Plumage imported before October, 1913, was still being sold legally. Feathers for fishing flies were also unrestricted and had taken an uncommon increase about 1937, when feather millinery began to come back into fashion. Finally, customs regulations permitted entry of feathers of domestic (interpreted by

for hats had been "very fruitful" in the past. As late as 1934 a deputy in New York was instrumental in having $850 worth of bird of paradise plumage seized by customs officers. Much of this contraband plumage found its way to educational institutions. A list dated 23 June, 1925, had in excess of 4,000 plumes of bird of paradise, 400 bunches of American egret, 38 bunches of snowy egret and other herons and was turned over to the Division of Textiles, the U.S. National Museum.

100. Richard H. Pough, "Massacred for Millinery," *BL* 42 (1940): 395–404. The list included: "The Jabiru, Maribou and Japanese Storks, the Steppe Eagle . . . Great Bustard, Indian Kinghunter, Red and Blue Macaw, Common Roller, Crested Screamer, Common Crane . . . the Short-tailed, Black-footed and Laysan Albatrosses," p. 396.

101. Ibid., p. 396.

some as domesticated) birds, even of species normally prohibited. This clause invited subterfuge.

In February, 1941, a satisfactory agreement was achieved by an accord with the feather importers, dealers and jobbers. The feather industry, mostly centered in New York, agreed to make full inventories of eagle, egret and bird of paradise plumage, and to file tallies of plumage in stock with the New York State Department of Conservation. For its part, the Audubon Society agreed to allow six years to elapse for the sale and disposal of such millinery before it could begin to lobby to terminate all traffic in wild bird plumage.[102]

New York passed a law in 1941 to end traffic (after 15 April, 1947) in wild bird plumage from any source, but the law was amended in 1942 to allow sales of plumage for fly-fishing purposes. In 1946, the state legislature further extended the original deadline for another three years. In 1947, further amendments permitted seven species of pheasant to be offered for sale if taken from captive birds raised in the United States. In 1951, wildlife groups—including the Izaak Walton League (which had opposed limits on trade in the feathers of game and harmful birds), fishing interests and a feather association—joined to eliminate abuses of the affidavit system relating to artificial flies. They agreed to quotas on imports of several species, and renounced the sale of plumage of native game birds. The Audubon Society and other organizations also proposed amendments to the Tariff Act by naming certain domestic fowl, waterbirds and pheasants that were to be imported only under the jurisdiction of the Department of Interior. This proposal was incorporated into congressional legislation in 1952 and has since been slightly amended.[103]

Summary

The year 1886 proved crucial for bird protection interests in the United States. In February of that year, George Bird Grinnell founded the Audubon Society; and in March, the AOU bird protection committee published its Model Law. This measure distinguished game birds from non-game birds and promised relief

102. John Baker, "An End To Traffic in Wild Bird Plumage," *Trans. Sixth North American Wildlife Conference* (1941): 16–19.

103. See various "Director's Reports," BL 43 (1941): 63–64, 198, 200, 370–373, 546–551; 44 (1942): 54–55, 117–118, 178, 243; 45 (1943): 183; 51 (1949): 109–110; and 53 (1951): 124–127.

for birds of prey, insectivorous warblers, herons, gulls, and terns. These and other species, long neglected or unevenly treated by state legislators, were vulnerable to mischievous boys, market and pot hunters, sportsmen, collectors and millinery agents.

New York was the first state to pass a bird law following AOU guidelines. It prohibited destruction of small birds for ornamental purposes. The law was, however, repealed; and late in 1886, a fashion for "snipe" feathers redoubled pressures on shorebirds, termed "game" under Model Law provisions. The AOU law did not explicitly object to the use of plumage taken from domestic fowl or to that of other birds lawfully killed as game. Nor did the Model Law address itself to the problem of foreign birds killed for the American millinery industry.

Grinnell's Audubon Society took an extreme stand on feather wearing. It opposed the use of any wild bird feathers. Pledges of membership did not permit game bird trim to be worn, whereas the AOU-sponsored law did. When the Audubon movement was revived in the 1890's, however, moderates believed it was appropriate to don the plumage of game and "food" birds, much to the distaste of the Society's more conservative elements, who eschewed the use of feathers *in toto*. Mabel Osgood Wright, co-editor of *Bird-Lore,* took the extreme position that Audubon members should, "join the total abstainers, or . . . devote enough time to bird study to be consistent in your actions." [104] Feather wearing, she believed, gave at least indirect credence to trade stories of moulted and artificial plumage. She later drew up a "Milliner's White List" of firms prepared to forego feather trim entirely, and recommended that every lady with the interests of birds at heart should wear the "Audubon Hat" with ribbons or lace but no plumes.

In the United States, the year 1913 was the high point in the history of the protection of plume birds. Congressional hearings brought both sides of the issue to the attention of the nation. Hornaday, assuming the abstainer position, took exception to Senator Clapp's proposal to exempt pest species and others used as food from prohibition under the Underwood Tariff Bill. In its final form, the plumage clause in this Act reflected the ardent hopes of bird protection elements. Loopholes in it resulted from uses to which feathers were put (educational, scientific and fly-

104. *BL* 1 (1899): 170–172, 172; 3 (1901): 40–41.

tying), and from the affidavits claiming that birds had been "raised in domesticity." While revisions to the Act in 1922 permitted travelers to bring feathers on personal effects into the country, this new tariff law was in fact a stronger measure than its predecessor because it empowered inspectors to seize stocks of feathers which lacked proper documentation.

In England, after the Plumage Act (1921) had circumscribed feather imports, the possession and sale of plumes was continued with only minimal risk of confiscation or prosecution. The years 1889 and 1921 are key dates in the British plumage campaign. The first marked the founding of the RSPB and the second celebrated the final passage of a long-delayed and overdue Plumage Act. Although the RSPB opposed feather fashions, generally it did not object to wardrobe items made from game species. Reflecting this position, the 1921 Act admitted into the country "birds ordinarily used as articles of diet," which applied to over 15 different types of birds. A Game Act of 1831 had included pheasants, partridges, grouse, heath or moor grouse and black game, in its provisions. A Poaching Prevention Law (1862) added woodcock and snipe. These game birds and common barn-door fowl, capercailles, ptarmigan, quails, pigeons, plovers, ducks, larks, guinea fowl and a bunting could be additionally defined as dietary items and therefore were exempt from 1921 Plumage Act restrictions. This law remained operative until the outbreak of World War II when it was suspended by an Import of Goods (Prohibition) Order.[105] Today, licenses are still issued in accordance with the 1921 Act. The Board of Trade continues to follow the Act's spirit and purpose, but without the help of a Plumage Advisory Committee, as the Act had required.

By focusing upon allegations of cruelty and bird destruction, the plumage debate stirred the English-speaking people on both sides of the Atlantic to take an interest in the status of their birdlife and that of colonies and foreign countries. The feather issue fostered a dramatic upsurge of interest in birds between 1880 and 1920. Who can be singled out as responsible for championing the bird cause? Grinnell, Dutcher, Hornaday, Chapman and Pearson in the United States; Newton, Hudson, Avebury, Buckland and Massingham in England. All worked unstintingly for effective

---

105. See T. S. Palmer, Papers, Game Laws, Box 66, Ms. Division, Lib. Congress, D.C., and M. G. Mecham, personal communication, 23 June, 1970.

bird laws in their respective countries. Until most recently these figures have been given merely a paragraph or two in histories of the conservation movement. Hornaday, for example, was applauded for his work for wildlife thirty years ago by Aldo Leopold, who stated:

> Dr. Hornaday's challenge to the Victorian fatalists is of wide philosophical significance. It is one of a series of challenges which have gradually undermined the glib assumption that all economic expansions are beneficent. We are now waking up to the fact that it is sometimes necessary for the public to protect itself against the unguided play of hostile economic forces.[106]

The outdoor literature of the 1870's and 1880's, according to Leopold, had been imbued with a sense of hopelessness about the inevitability of wildlife extinction. But while it was dismissed as "whipped before it was fairly born," bird preservation was able to develop and flourish through the single-minded and energetic pursuits of men like Hornaday, Dutcher, Chapman, and Pearson. As Secretary of the National Association of Audubon Societies, Pearson lectured widely on bird protection during the first decade of this century to women's groups and sportsmen's organizations. He urged politicians and officials to safeguard wild birds. Dutcher, whom Hornaday much admired, occupied a pivotal position in the drive to end plumage use. As President of the National Association of Audubon Societies, Dutcher urged Pearson, Palmer and others to drum up support for the bird movement in influential circles. A definitive history of the Audubon Society would illuminate the activities and relationships of these individuals with other bird and wildlife personalities and organizations. A recent essay on this subject provides useful guidance.[107] It would be unjust to single out any one person as the preeminent figure in the plumage movements of England or America, so widely treated were they in the literature of the day.

The relationship of the plumage debate to broader environmental attitudes of the time brings to mind Peter Schmitt's [108]

106. Hornaday, "Introduction" to the *Past, Present and Future of the Permanent Wildlife Protection Fund,* in *The Colorado State Forester,* Colorado State College (Fort Collins, 1935), p. 12.

107. Buchheister and Graham, "A Concise History of the Audubon Movement," *BL* 75 (1973): 4–45.

108. *Back to Nature: The Arcadian Myth in Urban America* (New York, 1969).

recent study of urban or suburban attitudes to nature in late-nineteenth century America. This historian of ideas has perceptively interpreted the "back to nature" movement of that era, not so much as a return to Jeffersonian agrarianism or Romantic primitivism, but as something rooted in the tamed wilderness of ruralized suburbia. Bird watching was important in this Arcadia just beyond the urban fringe. Weekend rambles, buggy or automobile drives, as well as literary voyages to the countryside with John Burroughs and Ernest Thompson Seton were fashionable and virtuous activities. To the city dweller seeking rural ideals, birds were his friends and teachers, a source of inspiration and a delight to his children. They instructed him with their antics, charmed him with their songs and colors, and awoke in him a love of nature.

The first decade of the twentieth century was witness to many bird books intended by ornithologists, nature lovers and clergymen to instruct and to amuse. Never before had wild creatures been written about so voluminously or with so much popular success. Never before had city folk so enthusiastically embraced the rural values and landscapes. At the same time, it was fashionable, even urbane, to be a "bird watcher" and "bird lover" early in this century. Anti-plumage groups were demanding behavior described as "proper," "decent" and "civilized." Legislatures inevitably felt the pressure of this groundswell of sentiment in support of birds. Newspapers clarioned protection principles and showed concern for cruelty to "our feathered friends." Professional ornithologists joined with nature lovers and sentimental bird lovers to render aid to beleaguered bird populations and to help preserve them for their children's children. In this they succeeded.

Conclusion

Bird preservationists claimed that upwards of 200 million birds were being killed for their feathers each year at the beginning of the twentieth century. The feather trim that millinery establishments turned out was only the conspicuous end-product of a process that led back to remote swamps and jungles. How many birds, the preservationists asked, fluttered away maimed by a gun blast and died a lingering death? How much more plumage was left uncollected as herons kicked in convulsions in a rookery thicket or on a distant part of a marsh? There is no doubt that wings, tails and ornamental plumes were but a small fraction of a greater quantity left to rot or to be discarded as soiled or (once on the market) out of style.

Whatever the absolute quantity of plumage utilized for trade purposes, the birds from which it was taken could be numbered by the scores. Birds of all sizes from the fields, hedgerows, mountains, forests and even open seas were shipped to fashion centers located in Western Europe and the United States. Tiny sunbirds, scavenging vultures and storks, predatory hawks, eagles and owls from British, Dutch, French and German colonies went into dress accessories displayed by London, New York and Parisian fashion houses. Parts of various birds appeared on the pages of a growing number of journals which acclaimed them as elegant and novel. Mail-order firms facilitated the distribution of ornamental plumage to style-conscious ladies. Frequent changes in the texture, shape and color of head ornament made the quest of hunters that much more intensive.

In the United States a number of well-documented stories described the methods of plume hunters and attested to a dramatic decline in the populations of sea, shore and marsh birds. Gulls, terns and herons suffered enormous losses to pluming in the 1880's and 1890's. Dutcher and Thayer took an important hand in protecting and rehabilitating breeding colonies of these birds from Maine to Louisiana. The egret became the symbol to many bird lovers of a need to save native species endangered by the feather trade. Before World War I estimates of an egret population of only 5,000 in the southern states raised real fears about the species' future survival. At the same time, contraband aigrettes were selling for as much as $80 an ounce in New York City. By the 1930's however, released from hunting pressures, the numbers of egrets had rebounded dramatically.

The American Audubon movement, AOU, the British Plumage Group, and the RSPB and its affiliates in Ireland, India, Australia and Western Europe, campaigned to bring the facts of endangerment, cruelty and ecological damage to the attention of the public. Members of these organizations contacted hundreds of newspaper editors about the need for public support of bird protection. They lobbied politicians at the state and national level about laws that would effectively combat the plumage fad. Through local and junior societies, and in the pages of *Bird-Lore* and *Bird Notes and News,* preservationists instructed children in a sense of wonder about animal creation. They encouraged youngsters to feed birds and to construct nesting places for them.

The cause of bird groups received sympathetic attention from the highest social circles on both sides of the Atlantic. Queen Victoria and Queen Alexandra of England made it known publicly that they approved of efforts to discourage ornamental feather use. As Governor of New York State and then, as President, Theodore Roosevelt lent his prestige to the bird cause, and acted to set up a Federal Reserve for brown pelicans on the Indian River, Florida, to offset threats from plume agents.

The plumage campaign lasted nearly fifty years. At various times, moves were made to halt the importation, sale and even possession of wild bird skins and feathers. Precisely how effective federal legislation in the form of the Lacey Act (1900), the Tariff Act (1913) and Migratory Bird Treaty Act (1916) were in settling the plumage issue is arguable; but these laws, in amended form, are clearly the basis for current wildlife legislation in the United States.

Despite the existence of protective bird legislation, enforcement agencies admitted that a good deal of contraband material was entering the United States and the United Kingdom. Some people even stated that the British 1921 Act was honored more in its breach than observance. Bird skins, like the expensive predatory cat skins of the late 1960's, could be carried in luggage or concealed on the person. Once supplies had become curtailed, the incentive to smuggle goods to support continuing feather fashions became greater. Officials in the Division of Enforcement of the United States Fish and Wildlife Service have commented that no amount of legislation can save wildlife if it can be exploited for commercial purposes. In the matter of ornamental plumage, a recent fine of $15,000 on a firm for smuggling grey jungle fowl skins into this country for fly-fishing purposes proves that contraband feathers are still worth something. Within the last three years a run has been made on pheasant plumage for collars, hats and head bands. Souvenirs, bric-a-brac, even lampshades have been seen to contain various kinds of pheasant plumage and have created problems of identification at ports in this country. Every amateur sportsman has the right to utilize feathers from game killed legally, but not to sell feathers or birdskins

The profusion of plumage in ladies' fashions at the turn of the century is likely to remain a thing of the past. According to Claudia Kidwell of the Smithsonian's Division of Costume and Furnishings, the role and corresponding image of woman has been altered profoundly. World War I was an occasion for women to devote themselves to the tasks of tending sick and wounded soldiers, and to performing daily tasks that had until then appeared largely masculine. In the 1920's, having won social and political equality, women slowly became equals in business and career professions. The increased mobility and speed associated with the automobile, together with the austerity engendered by the War, helped make billowing trimmings inconvenient and out of place. Some people even argued that feather millinery (known also as "hun headgear") was unpatriotic.

With woman's role in society changing and the simpler, more functional styles in daily dress, the decorative array of birds, wings, tails and heads so much admired in the 1880's had become bizarre by 1920. Laws undoubtedly have had a persuasive effect upon the choice and range of millinery ornaments. The widespread publicity that the issue of feather wearing received must also have changed a good many people's minds about the propriety of feather millinery.

The previous pages have described the first steps in England and the United States to drum up widespread concern for wild bird protection. What has been described as the "Age of Extermination" in the 1870's and 1880's made a number of sportsmen, scientists and others stop to think about the future of many waterfowl and shorebird populations. The conspicuous numbers of birds and their parts seen along the sidewalks of fashionable quarters angered many people because the motives for using them appeared to be paltry and inexcusable.

The sight of a white tern affixed to the crown of a lady's hat made patently clear to some that mankind had not merely betrayed his dominion over creatures, but had done so with gusto and with an eye only for immediate gain. In contemporary parlance the call to "lower the profile" in treatment of nature spelled a need to increase human sensitivity to wild things. That some women chose to abrogate to themselves the harlequin colors and shapes of feathered creatures made the picture of diminishing wildlife resources the more poignant.

In today's concern for environmental problems, themes are being repeated that were clarioned in the debate over feather wearing two generations ago. "Humility before nature" appears to be a guiding principle and the news media has been quick to continue the tune, sometimes off-key. One recent television program about wild northlands contained pictures of a man astride a partially submerged beluga whale, commenting that scientists like to have fun out of doors. Presumably there were thrills and excitement for some in shooting and skinning wild birds, and fun for many in wearing their feathers, but not for the bird, nor for the whale. How long the message of sensitivity to nature will take to sink into the minds of people is impossible to say. Some would have us believe it will take an eternity; others consider that the plumage crusade was a start.

Appendix I
Milestones in British and American Bird Protection

1868 (UK) Alfred Newton's address, "The Zoological Aspect of Game Laws," to a British Association meeting highlighted gull destruction in Britain.

1869 (UK) Sea Birds' Preservation Act passed.

1883 (US) Formation of the American Ornithologists' Union.

1884 (US) William Brewster, at the second annual meeting of AOU, moved for appointment of a Committee for the Protection of North American Birds.

1885 (UK) "Plumage League" founded by Rev. Francis O. Morris, Lady Mount-Temple and others.

1886 (US) Formation of an Audubon Society by George Bird Grinnell announced in *Forest and Stream* (11 February).

(US) Sixteen page supplement to *Science,* no. 160 (26 February), on bird destruction for plumage purposes; Allen, Dutcher, Sennett, Chapman co-authors (AOU, Bulletin One).

1888 (US) Audubon Society dropped by *Forest and Stream.*

1889 (UK) Society for the Protection of Birds (SPB) formed as an anti-plumage group.

1894 (US) C. A. Babcock, Superintendent of Schools, Oil City Pa., established "Bird Day" among children.

1896 (US) Audubon Society revived by William Brewster in Massachusetts.

1898 (US) Senator Hoar of Massachusetts introduced a bill to restrict trade in birds for millinery use. Failed to pass.

1899 (UK)	Order issued for the discontinuance of "osprey" wearing by officers of the British Army.
(US)	*Bird-Lore* published as the official organ of Audubon Societies. Chapman editor and owner.
1900 (UK)	SPB branch established in India.
(US)	Thayer Fund inaugurated to protect plume bird colonies.
(US)	Lacey Act passed (25 May).
1901 (US)	National Committee of Audubon Societies set up.
1902 (UK)	All wild bird skins and feathers forbidden export from British India.
(US)	National Association of Audubon Societies formed (in New York) by William Dutcher. Incorporated in 1905.
1903 (US)	First national bird reservation set up on Pelican Island, Florida, by Presidential Executive Order (14 March).
(US)	AOU-Audubon agreement with millinery interests.
1906 (UK)	Queen Alexandra permits the RSPB to use her name in support of its plumage campaign.
1908 (UK)	Lord Avebury introduced the first plumage bill into the House of Lords. It died in the Commons.
1910 (US)	Shea-White plumage bill passed in the State of New York curtailing by 1911 millinery activities in New York City.
	International Ornithological Congress supported a resolution favoring plumage prohibition.
(UK)	Inter-Departmental Government Committee inaugurated to discuss plumage problems.
1913 (US)	Federal Tariff Act with plumage import prohibitions signed into law (3 October).
1917 (UK)	Board of Trade passed an importation of plumage regulation (23 February).
1918 (UK-US)	Migratory Bird Treaty Act became law between United States and the United Kingdom for Canada (3 July).
1921 (UK)	Passage of Importation of Plumage (Prohibition) Bill (Royal Assent 1 July).
1922 (US)	Amendment of 1913 Tariff Act to change regulations on plumage importation and possession.

Appendix II
Plume Birds Protected in the United States in 1902

States	Grebes	Gulls	Terns	Pelicans	Egrets
Arkansas	X	X	X	X	X
California		X			
Connecticut	X	X	X	X	X
Delaware	X	X	X	X	X
District of Columbia	X	X	X	X	X
Florida	X	X	X	X	X
Illinois	X	X	X	X	X
Indiana	X	X	X	X	X
Maine	X	X	X	X	X
Maryland		X	X		
Massachusetts	X	X	X	X	X
Michigan	X	X	X	X	X
Minnesota	X	X	X	X	
Nevada	X	X	X	X	X
New Hampshire	X	X	X	X	X
New Jersey	X	X	X	X	X
New York	X	X	X	X	X
Oregon		X			
Pennsylvania		X	X	X	
Rhode Island	X	X	X	X	X
Texas		X	X	X	X
Utah		X			
Vermont	X	X	X	X	X
Virginia		X			
Wisconsin	X	X	X	X	X
Wyoming	X	X	X	X	X

Appendix III
List of Bird Plumage Used for Millinery Purposes

A "Revised List of Salable and Nonsalable Bird Plumage" in New York State, 1911, appeared in a millinery journal. It purported to be "a reliable and safe list from which are produced all the fancy feathers now being sold by the trade everywhere." An admixture of trade, popular and ornithological nomenclature, it covers a broad spectrum of bird families and species and is quoted in full.

Birds and Bird Plumage, The Sale and Possession of
Which is Permitted by Law

Senegal Rolliers—Commonly called rollers,
Guepiers
Large red parrots
Satyr—a species of pheasant
Japanese green pheasant
Goura—commonly called crown pigeon
Grand Duc Owl
Harphang—commonly called snowy owl
Velvet bird
Six filet—paradise bird
Pilet—species of duck
Duck
Partridge
Tetras Lyre—European black cock
Grouse—partridge tail

Aras—commonly called Macaw
Outarde—commonly called bustard
Forest pigeon
Faisanes—European pheasant
Japanese brown pheasant
Impeyan
Guinea fowl
Rhea—South American ostrich
Touroucon
Peacock
Tetras
Plover tail
Partridge wing
Crossoptilon pheasant
Junglecock
Hawk
Male Loriet
Numidie

Merle
Magpie
Snipes—marsh sandpiper
Ignicolores—weaver bird
Calfats Brun—weaver bird
Yellow head manakin
Ring neck plover
Touracco rouge—plantain bird
Breves—pitta
Red head blue body manakin
Small ring neck plover
Dark snipes—green sandpiper
Green parrots
Choucas—jackdaw
Snipe—green plover
Figuier—black head honey creeper
Becassine a piox—painted snipe
Calfat Isabelle—weaver bird
Parrots ailes striees
Touracco verts—plaintain eater

Grives, Grises, Hypsipetes
Golden oriole
Chicken feathers of all kinds
English pheasant plumage of all kinds
Chinese golden pheasant
Chinese silver pheasant
Turkey plumage of all kinds
Goose plumage of all kind
Swan plumage of all kinds
Grouse plumage of all kinds
Woodcock
East India fruit pigeon
Calfats gris—European sparrow
Blue Guepier—honey creeper
Red head manakin
Jap. hawk quills
Vulture
Bearded Vulture
Rooster tails of all kinds

Birds and Bird Plumage, The Sale and Possession of
Which is Not Permitted by Law

Pigeon—dark
Garnet dull tanager
Red tanager
Blue jays
Hirondelle Formosa swift
Etourneaux—starling
Bergonnettes Marron—bunting
Griselle—tern
Tourterelle Collier Espagne—turtle dove
Petit Hirondelle de Cheminee—swallow
Pies Bleues—blue jay
Petit Bouvreuil—bull finch
Starlings
Grey heron
Alouttes—skylark
Green ibis
Small owls—commonly called screech owls

Night heron
Figuier brown head Tanager
Verdiers—green finch
Eveques—starling
Dominoes—sooty tern
Petit—Martin pecheur
Eagle
Pelican
Condor
Tourterelle des Bois
Owls, Russie
Hawk Owl
Yellow finches—commonly called goldfinch
Yellow heron
Booby
Snow birds—bunting
White foot eagle
Marabout
Black Tanager

Red ibis
Quail wings
Gros Bouvreuil—haw finch
Jaseur quene jaune—wax
Petit Hirondelle swift
Pinson des ardonnes brambling
Bruants—bunting
Pincon male chaffinch
Pigeons bronze Malacca
Albinos—white tern

Brown heron
Grives royal—thrush
Chardonnerets—goldfinch
Blue Manakin
Grives marron—thrush
Egret
Turkey Buzzard
Grebes skins
Garnet Tanager

SOURCE: *The Millinery Trade Review* 36:10 (October, 1911) 49.

Bibliography

1. *Selected Unpublished Sources*

American Museum of Natural History, Audubon Society Correspondence, New York.

Doughty, Robin W. "Feather Fashions and Bird Preservation: A Study in Nature Protection," unpublished Ph.D., University of California, Berkeley, California, 1971.

Englebert, Ernest A. "American Policy for Natural Resources: A Historical Survey to 1862," unpublished Ph.D. thesis, Harvard, Cambridge, Mass., 1950.

The Feathers, A Tale; Or Venus Surpassed by a Beauty in Grosvenor Square. Inscribed to a Certain Fair Plumed Duchess. London, 1775(?), British Museum.

Hornaday, William T. Papers. Ms. Division, Library of Congress, Washington, D.C.

International Council for Bird Preservation. Presidential Correspondence about Grey Jungle Fowl, (*Gallus sonnerati*), February and July, 1969. Smithsonian Institution, Washington, D.C.

Kranz, Marvin W. "Pioneering in Conservation: A History of the Conservation Movement in New York State, 1865–1903," unpublished Ph.D., Syracuse, 1961.

National Audubon Society. Archives, Correspondence, etc. Ms. Division, New York Public Library, New York.

Palmer, Theodore S. Papers (especially Game Laws, Box 66–67), Ms. Division, Library of Congress, Washington, D.C.

RSPB. Correspondence Files, The Lodge, Sandy, Bedfordshire, England.

RSPCA. Files of Plumage Groups Covering British Bills, Jermyn Street, London.

Sennett, George B. "Report of the A.O.U. Committee on the Protection of North America Birds," unpublished manuscript dated 12 November, 1886, and housed with AOU material (% Alexander Wetmore) Division of Birds, Smithsonian Institution, Washington, D.C.

Swanson, E. B. "Use and Conservation of Minnesota Game, 1850–1900," unpublished Ph.D. thesis, Minneapolis, 1940.

United Kingdom, Board of Trade. Plumage (Prohibition) Advisory Committee, Minutes of 1st to 18th meetings, and Hearings 1921–37. Custom House Library, London.

————. Plumage Act Advisory Committee, India. Office Correspondence, Memorandum from the Commissioners in Sind no. 41, January 1918. Custom House Library, London.

United States, Dept. of Agric. Bur. Biol. Survey, Records 1902–41. Game Protection—Miscellaneous and Reservations by name RG 22, National Archives, Washington, D.C.

U.S. Congress, Senate. Committee on Finance, Tariff Schedule N-Sundries. Petitions in favor of House amendment and against Senator Clapp's amendment allowing game birds and pest birds for millinery use. Sen. 63A-J23 (Schedule N) Two bundles, National Archives, Washington, D.C., 1913.

University of California, Museum Vertebrate Zoology. Material confiscated by U.S. Treasury Dept., San Francisco. Accession no.'s 801, 934, 2432, 5600. Berkeley, California, 1914–1915.

2. *Selected Published Sources*

"A. D. 1950," *Forest and Stream* (17 September, 1885).

Adams, Alexander B. *John James Audubon: A Biography*. New York, 1966.

Aiken, Charlotte Rankin. *Millinery*. New York, 1922.

Ali, Salim A. and S. Dillon Ripley. *Handbook of the Birds of India and Pakistan*. 9 vols. in press. Bombay, London, 1968, etc.

Allen, J. A. "Decrease of Birds in Massachusetts," *Bull. Nuttall Ornith. Club* 1 (1876): 53–60.

————. "On the Decrease of Birds in the United States." *The Penn Monthly* 7 (1876): 931–944.

————. "Insectivorous Birds in Their Relation to Man." *Bull. Nuttall Ornith. Club* 6 (1881): 22–27.

————. *The American Ornithologists' Union; A Seven Years' Retrospect*. New York, 1891.

————. "An Ornithologist's Plea." *New York Times*, 25 November, 1897, p. 6, col. 6.

Allen, Robert P. "The Wild-Life Sanctuary Movement in the United States." Part One, *BL* 36 (1934): 80–84.

American Ornithologists' Union. Various reports in *The Auk* 1 (1884), etc.

Argentine Republic. *Anuario de la Direccion General de Estadistica.* Buenos Aires, 1896, etc.

Audubon, John James. *Ornithological Biography, or an Account of the Habits of the Birds of the United States of America. . . .* 5 vols. Edinburgh, 1831–1839.

"Audubon Society for the Protection of Birds." *The Audubon Magazine* 1 (1887): 20–21 and other articles.

Austin, Elizabeth S. *Frank M. Chapman in Florida: His Journals and Letters.* Gainesville, 1967.

Baker, E. C. Stuart. *The Fauna of British India, Including Ceylon and Burma.* 2nd edition, 8 vols. London, 1929.

Baker, John. "An End to Traffic in Wild Bird Plumage." *Trans. Sixth North American Wildlife Conferences.* (1941): 16–19.

Barr, Estelle De Young, "A Psychological Analysis of Fashion Motivation." *Archives of Psychology* 171 (1934).

Barrows, Walter. "The English Sparrow (*Passer domesticus*) in North America, Especially in Relation to Agriculture." *U.S.D.A., Div. Economic Ornith. and Mammalogy, Bull.,* I. Washington, D.C., 1889.

Barrus, Clara. *The Life and Letters of John Burroughs.* 2 vols. Boston, 1925.

Barton, Lucy. *Historic Costume for the Stage.* Boston, 1935.

Bartram, William. *Travels Through North and South Carolina, Georgia, East and West Florida. . . .* Philadelphia, 1791.

Bastide, Roger. "Brazil." *Encyclopedia of World Art.* 15 vols. New York, 1960.

Batchelder, Charles F. "An Account of the Nuttall Ornithological Club." *Memoirs of the Nuttall Ornith. Club.,* 8. Cambridge, Mass., 1937.

Beebe, Charles William. *A Monograph of the Pheasants.* 4 vols. London, 1918–1922.

Bell, Quentin. *On Human Finery.* London, 1947.

Ben Yusuf, Anna. *The Art of Millinery.* New York, 1909.

Bennett, David W. "Hunting the Egret," *San Francisco Call.,* 3 April 1898. p. 18, cols. 1–7.

———. "An Egret Hunter's Narrative." SPB *Leaflet* 26. London, n.d.

Benson, C. E. "Egret Farming in Sind." *Journal Bombay Nat. Hist. Soc.* 28 (1922): 748–750.

Bidie, G. "The Protection of Wild Birds in India." SPB *Leaflet* 37. London, 1901.

Birch, George. "Egret Farming in Sind." *Journal Bombay Nat. Hist. Soc.* 23 (June, 1914): 161–163.

Bird Lover. "Milliners' Claims Absurd." *New York Times,* 28 September, 1913. p. 6, col. 5.

Bock, Walter J. "A Generic Review of the Family Ardeidae (Aves)." *American Museum Novitates* 1779 (1956): 1–49.

Boucard, Adolphe. "What is to be Seen Everywhere in London." *The Humming Bird* 1 (1891): 1–2, 9–10.

Boussac, P. Hippolytée. "L'Autruche Dans la Civilisation Egyptienne." *La Nature* 34 (1906): 194–199.

Boutard, L. E. "Aigrettes Domestiquées dans la Republique Argentine." *Bull. Soc. d'Acclimatation* 44 (1897): 270.

Braum-Ronsdorf, Margarete. *Mirror of Fashion; A History of European Costume, 1789–1929.* trans. from German by Oliver Coburn. New York, 1964.

Brazil, Serviço de Estatistica Economica e Financeira do Tesouro Nacional, *Comercio Exterior do Brasil.* Rio de Janeiro, 1940, etc.

Brehm, Alfred E. *Bird Life; Being a History of the Bird, Its Structure and Habits.* trans. from German by H. M. Labouchere and W. Jesse. London, 1874.

Brewster, William. "The Terns of the New England Coast." *Bull. Nuttall Ornith. Club* 4 (1879): 13–22.

———. "The Present Status of Forster's Tern as a Bird of New England." *The Auk* 6 (1889): 66–67.

Brigham, William T. "Hawaiian Feather Work." *Memoirs Bernice P. Bishop Museum* 1 (1899): 1–81.

———. "Additional Notes on Hawaiian Feather Work." *Memoirs Bernice P. Bishop Museum* 1 (1903): 437–453.

———. "Additional Notes on Hawaiian Feather Work, Second Supplement." *Memoirs Bernice P. Bishop Museum* 7 (1918): 1–64.

Brooke, Iris. *English Costume of the Later Middle Ages: The Fourteenth and Fifteenth Centuries.* London, 1935.

———. *English Costume from the Fourteenth through the Nineteenth Century.* New York, 1937.

———. *Dress and Undress, the Restoration and Eighteenth Century.* London, 1958.

Brookfield, Charles M. "The Guy Bradley Story." *BL* 57 (1955): 170–174.

Buchheister, Carl W. and Frank Graham. "From the Swamps and Back—a Concise and Candid History of the Audubon Movement." *BL* 75 (1973): 4–45.

Buck, Anne. *Victorian Costume and Costume Accessories.* London, 1961.

Buckland, James. *Pros and Cons of the Plumage Bill.* London, 1911.

———. Testimony before U.K. Colonial Office Conference on the Destruction of Plumage Birds, 27 February, 1911. U.K. *Colonial Office, Miscellaneous,* no. 263. Public Record Office C. O. 885/21. London, 1911.

―――. "The Value of Birds to Man." *Journal Royal Soc. Arts,* 63 (1915): 701–711.

Buffon, Georges Louis Leclerc comte de. *Natural History, General and Particular.* trans. from French by William Smellie. New edit. 20 vols. (Birds. vols. 11–20), London, 1812.

Burroughs, John. "Real and Sham Natural History." *Atlantic,* 91 (1903): 298–309.

―――. *Signs and Seasons.* Boston, (1st edit. 1886), 1914.

―――. *Wake-Robin.* New York, (1st edit. 1871), 1877.

Cameron, Jenks. *The Bureau of Biological Survey: Its History, Activities and Organization.* Instit. Gov't Res., Service Monogr. U.S. Gov't, 54. Baltimore, 1929.

Cantwell, Robert. *Alexander Wilson: Naturalist and Pioneer, a Biography.* Philadelphia, 1961.

Cart, Theodore W. "The Lacey Act: America's First Nationwide Wildlife Statute," *Forest History* 17 (1973), 4–13.

Carvalho, Jose Candido de Melho. "Notas de Viagem ao Rio Negro," *Public. Avulsas do Museum Nacional,* no. 9. Rio de Janeiro, 1952.

Challamel, Augustin. *The History of Fashion in France; or, The Dress of Women From the Gallo-Roman Period to the Present Time.* trans. from French by Cashel Hoey and John Lillie. London, 1882.

Chapman, Frank M. Various articles and editorial comments in *BL* 1 (1899), etc.

―――. *Autobiography of a Bird-Lover.* New York, 1933.

Chesterton, G. K. *G. F. Watts.* London, 1904.

Coleman, Sydney H. *Humane Society Leaders in America.* Albany, New York, 1924.

Collette, J. R. "House Sparrow." *American Naturalist* 4:1 (March 1870), 54–55.

Cooke, W. Wells. "Distribution and Migration of North American Herons and Their Allies." U.S.D.A. *Biol. Survey, Bull.* 45. Washington, D.C., 1913.

Coues, Elliot *Key to North American Birds* . . . 3rd ed. Boston, 1887.

Courrier de Saigon. "Des Oiseaux du Huyen de Kien-Giang et des Eventails Fabriqués Avec Leurs Plumes." *Bull. Soc. d'Acclimatation,* 2nd série, vol. 10 (1873): 289–295.

Cunnington, Cecil Willett. *Feminine Attitudes in the Nineteenth Century.* New York, 1936.

Cunnington, Cecil Willett. *English Women's Clothing in the Nineteenth Century*. London, 1937.

Davenport, Millia. *The Book of Costume*. 2 vols. New York, 1948.

Dearborn, George Van Ness. *The Psychology of Clothing*. Princeton, N.J., and Lancaster, Pa., 1918.

Delacour, Jean T. *The Pheasants of the World*. London, 1951.

Denis, Ferdinand. *Arte Plumaria*. Paris, 1875.

"Destruction of Small Birds." *Forest and Stream* 23 (1884): 24.

Dewar, Douglas. *Indian Bird Life*. London, 1925.

————. *Game Birds*. London, 1928.

Dill, Homer R. and William A. Bryan. "Report of an Expedition to Laysan Islands in 1911." U.S.D.A., *Biol. Survey, Bull.* 42. Washington, D.C., 1912.

Dodsworth, P.T.L. "Protection of Wild Birds in India and Traffic in Plumage." *Journal Bombay Nat. Hist. Soc.* 20 (1911): 1103–1114.

Downham, Charles F. Testimony before U.K. House of Lords—Select Committee. *Report on the Importation of Plumage Prohibition Bill, with Minutes of Evidence*, 24 June, 1908, London, 1908.

————. "The Trade in Feathers." *The Times*, 4 November, 1910. p. 16, col. 3.

————. *The Feather Trade: The Case for the Defence*. London, 1911.

————. "The Plumage Trade." *The Times*, 4 April, 1913. p. 5, col. 6.

————. "Wild Birds and Millinery." *The Times*, 3 January, 1914. p. 4, col. 2.

————. "Plumage Trade." *The Times*, 6 March, 1914. p. 10, col. 5.

"Drummers in Flowers and Feathers." *The Millinery Trade Review* 25 (1900): 111–112.

Dubos, René Jules. *A Theology of the Earth*. Lecture Smithsonian Instit., October 1969. Washington, D.C., n.d.

Duerden, James Edwin. "Ostrich Farming in South Africa. Successful Results Suggesting the Possibility of Saving Other Wild Birds Thro' Domestication." *American Mus. Journal* 17 (1917): 367–375.

Dutcher, William. Various comments, articles and reports in *The Auk* and *BL*.

————. "Destruction of Bird-Life in the Vicinity of New York." Science-supplement 7:160 (25 February, 1886): 197–199.

Earle, Alice Moorse. *Two Centuries of Costume in America: 1620–1820*. 2 vols. New York, 1903.

"Egret Farming in Sind." *Journal Bombay Nat. Hist. Soc.* 27 (1921): 944–947.

Ely, C. A. and Roger Clapp. "Natural History of Laysan Island. . . ." *Atoll Research Bull.* No. 171 (1973).

Evans, Mary. *Costume Throughout the Ages*. Philadelphia, 1930.

Fairholme, Edward G. *A Century of Work for Animals: the History of the R.S.P.C.A., 1824–1934.* London, 1934.

"Feathers—Their Nature and Uses." *Penny Magazine* 10 (1841), 357–358, 363–364.

Feiner and Maas. "Aigrette Dealers Not Involved." *New York Times,* 4 June, 1913. p. 10, col. 5.

———. "Foreign Wild Birds." *New York Times,* 29 May, 1913 p. 10, col. 6.

"Firm Admits it Smuggled Bird Feathers." *Minneapolis Tribune,* 3 December, 1970.

Fisher, Arthur H. "Marajó—Paradise of Bird Life and Lesson in Protection." *Nature Magazine* 32 (1939): 35–38.

Fisher, James. *The Shell Bird Book.* London, 1966.

Fisher, Joseph L. "New Perspectives on Conservation." *Biological Conservation* 1 (1969): 111–116.

Flagg, Wilson. "The Birds of the Pasture and Forest." *Atlantic Monthly* 2 (1858): 863–875.

———. *The Birds and Seasons of New England.* Boston, 1875.

Flower, Sir William H. "Artificial Plumes." SPB *Leaflet* no. 27. 1903 edition, London, 1903.

Flower, W. H. "Feathers in Ladies Hats." *The Times,* 25 June, 1896. p. 12, col. e.

Flügel, John Carl. *The Psychology of Clothes.* London, 1930.

Foerster, Norman. *Nature in American Literature; Studies in the Modern View of Nature.* New York, 1923.

Forbush, Edward H. *Decrease of Certain Birds and its Causes with Suggestion for Bird Protection.* (Special Report), 2nd edition, revised. Boston, 1908.

Forest, Jules. Various articles on plumage in *Bull. Soc. d'Acclimatation* 40 (1893), 44 (1897), and in *Revue Scientifique* 35 (1898) and 38 (1901).

"Friends of Birds Victors." *Washington Post,* 3 September, 1913, p. 2, col. 5.

Geay, F. "Observations Faites sur les Aigrettes Dans l'Amérique Tropicale." *Bull. Soc. d'Acclimatation* 44 (1897): 205–209.

Gilliard, Ernest Thomas. *Birds of Paradise and Bower Birds.* London, 1969.

Glacken, Clarence J. "The Origins of the Conservation Philosophy." *Journal Soil and Water Conservation* 11 (1956): 63–66.

———. *Traces on the Rhodian Shore.* Berkeley, Los Angeles, 1967.

———. "Man's Place in Nature in Recent Western Thought." in Michael Hamilton (ed.) *The Little Planet.* New York, 1970, 163–201.

Goeldi, Emilio A. *Against the Destruction of White Herons and Red Ibises on the Lower Amazon, Especially on the Island of Marajó.* trans. from Portuguese by W. H. Clifford. Pará, 1902.

Graham, Edward H. *The Land and Wildlife.* New York, 1947.

Graham, Frank. *Man's Dominion: the Story of Conservation in America.* New York, 1971.

Grant, Madison. "France Awards a Medal for Bird Protection." *Statement of the Permanent Wild Life Protection Fund. 1913–1914,* 89–92, New York, 1915.

Greene, Rev. H. "As in a Mirror." SPB *Leaflet* no. 2, 4th edition, London, 1898.

Greenway, James C. *Extinct and Vanishing Birds of the World.* New York, 1958.

Hayden, Sherman Strong. *The International Protection of Wild Life* New York, 1942.

Haymaker, Richard E. *From Pampas to Hedgerows and Downs; A Study of W. H. Hudson.* New York, 1954.

Hehn, Victor. *The Wanderings of Plants and Animals From Their First Home.* James S. Stallybrass (ed.). London, 1885.

Hemming, Kingdon B. and Hal Sorenson. "Hats Bonnets and Decoys." *Decoy Collector's Guide 2* (1964).

Herrick, Francis Hobart. *Audubon the Naturalist; A History of His Life and Time.* 2 vols. New York, 1917.

Hickey, Joseph J. (ed). *Peregrine Falcon Populations; Their Biology and Decline.* Madison, 1969.

Hicks, Philip M. *The Development of the Natural History Essay in American Literature.* Philadelphia, 1924.

Horn, Marilyn J. *The Second Skin: An Interdisciplinary Study of Clothing.* New York, 1968.

Hornaday, William T. "Destruction of our Birds and Mammals." *New York Zool. Soc. Second Annual Report* (March 1898): 77–107.

———. "Feather Trade 'Fakes'." *New York Times,* 30 September, 1913. p. 12, col. 6.

———. "Foreign Wild Birds." *New York Times,* 31 May, 1913. p. 10, col. 6.

———. *Our Vanishing Wild Life; its Extermination and Preservation.* New York, 1913.

———. *The Statement of the Permanent Wild Life Protection Fund, 1913–1914.* New York, 1915.

———. *Thirty Years War for Wild Life; Gains and Losses in the Thankless Task.* Stamford, Conn., 1931.

Hudson, William H. "Feathered Women," SPB *Leaflet* no. 10. London, 1902.

———. "Letter to the Clergy." SPB *Leaflet* no. 25. London.

———. "On Liberating Caged Birds." SPB *Leaflet* no. 73. London.

———. "Lost British Birds." SPB *Leaflet* no. 14. London.

———. "Osprey; Or, Egrets and Aigrettes." SPB *Leaflet* no. 10. London, 1902.

———. "The Trade in Birds' Feathers." SPB *Leaflet* no. 28. London, 1903.

Hurlock, Elizabeth B. "Motivation in Fashion." *Archives of Psychology* no. 111 (1929): 1–71.

———. *The Psychology of Dress; an Analysis of Fashion and Its Motive.* New York, 1929.

Ingersoll, Ernest. *Birds in Legend, Fable and Folklore.* New York, 1923.

———. "Specious Arguments Veil Feather Trade's Real Purposes." *New York Times,* 25 March, 1914. p. 10, col. 6.

International Council for Bird Preservation. "India—The Case of the Indian Grey Jungle Fowl." *Asian Section News* 1 (February 1968): 1–2.

———. "India—The Indian Grey Jungle Fowl." *The President's Letter* 17 (July 1969): 1–2.

International Union for the Conservation of Nature and Natural Resources. *Red Data Book.* 4 vols. Morges, Switzerland, 1967 etc.

Jamison, H. K. "Some Rookeries on the Gulf Coast of Florida." *The Auk* 8 (1891): 233.

Kennedy, William Sloane. *The Real John Burroughs: Personal Recollection and Friendly Estimate.* New York, 1924.

Kimball, David and Jim. *The Market Hunter.* Minneapolis, 1969.

Koebel, William H. (ed.). *Enciclopedia de la América del Sur . . .* 4 vols. "Matto Grosso," vol. III, 1249–1250; "Plumas," vol. IV, 1542–1544. Buenos Aires (1912?).

Langlade, Emile. *Rose Bertin the Creator of Fashion at the Court of Marie-Antoinette.* Adapted from French by Angelo S. Rappoport. London, 1913.

Larousse, Pierre. *Grand Dictionnaire Universel du XIX Siècle, . . .* 17 vols. Paris, 1866–1890.

Lavauden, L. "Domestication du Marabout." *Revue Française d'Ornith.* 37 (May 1912) 310.

Lawson, Sir Charles. "India and Her Wild Birds." SPB *Leaflet* no. 36. London (1901?).

Laycock, George. *The Alien Animals.* New York, 1966.

Lefèvre, Edmond. *Le Commerce et l'Industrie de la Plume Pour Parure.* Paris, 1914.

Lemon, Mrs. Frank E. "Dress in Relation to Animal Life." SPB *Leaflet* no. 33. London (1899?).

Lloyd, Helen B. "Fashions in New York." *The Delineator* 67 (1906): 7–11.

Lovejoy, Arthur O. *The Great Chain of Being: The Study of the History of an Idea.* Cambridge, Mass., 1948.

Mackey, William J. *American Bird Decoys.* New York, 1965.

Magnien V. and Deu. L. J. *Dictionnaire des Productions de la Nature et de l'Art.* . . . 2 vols. Paris, 1809.

Maigne, W. *Nouveau Manuel Complet du Pelletier Fourreur et du Plumassier.* Paris, 1881.

Marling, Joseph M. *The Order of Nature in the Philosophy of St. Thomas Aquinas.* Washington, D.C., 1934.

Marsh, George P. *Man and Nature; Or, Physical Geography as Modified by Human Action.* New York, 1864.

Massachusetts Society for the Prevention of Cruelty to Animals. *Our Dumb Animals* 1:1 (June 1868), etc.

Matthiessen, Peter. *Wildlife in America.* New York, 1959.

Mattingley, A.H.E. "A Visit to Heronries." *The Emu* 7 (1907): 65–73.

Maughan, Cuthbert. *Markets of London.* London, 1931.

Maxwell, Herbert Sir. "Fowls of the Air." SPB *Leaflet* no. 23. London, 1896.

McAtee, W. L. "Economic Ornithology." *Fifty Years' Progress of American Ornithology 1883–1933.* Lancaster, Pennsylvania, 1933, 111–129.

McClellan, Elisabeth. *History of American Costume 1607–1870.* New edit. New York, 1937.

McCrea, Roswell C. *The Humane Movement.* New York, 1910.

McIlhenny, Edward A. *The Autobiography of an Egret.* New York, 1939.

———. *Bird City.* Boston, 1934.

Ménégaux, A. *Bird Protection and the Feather Trade.* Paris, 1911.

———. Articles on heron hunting and Wearing in *La Nature* (1909, 1914) and *Revue Française d'Ornith.* (1913–1916).

Michelet, Jules. *The Bird.* Trans. from French by A. E., 1st edition, 1856, New York, 1869.

Miller, Leo E. "Destruction of the Rhea, Black-Necked Swan, Herons, and Other Wild Life in South America." *BL* 16 (1914): 259–262.

———. *In the Wilds of South America.* New York, 1918 and London, 1919.

Millinery Trade Review. Vols. 1–63 (1876–1938).

Mitchell, Elizabeth K. *The Ostrich and Ostrich Farming; A Bibliography.* Cape Town, 1960.

Montillot, Justin Marie N. *La Plume des Oiseaux, Histoire Naturelle et Industrie.* Paris, 1891.

Morin, E. *La Plume des Oiseaux et l'Industrie Plumassière*.Paris, 1914.

Morrell, William. " 'New England' in 'New England's Plantation'." *Collections of the Massachusetts Historical Society*, 1–2 (1792): 126–139.

Morris, F. O. "A Plumage League." *The Times* (London), 18 December, 1885, p. 14, col. 1.

———. " 'The Skout, the Skort, the Kittiwake'." *The London Times*, 17 August, 1885, p. 6, col. 5.

Mosenthal, Julius de and James E. Harting. *Ostriches and Ostrich Farming*. London, 1876.

Mott, Frank Luther. *A History of American Magazines*, 5 vols. Cambridge, Mass., 1938–1968.

Moule, C.F.D. *Man and Nature in the New Testament*. Philadelphia, 1967.

Muhlberg, C. M. "How Fur-Bearing Mammals and Plumage Birds are Being Saved from Undue Diminution." *Selborne Magazine and Nature Notes* 25 (1914): 8–14, 26–30.

Murphy, Robert Cushman. "John James Audubon (1785–1851): An Evaluation of the Man and His Work." *New York Historical Society Quarterly* (1956): 35.

Musgrave, George A. "The Destruction of Birds of Beautiful Plumage." *The Times* (London), 17 August, 1885, p. 6, col. 4.

National Audubon Society. *Bird Lore* 1 (February, 1899, abbreviated in the text to *BL;* now called *Audubon*).

Newton, Alfred. *A Dictionary of Birds*. London, 1893.

———. "The Zoological Aspects of Game Laws." Address to British Assoc., Section D, (1868) reprinted by RSPB *Third Annual Report*, Appendix pp. 24–31. London, 1893.

Niven, Charles D. *History of the Humane Movement*. New York, 1967.

Nystrom, Paul H. *Economics of Fashion*. New York, 1928.

Oldys, Henry. "Audubon Societies in Relation to the Farmer." U.S.D.A., *Yearbook for 1902*. Washington, D.C., 1903.

Oliver, Ernest. "Un Parc à Aigrettes en Tunisie" *Bull. Soc. d'Acclimatation* 43 (1896): 302–305.

Palmer, Ralph S. (ed.). *Handbook of North American Birds*. New Haven, London, 1962.

Palmer, Theodore S. "Bird Day in the Schools." U.S.D.A. *Div. Biol. Survey, Circular* no. 17. Washington, D.C., 1896.

———. "A Review of Economic Ornithology in the United States." U.S.D.A., *Yearbook* (1899): 259–292.

———. "Legislation for the Protection of Birds Other Than Game

Birds." U.S.D.A., *Biol. Survey Bull.* 12, Revised edition. Washington, D.C., 1902.

———. "Chronology and Index of the More Important Events in American Game Protection, 1776–1911." U.S.D.A., *Biol. Survey Bull.* 41 Washington, D.C., 1912.

Palmer, Theodore S. Various reports and comments about the plumage trade in BL (particularly, 1921) and *The Auk* (1901).

Parmalee, Paul W. *Decoys and Decoy Carvers of Illinois.* DeKalb, 1969.

Paul, Alexander. *The Practical Ostrich Feather Dyer.* Philadelphia, 1888.

Pearson, Thomas Gilbert. *Adventures in Bird Protection.* New York, 1937.

———. "The White Egrets and the Millinery Trade." *The Craftsman* 22 (1912): 417–424.

———. "The Passing of the Feather Trade." *The Craftsman* 24 (1913): 303–308.

Pellew, Charles E. *Dyes and Dyeing.* New York, 1918.

Penry-Jones, J. "Feathers." *Port of London Authority Monthly* 33 (1958): 91–94.

Percival, MacIver. *The Fan Book.* London, 1920.

Perry, Lorinda. *The Millinery Trade in Boston and Philadelphia.* New York, 1916.

Peterson, Theodore Bernard. *Magazines in the Twentieth Century,* 2nd edition. Urbana, 1964.

Phillips, John C. "Migratory Bird Protection in North America." *Special Public American Committee International Wild Life Protection* 1 (1934): 3–38.

Planché, James Robinson. *A Cyclopedia of Costume; Or, Dictionary of Dress,* . . 2 vols. London, 1876–1879.

Price, Julius M. *Dame Fashion.* London, 1913.

———. "President Watches Daughter in Play." *New York Times,* 13 September, 1913, p. 11, col. 1–2.

Quicherat, Jules E. J. *Histoire du Costume en France.* . . . Paris, 1875.

" 'Report of an Expedition to Laysan Islands in 1911'." *BL* 14 (1912): 279–283.

Repton, John Adey. "Observations on the Various Fashions of Hats, Bonnets, or Coverings for the Head . . . from . . . King Henry VIIIth to the Eighteenth Century." *Archaeologia* 24 (1832): 168–189.

Roach, Mary Ellen and Joanne Bubolz Eicher. *Dress, Adornment, and the Social Order.* New York, 1965.

Rook, Dorothy. "Protecting Britain's Birds." *BNN* (1966): 65–69.

Royal Society for the Protection of Birds, *Annual Report* (espec. 1st, 12th, 14th, 15th, 19th, 22nd, 27th, 30th) London, 1902, etc.

————. *Bird Notes and News* 1 (1901) now *Birds,* a publication of the Royal Society for the Protection of Birds, abbreviated herein as BNN).

————. *Feathers and Facts.* London, 1911.

Scott, William E. D. Reports and articles on the state of plume birds in Florida in *The Auk* (1887–90).

————. *The Story of a Bird Lover.* New York, 1903.

Sennett, George B. "The Audubon Society." *Forest and Stream* 26 (1886): 124.

Serre, Paul. "Aigrettes de l'Orénoque et Colibris de la Trinité." *Bull. Soc. d'Acclimatation* 62:7 (July, 1915): 219–221.

Sittler, Joseph. "A Theology for Earth." *The Christian Scholar* 37 (1954). 367–374.

Smallwood, William. *The Development of the Natural History Essay in American Literature* (Ph.D. dissertation) Philadelphia, 1924.

Smallwood, William M. and Mabel S. *Natural History and the American Mind.* New York, 1941.

Smith, Harold Hamel. *Aigrettes & Birdskins.* London, 1910.

[Smuggling]. "Hold Up of Five Hats." *New York Times,* 9 January, 1914, p. 1, col. 7.

————. "Traced Plume to Hotel." *New York Times,* 10 January, 1914, p. 2, col. 3.

————. "Sends $1,000 to Huerta." *New York Times,* 18 April, 1914, p. 1, col. 7.

————. "Dancer's Aigrets Banned." *New York Times,* 20 June, 1914, p. 3, col. 2.

————. "Aigrettes Smuggled Here." *New York Times,* 26 July, 1915, p. 11, col. 4.

————. "Importer Admits Frauds." *New York Times,* 16 December, 1915, p. 7, col. 6.

————. "Court May Decide White Heron Home." *New York Times,* 19 December, 1915, VI, p. 12, col. 4–7.

————. "For Customs Fraud." *New York Times,* 21 December, 1915, p. 14, col. 3.

————. "Plumage Prohibition Act." *Parliamentary Debates—Commons,* 180, 10 February, 1925, pp. 9–11.

South Africa. Department of Agriculture. "Breeding Experiments With North African and South African Ostriches." *Bulletin* no. 3 of 1919. V. *Crossing the North and South African Ostriches.* Pretoria, 1919.

Steele, Zulma. *Angel in Top Hat.* New York, 1942.

Stone, Witmer. "Past and Present Bird Life of the Southern New Jersey Coast." *Yearbook, Acad. Nat. Sci. Philadelphia for 1895.* Philadelphia, 1896: 19–29.

———. "Report of the Committee on the Protection of North American Birds for the Year 1900." *The Auk* 18 (1901): 68–76.

Stresemann, E. "Die Enteckunsgeschichte der Paradiesvogel." *Journal für Ornithologie* 95 (1954): 263–291.

Syrett, Herbert. "Plumage Save Birds." *New York Times,* 13 September, 1913, p. 10, col. 7.

"Technology—Feather-work." *Catalogue Peabody Museum of Archaeol. and Ethnology.* Boston, 1963.

Textile Colorist. *A Monthly Journal Devoted to Practical Dyeing, Bleaching, Printing and Finishing* . . . vol. 1 (1879) Philadelphia, 1879–1914.

Trefethen, James B. *Crusade for Wildlife; Highlights in Conservation Progress.* Harrisburg, Pa., 1961.

Trench, C. C. Chevenix. "Egret Farming in India." *Journal Bombay Nat. Hist. Soc.* 28 (1922): 751–752.

Trevor-Battye, Aubyn B. R. (ed.). *Lord Lilford on Birds.* London, 1903.

Turner, Ernest S. *All Heaven in a Rage.* New York, 1965.

United Kingdom, Colonial Office. "Inter-Departmental Conference on the Destruction of Plumage Birds." Miscellaneous no. 263. Minutes of Evidence, Public Record Office, 885/21. London, 1911.

———. "Report of an Inter-Departmental Conference With Subsequent Correspondence Relating to the Destruction of Plumage Birds." Public Record Office, 885/23. London, 1912.

———. House of Lords-Select Committee. Report on the Importation of Plumage Prohibition Bill, with Minutes of Evidence, July, 1908. London, 1908.

———. Parliamentary Debates, Commons. 3rd series, 194. Sea Birds Preservation Bill. 26 February, 1869, par. 404–406, etc.

———. *Statistical Abstract.* London, 1876, etc.

———. Customs Statistical Office, *Annual Statement of the Trade* . . . *With Foreign Countries.* London, 1889, etc.

———. *Board of Trade.* Import Licensing Branch. "Summary of Import Licensing Regulations." Notice to Importers no. 1180. Mimeographed.

United States. Bureau of Manufactures. "Feathers and Bristles. Chinese Feather Trade." Department of Commerce and Labor *Monthly Consular and Trade Reports* 340 (1909): 229–232.

———. Bureau of Statistics, Department of Commerce and Labor. *The Foreign Commerce and Navigation of the United States.* Washington, D.C., 1870, etc.

———. U.S. Congress, Senate. Committee on Finance, *Hearings on Tariff Schedule N.* 63rd Congress, 1st session. Washington, D.C., 1913.

———. U.S. Congress, House of Representatives, Committee on Ways and Means. *Hearings on Tariff Schedule N-Sundries.* 62nd Congress, 3rd session. Washington, D.C., 1913.

———. Department of Interior, Bureau Sport Fisheries and Wildlife, Management and Enforcement. "Provisions of the Tariff Act of 1930, as Amended, Regulating the Importation of Plumage, Game, etc.," n.p., 1962. Mimeographed.

Uzanne, Louis O. "Weapons and Ornaments of Women." *Cosmopolitan* 41 (1906): 405–414.

Van Kleeck, Mary. *A Seasonal Industry; a Study of the Millinery Trade in New York.* New York, 1917.

Venezuela. Department of Fomento. *Law on the Gathering and Exploitation of Heron Feathers of June 26, 1917.* Caracas, 1920.

———. Ministerio de Fomento. *Anuario Esdatistico de Venezuela.* Caracas, 1912, etc.

Voitkevich, A. A. *The Feathers and Plumage of Birds.* New York, 1966.

Wagner, E. R. "Chasse à l'Aigrette Dans l'Amérique de Sud." *Revue Française d'Ornith.* 52 (1913): 132–135.

Warwick, Edward. Henry C. Pitz and Alexander Wyckoff. *Early American Dress. The Colonial and Revolutionary Periods.* New York, 1965.

Watts, Mary S. *George Frederic Watts.* 3 vols. London, 1912.

Welker, Robert H. *Birds and Men.* New York (1st edition, 1955), 1966.

White, Lynn. *"The Historical Roots of Our Ecologic Crisis." Science* 115 (1967): 1203–1207.

Whitney, Caspar. *The Flowing Road; Adventuring on the Great Rivers of South America.* Philadelphia, London, 1912.

Wilcox, R. Turner. *The Mode in Hats and Headdress.* New York, 1945.

Wilson, Alexander. *American Ornithology; Or, The Natural History of the Birds of the United States.* 9 vols. Philadelphia, 1808–1814.

Wood, James Playsted. *Magazines in the United States, Their Social and Economic Influence,* 2nd edit. New York, 1956.

Wright, Mabel Osgood. Reports, articles and comments in *BL* (1899–1906).

Zeuner, Frederick. *A History of Domesticated Animals.* New York, 1963.

Ziswiler, Vinzenz. *Extinct and Vanishing Animals.* New York, 1967.

Index

Act to Prohibit the Importation of Plumage. *See* Plumage Act

Agriculture, U.S. Department of: Bureau of Biological Survey in, 59, 63, 87, 107, 112 (*see also* Biological Survey, U.S. Bureau of); Lacey Act and, 109

Aigrettes: Alexandra protects, 116–17; "artificial," 67, 68; contraband, 61, 146, 154 (*see also* Smuggling); defined, 10–11; fashions employing, 12, 18, 20–22, 24; Underwood Tariff Bill and, 128, 131, 132; Victoria bans, 12, 115–16, 154. *See also* Egret

Alden, Percy, 118, 119, 122

Alexandra, Queen, 116–17

Allen, Joel A., 53, 58, 80, 90, 113

American Ornithologists' Union, 37, 53, 113–14, 154. *See also* American Ornithologists' Union Committee on the Protection of North American Birds; *Auk*

American Ornithologists' Union Committee on the Protection of North American Birds: Audubon Society and, 98, 100, 103–104; Model Law proposed by, 92, 104–105, 107–108, 148–49; origin and early work of, 58–59, 98, 103–104; protects seabirds, 110–12. *See also* names of individual members

American Society for the Prevention of Cruelty to Animals, 43, 45

André, Eugene, 71

Angell, George T., 43, 45, 47

Anson, Sir William, 118, 122

Anti-plumage groups in England and the United States, 93–104. *See also*

American Ornithologists' Union Committee on the Protection of North American Birds; Anti-plumage movement; Audubon Society; Humane organizations interested in birds; Royal Society for the Protection of Birds; Selborne Society

Anti-plumage movement: achievements of, summarized, 148–56; and back to nature movement, 31–33, 49–50; supporters of, 43–49, 52–55; in the United States, origins of, 33–40. *See also* Anti-plumage groups in England and the United States; Bird protection legislation; and names of individuals and groups

AOU. *See* American Ornithologists' Union

Archer-Shee, Lt. Col., 66, 135

Ardeidae. *See* Egret; Heron

ASPCA, 43, 45

Association for the Protection of British Birds, 93

Association of Feather Merchants and Manufacturers of Paris, 55

Auction sales, London, RSPB statistics on, 30–31

Audubon, John James, 36–39, 81

"Audubon Hat," 149

Audubon Magazine, 100–103

Audubon Society: AOU Committee and, 98, 100, 103–104; on birds in ecology, 59–60; contributions of, summarized, 57, 127, 149, 151, 154; on egret farming, 76; legislation supported by, 92, 128, 132, 133, 147–48; membership data for, 101, 102; millinery agreements and, 113–15; origins and early

179

United States (*continued*)
also American Ornithologists' Union;
American Ornithologists' Union Committee on the Protection of North
American Birds; Audubon Society
U.S. Department of Agriculture. *See* Agriculture, U.S. Department of

Vanity Fair, 116
Victoria, Queen: bans osprey wearing,
12, 115–16, 154; patron of RSPCA, 45
Vogue, 15

Watts, George F., 48–49
Welker, Robert, 48, 54, 102

White, Lynn, 89
Whitney, Caspar, 71
Whittier, John Greenleaf, 102
Wild Birds Protection Act (1887), 61
Williamson, Mrs. Robert W., 96
Willis, Nathaniel P., 40
Wilson, Alexander, 11, 34–36, 49
Wilson, Woodrow, 131–32
Women's National Liberation Federa-
tion, 135
World, 116
Wright, Mabel Osgood, 113, 149

Yate Bill, 120, 135
Youth's Companion, 48